MW00856567

STORIES OF
PEOPLE & CIVILIZATION

NORSE

ANCIENT ORIGINS

FLAME TREE PUBLISHING
6 Melbray Mews, Fulham,
London SW6 3NS, United Kingdom
www.flametreepublishing.com

First published and copyright © 2023
Flame Tree Publishing Ltd

23 25 27 26 24
1 3 5 7 9 10 8 6 4 2

ISBN: 978-1-80417-578-1

Cover and pattern art was created by Flame Tree Studio, with elements courtesy of
Shutterstock.com/svekloid/Bourbon-88. Additional interior decoration courtesy of
Shutterstock.com/Anne Mathiasz.

Special thanks to Jason Emerson.

Judith John (lists of Ancient Kings & Leaders) is a writer and editor specializing in
literature and history. A former secondary school English Language and Literature
teacher, she has subsequently worked as an editor on major educational projects, including
English A: Literature for the Pearson International Baccalaureate series. Judith's major
research interests include Romantic and Gothic literature, and Renaissance drama.

The text in this book is compiled and edited, with a new introduction, from elements of
the following: *History of the Norwegian People*, by Knut Gjerset, Volume 1 (The Macmillan
Company, 1915), with portions coming from *The Story of Norway*, by Hjalmar H. Boyesen
(G.P. Putnam's Sons, 1886), and a small amount from *Norway: The World's Best Histories*, by
Sigvart Sörensen (The Co-Operative Publication Society, 1899).

A copy of the CIP data for this book is available
from the British Library.

Designed and created in the UK | Printed and bound in China

COLLECTOR'S EDITIONS

STORIES OF
PEOPLE & CIVILIZATION

NORSE

ANCIENT ORIGINS

With a New Introduction by
BETH ROGERS
Further Reading and
Lists of Ancient Kings & Leaders

FLAME TREE PUBLISHING

CONTENTS

STORIES OF
PEOPLE & CIVILIZATION
NORSE
ANCIENT ORIGINS

SERIES FOREWORD

Stretching back to the oral traditions of thousands of years ago, tales of heroes and disaster, creation and conquest have been told by many different civilizations, in ways unique to their landscape and language. Their impact sits deep within our own culture even though the detail in the stories themselves are a loose mix of historical record, the latest archaeological evidence, transformed narrative and the unwitting distortions of generations of storytellers.

Today the language of mythology lives around us: our mood is jovial, our countenance is saturnine, we are narcissistic and our modern life is hermetically sealed from others. The nuances of the ancient world form part of our daily routines and help us navigate the information overload of our interconnected lives.

The nature of a myth is that its stories are already known by most of those who hear or read them. Every era brings a new emphasis, but the fundamentals remain the same: a desire to understand and describe the events and relationships of the world. Many of the great stories are archetypes that help us find our own place, equipping us with tools for self-understanding, both individually and as part of a broader culture.

For Western societies it is Greek mythology that speaks to us most clearly. It greatly influenced the mythological heritage of the ancient Roman civilization and is the lens through which we still see the Celts, the Norse and many of the other great peoples and religions. The Greeks themselves inherited much from their neighbours, the Egyptians, an older culture that became weary with the mantle of civilization.

Of course, what we perceive now as mythology had its own origins in perceptions of the divine and the rituals of the sacred. The earliest civilizations, in the crucible of the Middle East, in the Sumer of the third millennium BCE, are the source to which many of the mythic archetypes can be traced. Over five thousand years ago, as humankind collected together in cities for the first time, developed writing and industrial scale agriculture, started to irrigate the rivers and attempted to control rather than be at the mercy of its environment, humanity began to write down its tentative explanations of natural events, of floods and plagues, of disease.

Early stories tell of gods or god-like animals who are crafty and use their wits to survive, and it is not unreasonable to suggest that these were the first rulers of the gathering peoples of the earth, later elevated to god-like status with the distance of time. Such tales became more political as cities vied with each other for supremacy, creating new gods, new hierarchies for their pantheons. The older gods took on primordial roles and became the preserve of creation and destruction, leaving the new gods to deal with more current, everyday affairs. Empires rose and fell, with Babylon assuming the mantle from Sumeria in the 1800s BCE, in turn to be swept away by the Assyrians of the 1200s BCE; then the Assyrians and the Egyptians were subjugated by the Greeks, the Greeks by the Romans and so on, leading to the spread and assimilation of common themes, ideas and stories throughout the world.

The survival of history is dependent on the telling of good tales, but each one must have the 'feeling' of truth, otherwise it will be ignored. Around the firesides, or embedded in a book or a computer, the myths and legends of the past are still the living materials of retold myth, not restricted to an exploration of historical origins. Now we have devices and global communications that give us unparalleled access to a diversity of traditions. We can find out about Indigenous American, Indian, Chinese and tribal African mythology in a way that was denied to our ancestors, we can find connections, plot the archaeology, religion and the mythologies of the world to build a comprehensive image of the human experience that is both humbling and fascinating.

The books in this series introduce the many cultures of ancient humankind to the modern reader. From the earliest migrations across the globe to settlements along rivers, from the landscapes of mountains to the vast Steppes, from woodlands to deserts, humanity has adapted to its environments, nurturing languages and observations and expressing itself through records, mythmaking stories and living traditions. There is still so much to explore, but this is a great place to start.

Jake Jackson
General Editor

STORIES OF
PEOPLE & CIVILIZATION
NORSE
ANCIENT ORIGINS

INTRODUCTION
& FURTHER READING

INTRODUCTION TO
NORSE ANCIENT ORIGINS

The people of ancient Norway were tired. Their bones ached as they rose each day to tend to their farms and care for their animals. Mountain peaks winked in the distance, promising rich soil, secret hot springs and green valleys fed by glacial meltwater. The deep fjords were full of fish and whales, thick with meat and fat to keep them warm through the winter. The forests were so plentiful with game that no huntsman's children would go hungry. But you had to work for them with your own two hands. If they toiled long and hard, men and women and children all together, they could build a life for themselves and their families, and their families' families, on the shores of this land. When each day's work was done, the beauty that surrounded them soothed their worries and sang songs of a green and prosperous spring.

In those early days the inhabitants cleared the land for their young herds of cattle and sheep, built houses of long, wooden trunks, held together with wattle and daub, and erected fences of stone and wood to cry out to the world 'This place is mine'. The people of Norway gazed upon trees and dewy fields, mountains and crystal blue lakes. But the land claimed them just as much as they claimed it. Year after year, as they sheared their sheep, gathered seagull eggs and herbs and bred horses packed with muscle for fighting games, their lives were bound up in the land, a thick gnarled root circled by the swirl of the blue sea. The hours of their lives were filled with the endless labour of milking the animals as the hay reserve ran low, making good cheese which would last through the winter, weaving wool to keep them dry in the rain and keeping the fire always warm and ready. These images of life and land coloured their nights when they went wearily indoors after feeding their animals and families for another day.

Inside at last, families huddled on the long benches in front of the firepit that filled the house with lazy wisps of smoke trying to find the hole in the roof. These people of Norway shared what they knew and what they imagined. They entertained themselves with the exploits of great kings and stories of their ancestors, telling of the deeds of legendary heroes and clever gods – a diversion on long cold nights from worrying about what might happen to their flocks if frost came early upon their fields. Now you too can cast your worries aside, put your feet up by the fire and relax into these absorbing tales.

THE LAND OF NORWAY AND THE MIGRATION OF ITS PEOPLE

The first love of a people is their land. The Norse-Icelandic poem *Hávamál*, containing what is thought to be some of the oldest folk wisdom of the North, declares:

> *'Fire is needed, by those who have come in, frozen
> at the knees. One needs food and clothing, by those
> who have passed through the mountains.*

The people who listened to this poem knew something about ice so thick and cold it burns like fire. In Neolithic times almost all the land we know as Scandinavia today (Norway, Sweden and only part of Finland, so-called because of their position on the Scandinavian peninsula), was covered in a rime of ice that obliterated even the memory of warmth. Yet nomadic hunters still braved the unforgiving weather to traverse this primeval frost, and the first elements of Norse culture blossomed in the dark and cold.

They left behind stories of frost giants (*jotun*) and of the first being, Ymir, who fed on milk flowing from the primordial cow, kept alive until she licked Búri, ancestor of the gods, from the salty hoarfrost. Búri's children, Odin and his sons, would use Ymir's mighty form to fashion the Earth and all its realms from his flesh. His blood is the ocean, his bones are visible in the mountain crags, the wind caresses his hair as it blows through the trees; even the realm of humanity, Middle Earth, was made from his body. Did you know you lived in the eyebrows of a god?

These people stayed, hunting and gathering and fishing, and made an enduring bond with the land. By the Bronze Age they had become great artisans and traders, taking inspiration for their pottery and weaving from such distant places as Egypt and Greece. Climate change at the end of the Bronze Age, though dangerous to a people who had grown comfortable enough on this chilly peninsula, inspired another story: that of a 'great winter' (*Fimbulvetr*), heralding the end of the world and the death of the gods (*Ragnarök*).

As the Germanic tribes ebbed and flowed across the continent, moving ever outward as the Roman Empire expanded and conflict arose between groups, trade continued to grow. Though many great writers of the ancient world, for example Tacitus and Jordanes, chose to scoff at these milk-drinking barbarians who stank of horse, drank too much and hardly knew how to grind grain for their daily bread, the people flourished. Large quantities of goods were imported from the Empire to these outlying lands, bringing items such as coins, vessels, bronze images, glass, silver buttons, enamelled buckles, weapons and more.

After the fall of the Roman Empire, and the division of its treasures – a process that the Nordic people knew very well – gold became scarce. To keep their farms prosperous, their servants fed and their children prepared to make the most advantageous marriages possible, the Norse people began to look elsewhere, wondering where they would find the wealth they needed. If the land could not sustain them, perhaps it would be best to travel again. Avoiding the chaos of trying to expand into the fallen Roman Empire, the people gave some thought to the whale-road (an Old Norse kenning – a poetic device describing an ordinary object metaphorically – for 'the sea', found in *Beowulf*) and where it might lead.

SAIL OUT ON AN EXPEDITION WITH THE VIKINGS

Now it is time to board a shallow-bottomed boat with a dragon at its prow and to go where the raven flies! Travelling both near and far, Norsemen dominated the globe during the

Viking Age. Scholars set the beginning of the era at 793 CE, the year that saw the burning of the Lindisfarne monastery on the north-eastern coast of England. In this section you'll read some excerpts from manuscripts such as *The Anglo-Saxon Chronicle*, a history of the Anglo-Saxon people dating to the ninth century. It mentions dire portents and evil signs slashing across the sky in wind and lightning in the months before the attack on the holy site, a powerful clash of Christian and pagan, the civilized and the barbarian. The Norsemen's actions on this day, killing defenceless monks and pouring the blood of saints stolen from the altar of the church on to the ground, would set the template for a Viking for centuries to come: a brutish, ignorant, violent raider. He (or, perhaps even more horrifyingly, she) trails blasphemy and blood with every trespassing footstep. What began in Lindisfarne expanded in every direction around the known world, as these Vikings (traders and sailors in the summers, but usually quite mild-mannered farmers for the rest of the year) looked for new opportunities to sell, buy and take. It was the way of the world.

The Vikings in Continental Europe

Once the treasures of the monastery were collected (for this was the object of the attacks, not Christianity itself), their pious protectors killed or enslaved, they were weighed and divided into various treasure hoards, then loaded on to the boats. The Norsemen understood that the foam and froth of rivers and the icy waves of the ocean could bring them wealth far beyond the toil of hard ground, poor growing seasons and a barn packed full of hay above a pen of fleecy sheep. The riches of a holy place were easily taken, poorly guarded and all around, for those who knew how to read the signs. They were a powerful incentive to sail tormented seas, and fight like *berserkers* (warriors in a trance-like state, who often wore bear furs or fought in a blind rage). No wonder that Viking raids were dreaded – imagine being a simple Anglo-Saxon farmer and seeing Norse warriors coming across the barley field one afternoon!

From the coast, the Norsemen went north to Scotland and Ireland, further horrifying early historians and giving rise to more grisly tales of barbarians intent on destroying their way of life and even God himself. However, their intent was not always to destroy. The Norsemen brought their stories with them – wherever their kindling would catch a spark, the scent of woodsmoke wafted on the air and a warm and calming wind blew through their camps as they plotted where to sail next. Sometimes they listened to the ravens when they told the Vikings to stop, establishing settlements in the Hebrides by 830 CE. Power struggles between the traditionally Scandinavian *Jarl* (Earl) of Orkney and the maritime empire of the Irish-ruled northern isles, such as the Isle of Man and the Hebrides, would continue until boundaries were established and proper ties to the Norwegian crown formalized in the eleventh century.

At that time the last of the Viking kings, Magnús Barefoot, a fellow you'll get to know in this work, decided to carry on the grand tradition of his ancestors and invade. (After 400 years or so the rulers of the Kingdom of Isles had decided that enough was enough with these Nordic upstarts and quickly reasserted their claim). As it says in *Laxdæla saga*, a story featuring an enterprising woman named Unnr who travels to Scotland and the Orkney and Faroe Islands before settling in

Iceland, 'A hungry wolf wages a hard battle'. After centuries
of conquest, subjugation, occupation, disputes, land claims,
outright thievery and general misbehaviour from these men of
the North, the people of the isles had learned to be hungry too.

Of course, not all territory was quite so stressful to conquer.
Among stories of the many kings and noblemen discussed in
this book, you'll find Rollo of Normandy. Near the end of
Charlemagne's reign, a string of Norse raids began in the area
of Rouen, using an estuary of the Seine. They would continue
to vex his sons and grandsons until the Franks capitulated,
allowing the Norsemen to settle the region now known as
Normandy in 911 CE. The French king Charles the Simple
granted the Duchy of Normandy to mighty Rollo in the hopes
of calming down these excitable, apparently unstoppable
Vikings. Charles appealed to Rollo's ego, bestowing the title
of duke upon him. In return Rollo swore fealty to Charles,
converted to Christianity and solemnly swore to *knock it off*.
Now, a wealthy man with land in Frankish territory, he had
to contend with other raids. By this time Europe had begun
to learn a valuable lesson: it takes a Viking to stop a Viking.
Normandy's influence in the politics and society of the Viking
Age would continue for decades until Rollo's descendant,
William, seized the throne of Anglo-Saxon England in 1066.

Everybody Back in the Boat! We're Taking England Again

The Norsemen had solved many of the problems that drove
them to the boats in the first place: the increasing population
in an overtaxed land had created a generation of landless men,
eager to prove themselves and make their own wealth. Vikings

who had come to plunder the British Isles found themselves comfortable in northern and eastern England; they began to build homes and have families there, returning to the plough to support themselves. The Danelaw was established as a separate cultural area, with its own society and laws. It was clearly distinct from the purview of Alfred the Great, who began his reign as King of the West Saxons in 871 CE, but became King of the Anglo-Saxons from 886 until his death in 899.

The Vikings in the East: Russia and Constantinople and Beyond

Still searching for relief from societies that now disinherited all but the oldest son, by order of the Norwegian king looking to solidify his authority, and confronted by new expectations to become Christian, the Vikings continued to sail in search of opportunity. If they longed to return home or ever grew tired of being called *outsiders* or *strangers* (among other things in this section of the book!) by others in their new communities, it is not known. What remains in the image of the Viking Age is a people with a zest for discovery, and a will to keep what they had found by any means necessary. They could burn it, plunder it or enslave it (especially if it had pretty red hair like the women of Celtic descent, who may have made up as much as 60 per cent of the original settlers of Iceland). They could guard a trade route as easily as they could – and did – guarantee the personal safety of Byzantine emperors as the Varangian Guard. These men (and, occasionally, women) made their mark upon Nordic culture in ways as transient as the food and drink on their tables and as enduring as graffiti found on the marble parapets of the Hagia Sophia. This was, at the time of the carvings, a Greek Orthodox church in Constantinople; the inscriptions referred to mention Halfdan and Ari, possibly members of the Varangian Guard, tasked with protecting the Byzantine rulers.

THE STORIES OF NORWEGIAN KINGS

The Norse-Icelandic *Kongesogur* as a Genre

As I'm sure you've noticed, most of the narratives in this book are historical chronicles collected from both the Old Norse-Icelandic corpus and those they invaded, such as the *Anglo-Saxon Chronicle*. This section, which illuminates the biographies of Norwegian kings, fits into a special genre of text: the *saga*.

While it is literally translated as 'story', this is a special word used often in discussions of narratives told by or about the Nordic people. Speakers of Old Norse used *saga* to mean a story that has a prose narrative and was found in manuscripts painstakingly written on vellum at royal courts and religious centres, or commissioned at the estates of wealthy landowners in the medieval period. This contrasts with an older form of storytelling: spoken-word poems or songs communicating myths, legends, law and literature in a way that depends on the memory of the storyteller (loftily called 'the oral tradition' in modern scholarship).

The Dynasty of the Ynglings (from Odin to Magnus Barefoot)

In the extracted text of *Ynglinga* saga, written by Icelandic poet and chieftain Snorre Sturlason in approximately 1225, we begin with the origin of a dynasty of Swedish and Norwegian kings. Their ancestor, so the story goes, is no less than the

Norse god Odin himself. The text moves swiftly from this to Halfdan the Swarthy, a ruler of the ninth century, charting his descendants all the way to Magnus Barefoot, who reigned until 1103. In the time between these monarchs unified Norway, converted Norway to Christianity (slaying a dragon in the process), and reached new heights of power in a combined throne of Denmark and Norway.

Heimskringla is also notable by saga scholars because it not only contains a wealth of knowledge about this era of Norse history and the men who ruled during it, but is also a contemporary work, meaning that the manuscript was produced roughly when the events described occurred. This is unlike most other Norse-Icelandic sagas, which recount history roughly spanning the Settlement of Iceland to the Conversion of Christianity in the year 1000 CE, yet were set down in writing mainly in the twelfth and thirteenth centuries. The gap of several centuries between the writing of the texts and the events they describe can be frustrating indeed – are they works of fact, fiction or something in between? Scholars in the modern era have very few resources to know for sure, though we try our best. In his book *Witchcraft and Magic in the Nordic Middle Ages*, Stephen A. Mitchell describes the difficulty in making sense of, or assigning truth to, these 'curious and unequal fragments of that universe that are passed on to us by random preservation'.

THE NEXT MILLENNIUM

The impact of the Norse people and the Viking Age on world history cannot be understated. These brutes, bandits, shepherds, sowers and sailors – for a Viking is all of these, all at once – expanded inward to the highlands of Norway in the ninth century; when that could not support them, they then went west to Iceland and then south to England and Scotland. By the tenth century they had pushed further west to Greenland and were settling more firmly than ever into the cultural fabric of England. Finally, in the eleventh century, they were to push the boundaries of the impossible, settling in Italy and Northern Africa, even discovering the New World. All this took place while the Norsemen were raiding and trading beyond Constantinople in the east and establishing contact with peoples further west than a Viking had ever been before.

However, it could not last for ever. The world was growing smaller as kings consolidated their realms under absolute power, and the Christian Church, an organization of considerable influence in all areas of medieval life, rose to monolithic status. No longer could a Viking go where the raven's portent told him to – not when merchants viewed pagans with suspicion. Society changed as well, as people became increasingly beholden to the land or the lords they served. These same lords, wealthy enough to pay trained soldiers to guard their riches, were no longer naïve enough to leave it on the windy shores of a simple holy isle in Northumberland, watched over by unarmed priests.

Eventually the tide of history turned against them. The Vikings could neither steal more wealth, as they had done in the Viking Age, nor apparently hold on to what they had. At the Battle of Stiklestad in 1030, King Olaf of Norway was killed. His younger half-brother, the ill-mannered Harald Hardrada ('Hard-rule'), took the throne in 1047. Not content with that – why should he be, when his forefathers had accomplished so much? – he died in a failed attempt to invade England at the Battle of Stamford Bridge in 1066. Victory was snatched away from him by a rival, also of Nordic blood, descended from the Norman duke Rollo. History calls him William the Conqueror although, as always, the English had another, blunter name for this foreigner who bashed his way to the throne.

The Viking Age was over, and the monarchs of the Nordic peoples settled down to see what would happen. Jockeying for position, they contented themselves by emulating the political and artistic innovations of the great courts in England and France. Famine and the Black Death, along with the Western Schism in the Roman Catholic Church and civil wars between nobles in these two countries, forced a rebirth – the Renaissance. It brought a new appreciation of the humanities, a celebration of the arts and, finally, the early modern era.

So, while this book contains stories from a variety of genres, retold by writers from an array of historical periods and cultural perspectives, its emphasis is steadfastly on one of the most intriguing aspects of Old Norse culture: the humble beginnings and violent exploits of a fierce and resourceful people – for ever known as both villeins and villains of the Viking Age – in the annals of history.

A NOTE TO READERS: SOURCES

The majority of the main text of this book (pages 38–157 and 285–352) is reprinted from the 1915 edition of *History of the Norwegian People* (Volume 1) by Knut Gjerset, presented here for your enjoyment. In his foreword, he mentions 'the preservation of the [Norwegian] people's personal freedom amidst general national decay' during the period of the Kalmar Union (1397–1593). In the next paragraph, Gjerset connects this emotion indelibly to 'Norway's long struggle for complete independence after 1814', while assuring his readers that the 'noble and heroic Swedish people' are, as ever, Norway's friends.

As you might guess from these charged statements, Gjerset's work is no longer representative of the latest attitudes towards compilation and the concept of 'historical authenticity', more of which below. However, the undeniable wealth of understanding that Gjerset provides about the chronology of Norwegian history and foundational concepts of Nordic culture – quite literally from the ground up – are compelling. They continue to be explored, enriched and expanded upon by scholars working in Scandinavian Studies today.

The second featured text in this work (pages 160–259) derives from *The Story of Norway* by Hjalmar H. Boyesen, reprinted from the 1886 edition. In the preface to his work, Hjalmar admirably acknowledges his desire to write a history of his native land, yet explains that he chose to write in a way that would allow him to 'dwell particularly upon the dramatic phases of historical events and concern itself but slightly with the growth of institutions and sociological phenomena'. In this way, like Gjerset above, his work is coloured by national pride and romanticism common to the era in which he worked, evidenced by his desire to speak of 'great deeds' of men such as 'the hero Olaf Tryggvasson' and ignore smaller events in which, in his opinion, nothing much happened. In so doing, Boyeson too does not represent the modern scholarly approach, which strives to contextualize cultural matters within a larger perspective of human society and place it upon that continuum in a useful way.

The final scholar whose work is showcased here (pages 262–85) is Sigvart Sörensen, who wrote *Norway: The World's Best Histories* (1899). Because of how much time has passed since he wrote this, he, like his fellow authors in this book, is missing more than a century of exciting developments, refinements and new understandings within the field of Scandinavian history. Most significantly, we have shed notions of nationalist pride which lead us to look at history with a jaundiced eye. We acknowledge our biases and do our best to question all evidence critically, especially insofar as we attempt to verify it through interdisciplinary work. For example, can the assertions of the text be corroborated by any other evidence, whether from archaeological samples, biological evidence, church inventories or annals? If so, you may just be able to support your point with such evidence, but you will probably want to say something more expansive than simply 'this evidence shows'. It may be more acceptable to your fellow scholars to observe, carefully and thoughtfully, 'this evidence suggests' instead.

You will note too that spellings, such as of names, vary – these authors used spellings derived from different transliterations of the Old Norse or Icelandic than is currently generally accepted, but we have retained them so as to keep the original flavour of the text. And a last, critical change to our perspective about the Old Norse-Icelandic literary corpus is that we no longer view these stories as indisputable fact, but rather as narrative creations. They create a beautiful fiction that bursts with vitality in its depictions of daily life, society and, occasionally, a historical figure in the Norse Middle Ages and Viking Age. Much may be gleaned from what they reveal, but they were written so long after the time periods in which they are set – in some cases more than four centuries later – that they cannot be accepted without intense critical analysis, aided by cross-confirmation of other disciplines. Unlike Gjerset, Boyesen and Sörensen, who speak to us from a century gone by, we cannot assert ourselves with the absolute conviction of a Viking of old.

FINAL WORDS

In the end, the histories in this book are interpretations of stories translated and adapted to thrill a Norwegian audience excited to revel in their newfound independence from Denmark, or a foreign audience just beginning to awake to an exciting bunch of world-travelling, empire-threatening seafarers. In this sense the long life of these sources, especially Snorre Sturlason and his works, cited by all three authors in our collection, continue to tell the history of the Norse people. Compelling and changeable by all who come into contact with them, these heroes and their deeds do not belong only to Vikings or medieval Old Norse speakers, to their modern descendants or scholarly experts. The struggle of the Norse people to survive, to succeed and never to stop until the day is done and you can rest your weary bones by the fire remains something innately felt by us all.

Beth Rogers, M.Ed., MA
PhD Candidate, University of Iceland
Reykjavík, Iceland

FURTHER READING

If you enjoyed the material presented here, I recommend you take a look at close translations of other saga genres. These, like the Kings' sagas included in this volume, have similar themes and descriptions of heroic historic events, such as the Legendary sagas and the Icelandic Family sagas. Some of the more well-known stories have been translated into high-quality and affordable English-language editions. These include:

Legendary Sagas

These stories are set in the 'ancient past', before the Viking Age. They often contain supernatural elements such as magic, dragons and the gods meddling in human affairs:

Byock, Jesse L. (translator), *The Saga of the Volsungs: The Norse Epic of Sigurd the Dragon Slayer* (Penguin Books, 1990)

Crawford, Jackson (translator), *The Saga of the Volsungs: With the Saga of Ragnar Lothbrok* (Hackett Publishing Company, 2017)

Kunz, Keneva (translator), *The Vinland Sagas* (Penguin Books, 2008)

Though the first two books here illuminate the same saga, the Jackson Crawford translation includes the *Saga of Ragnar*

Lothbrok, made popular by the historical drama television series *Vikings*, created and written by Michael Hirst for the History Channel. It tells the story of the hero Ragnar Lodbrok, whom you will meet in this volume, and his sons as they became kings of Sweden and Denmark.

A spin-off series, *Vikings: Valhalla*, continues with stories of famous figures such as Hardrada, William the Conqueror and Leif Erikson, who was the first European to set foot in the 'New World'. The story of Leif, his father Eirik the Red and their journey to Vinland is told in the third offering, *The Vinland Sagas*.

Icelandic Family Sagas

These are prose narratives mostly based on historical events that explore daily life in Iceland from the Settlement Period in the ninth century to the eleventh century. Two of the most popular are:

Cook, Robert (translator), *Njáls Saga* (Penguin Books, 2001)
Kunz, Keneva (translator), *The Saga of the People of Laxardal and Bolli Bollason's Tale* (Penguin Books, 2008)

Religious Figures

Influential scholarly works on religious leaders such as St Olaf Tryggvasson, who is a figure discussed in this book, and the Christianization of Northern Europe include:

Jochens, Jenny, 'Late and Peaceful: Iceland's Conversion Through Arbitration in 1000', *Speculum* 74, no. 3 (1999): pp621–55

Nordeide, Sæbjörg Walaker, *The Viking Age as a Period of Religious Transformation: The Christianization of Norway from AD 560–1150/1200* (Brepols, 2011)

Sanmark, Alexandra, *Power and Conversion: A Comparative Study of Christianization in Scandinavia.* Uppsala: Department of Archaeology and Ancient History (Uppsala University, 2004)

Life, Society and Literature

For general information about life, society and literature during the Viking Age and Nordic medieval period, I recommend:

Ármann Jakobsson and Sverrir Jakobsson, *The Routledge Research Companion to the Medieval Icelandic Sagas* (Routledge, 2017)

Byock, Jesse, *Viking Age Iceland* (Penguin Books, 2001).

Clover, Carol and John Lindow (eds.), *Old Norse-Icelandic Literature: A Critical Guide* (University of Toronto Press, 2005)

Clunies-Ross, Margaret, *Old Icelandic Literature & Society* (Cambridge University Press, 2009)

Clunies-Ross, Margaret, *A Cambridge Introduction to the Old Norse-Icelandic Saga* (Cambridge University Press, 2012)

History, Famous Figures and Epic Adventures

There are many reference guides for readers who thirst for history, famous figures of the past and their epic adventures, for example:

Brink, Stefan and Neil Price, *The Viking World* (Routledge, 2011)

McTurk, Rory (ed.), *A Companion to Old Norse-Icelandic Literature and Culture* (Wiley-Blackwell, 2005)

Bear in mind that these are thick volumes with hundreds of pages of knowledge, so may be expensive. They are available at university libraries in both print and digital editions.

More Specific History and Culture

Finally, for those interested in taking a look at Norse history and culture through a more specific lens, such as gender, pre-Christian religion or food, you'll find exciting material on a variety of topics collected in volumes such as:

Role of Women

Jesch, Judith, *Women in the Viking Age* (Boydell & Brewer, 1991)

Jochens, Jenny, *Women in Old Norse Society* (Cornell University Press, 1995)

Jóhanna Katrín Friðríksdóttir, *Women in Old Norse Literature: Bodies, Words and Power* (Palgrave Macmillan, 2013)

Pre-Christian Religion

Andrén, Anders, Catharina Raudvere and Kristina Jennbert (eds.), *Old Norse Religion in Long-term Perspectives: Origins, Changes and Interactions* (Nordic Academic Press, 2006)

Davidson, Hilda Ellis, *Roles of the Northern Goddess* (Taylor & Francis, 2002)

Mitchell, Stephen A., *Witchcraft and Magic in the Nordic Middle Ages* (University of Pennsylvania Press, 2011)

O'Donoghue, Heather, *From Asgard to Valhalla: The Remarkable History of the Norse Myths* (I.B. Tauris, 2008)

Tolley, Clive, *Shamanism in Norse Myth and Magic* (2 vols) (Academia Scientiarum Fennica, 2009)

For History So Good You Can Taste It

The authors of this work balance meal reconstruction from all over Northern Europe with careful descriptions of archaeological finds to support their recipes. Their research makes a feast fit for a modern scholar!

Serra, Daniel and Hanna Tunberg, *An Early Meal: A Viking Age Cookbook and Culinary Odyssey* (ChronoCopia Publishing, 2013)

Beth Rogers (Introduction) is an instructor and PhD student at the University of Iceland in Reykjavík, Iceland. She also has an MA in Medieval Icelandic Studies and an M.Ed in secondary education. Beth has written more than 30 popular and academic articles, including two book chapters, on such varied topics as Viking dairy culture, salt in the Viking Age and medieval period, and the literary structure of *Völsunga saga*. Her other research interests include medieval literature, military history, Old Norse mythology and folklore, and cultural memory. Beth has organized several workshops and conferences, including the 2019 NECRON (Network of Early Career Researchers of Old Norse) workshop in Bergen, Norway, and the Háskóli Íslands Student Conference on the Medieval North.

THE LAND & ITS PEOPLE

Modern **Norway** is a country in Northern Europe, located on the western and northern coasts of the Scandinavian peninsula on the edge of the Arctic Circle. It's known for its inscrutable weather patterns, rugged coastline, misty fjords and rugged mountains housing trolls. This unassuming nation is home to more than 5.4 million people, famous for their strong national consciousness and cultural heritage. The official language is Norwegian and much of the population belongs to the Evangelical Lutheran Church. Norway has a high standard of living and a strong welfare state, which provides its citizens with universal health care and other social services. The Norwegian economy is mainly driven by oil and gas production, fishing and shipping, as well as tourism and technology.

Historian Will Durant, however, would not be impressed with how far Norway has come. 'Civilization,' he wrote, 'is based upon the food supply ... The cathedral and the capital, the museum and the concert chamber, the library and the university are the façade; in the rear are the shambles.' In this section of our book, roll up your sleeves and dig through the rubble of a Germanic tribe eking out a life at the edge of the known world. The challenges they faced as they established the first farms, cultivated societies and went in search of more certainly led to some wreckage along the way. It also created a society with a strong sense of family and identity, a love of nature, a desire to help those in need and a willingness to work with others to reach a worthwhile goal. After all, no one can build a concert chamber, library or university all alone.

THE COUNTRY AND ITS RESOURCES

The **kingdom of Norway** forms a part of the Scandinavian peninsula, embracing its mountainous western slope. It consists of a rock-bound coast region 2,700 kilometres (1,700 miles) in length when measured along the outer belt of rocks. In the southern part it is about 418 kilometres (260 miles) wide, in the northern about 96 kilometres (60 miles), though the extreme northern province, Finmarken, is considerably wider. Measured in a straight line, the distance north and south from Vardø to Lindesnes is 1,700 kilometres (1,100 miles), so that if the country were swung around, its northern extremity would reach the Pyrenees [...]. The country consists of a mountain plateau broken by two larger depressions: one in the southwestern part; another, and smaller one, around the Trondhjemsfjord. These two tracts – Østlandet and Trøndelagen – consisting of undulating mountain slopes, contain extensive and valuable forests of coniferous trees, and are especially well adapted to farming and cattle raising. The southern coast region – Vestlandet – as well as the northern part – Nordland and Finmarken – is intersected by narrow fjords extending far into the country. These deep cuts in the rocky plateau continue inland as narrow, fertile valleys, abounding in streams and waterfalls, and are often of incomparable beauty and grandeur. Fringing these valleys are large mountain-tracts unfit for agriculture, bearing timber, grass, and wild berries. These tracts are valuable as pasture and timberlands, while an abundance of wild game lends them a special charm as excellent hunting grounds. The high inland plateau is uninhabitable, being for the most part covered by glaciers and perpetual snow. This is the undisputed domain of birds and wild deer, which exist here in such numbers as to render even these large areas of frozen desolation of considerable importance to domestic economy.

Norway lies north of the 58th parallel; its southern extremity, Lindesnes, being at 57° 59' N. L., while in the north it reaches a latitude of 71° 11'. If the country were applied to the North American continent in the same latitude, its southern part would be found to lie in the region of central Labrador, while its northern extremity would reach the magnetic pole. Considering its high latitude, the climatic conditions of the country are unique. The Gulf Stream, passing up through the Atlantic to the west of the Scandinavian peninsula, so affects conditions in this respect, that nowhere else in the world is the average temperature so high in the same latitude. The climate varies a great deal with the elevation above the sea, as well as with the latitude, but south of the arctic circle the average temperature is about the same as in our northern tier of states, being cooler in summer, and warmer in winter [...] Thunderstorms are rare, even in the southern part. The coast is often swept by strong winds or severe storms, especially in winter, but in the inland districts the air is almost always calm, owing to the uniform temperature. The winter is long and dark; in the northern part of the country an almost unbroken night. A deep covering of snow then spreads over mountains and woodlands, affording unequalled opportunity for sleighing and skiing, which form the most characteristic features of winter life in Norway.

The summer, with its almost continuous daylight, is very beautiful. From the last days of May till the end of July the sun never sets on northern Norway, and even in Christiania day fades so gently into night that they can scarcely be told apart. The summer landscape of fjords and wooded mountain sides, dark headlands and green islands, which break the evening sunlight into various hues and tints, has the ethereal mystic beauty peculiar to high latitudes.

Fishing, farming, and cattle raising were the chief occupations from early times, and they still continue to be the people's principal means of subsistence, though many new pursuits, such as lumbering, commerce, and manufacturing, have become of great importance in later years. According to the sagas, splendidly painted ships with many-coloured sails carried fish from Norway to England over 1,000 years ago, and fish still continues to be one of the chief articles of export. Especially important are the herring and cod fisheries, though mackerel, halibut, salmon, sea trout, sardines and lobster are also caught in large quantities. The most noted fishing grounds are the Lofoten Islands, [...] Agriculture is one of the leading pursuits in Norway, and is carried on in all parts, except in the extreme northern region north of the 70th parallel, where no grain can be raised [...].

Of the cereals wheat, barley, oats and rye are raised. Wheat and barley were cultivated on the Scandinavian peninsula as early as in the Younger Stone Age, prior to 1500 BCE. Oats were introduced in the Bronze Age (1500–500 BCE), and rye in the Iron Age (after 500 BCE) [...]. Fruit raising is carried on in many parts of Norway, but not on a very extensive scale. Apples, pears and cherries are raised, and berries, such as currants, gooseberries and raspberries, are grown in great abundance. Of wild varieties the blueberry, cloudberry and whortleberry are found in inexhaustible quantities in the mountain districts. The home market is often glutted with these delicacies at certain seasons of the year, and the export of berries is a growing source of income.

The raising of cattle and other domestic animals is of even greater importance than agriculture, because this branch of husbandry can be carried on with success in places where grain cannot be cultivated [...].

In olden times wild game was so plentiful in the mountain regions of Norway that hunting was an occupation of considerable importance. The Anglo-Norman historian Ordericus Vitalis, who visited Norway in the first part of the twelfth century, writes: 'Rural homesteads are found in large numbers around the lakes of the interior. The people have plenty of fish, fowl and meat of wild animals. They keep strictly the Commandments and strict laws of the Christian faith, and punish severely any violation of these. From all quarters their ships bring treasures into the country.' Hunting has lost its former significance, being now carried on mainly as a sport, but wild game is still very plentiful in all parts of the country, and a considerable income is derived from this source in many districts. The red deer, the elk, and the reindeer still inhabit the mountains and forests in large numbers [...]. Still greater are the number and varieties of birds and small game. The grouse is, no doubt, the most important wild game in the country [...]. The coast of Norway is yearly visited by hosts of wild geese, swans, eider ducks, and other aquatic fowl, and great quantities of eggs and down are gathered.

Commerce reached a high development in Norway in very early times. Through the Viking expeditions new trade routes were developed, and the Norsemen soon became clever merchants, as well as able seamen, and bold warriors. In *The King's Mirror* (*Kongespeilet*, or *Speculum Regale*), written in Norway about 1250 CE, a father gives advice to his son, who wishes to become a merchant. 'Both knowledge and experience is necessary,' says the father, 'as a merchant must travel in distant lands and among strange peoples. He should be courteous, pleasing in manners, generous, a good judge of goods and honest and upright in all his dealings. He should avoid gambling and bad company, and whatever might create the impression that he is a mere barterer and an uncultured person. He should set a good table, dress well, and seek the company of the best people wherever he comes.' 'Study carefully all laws,' says the father; 'but if you want to be a merchant, there is no law which you should study more carefully than the *Bjarkeyjarréttr*, or laws of trade.'

'Though I have been more a king's man than a merchant,' he says, 'yet I find no fault because you choose this occupation, for it is now chosen by many of our best men.' [...]

The forests of Norway are very extensive, covering about 24 percent of the entire area of the country. About three-fourths of this area is covered with coniferous, and one-fourth with deciduous trees [...]. Mining has not hitherto been engaged in on any extensive scale. [...] Iron ores occur in large quantities in many places, and the mining of this metal is rapidly increasing.

Manufacturing is of comparatively recent development in Norway. In olden times manufactured articles were either imported, or they were supplied through private industry carried on in the homes by members of the family or by skilled labourers. A high degree of skill and artistic taste had been developed in many handicrafts long before the times of recorded history. Weaving of homespun cloth, both of wool and linen, was common, and the farmers made their own tools and implements. It was the pride of the women then, as it is still in Norway, to embroider with taste, and there were artisans skilled in blacksmithing, wood carving, and in the making of ornaments of precious metals. Shipbuilding and the making of weapons were national arts which were held in high esteem, and were carried on with surprising skill in design and workmanship. With the development of towns and cities in the eleventh and twelfth centuries, and through the influx of skilled foreign artisans in the thirteenth, fourteenth, and fifteenth, a system of crafts and guilds originated which gained full control of the different lines of manufacture. This system of corporations produced a new industrial growth. Each guild had a monopoly on its specialty, to which the members were limited by strict laws, and which they did much to develop. The old native artisans, not able to compete with these new organizations, lost their importance, and also much of their former skill; but to some degree they have survived all industrial changes, so that even at the present time workers in wood, silver and brass can be found here and there in the rural districts, whose art seems to have been inherited through successive generations from those early times [...].

But hitherto, during all the centuries of the past, the location, as well as the general character of the country, has been favourable to the development of the seafaring life along the extensive coasts, and the husbandry in the inland districts which have given Norwegian national life its distinctive features, both economically and socially.

SCANDINAVIA IN PREHISTORIC TIMES

How long Scandinavia has been inhabited cannot be determined. When history, about 800 CE, first lifts the veil of darkness which envelops the remote past, we find a people far advanced in civilization, possessing a high social organization, art, laws and even some degree of luxury and refinement. No detailed account can be given of the people's life and development prior to this period, but archaeology has been able, through numerous finds of relics of antiquity, to establish some important data regarding prehistoric conditions which make it possible to trace in large outlines the greater phases of progress and the mode of life. Iron has been in use in Scandinavia since about 500 BCE, and the period from 500 BCE to 1050 CE is called by archaeologists the *Iron Age*. Other metals were in use earlier. Articles of gold, copper, and bronze were brought to Scandinavia from southern Europe as early as 2000 BCE.

About 1500 BCE bronze seems to have come into general use in the making of weapons and edged tools. The period from 2000 BCE to 500 BCE, when iron makes its appearance, is, therefore, known as the *Bronze Age*. Prior to this era weapons and implements were made of stone, wood, bone, and horn, and this earliest period is called the *Stone Age*. In this period two different epochs are noticeable; the *Older Stone Age*, and the *Younger Stone Age*. In the Older Stone Age people seem to have lived almost exclusively by hunting and fishing. Their clothes were made of skin; their tools and weapons of horn and bone. They had only one domestic animal, the dog, probably a domesticated jackal.

No graves have been found from this period. The most important remains are the great shell heaps (*avfaldsdynger, kjøkkenmøddinger*). These heaps consist of mussel and oyster shells, and of bones of fish, birds and animals, such as the bear, aurochs, wild boar, deer, wolf, fox, etc.; embedded in which are found arrowheads, spear points and other stone weapons and implements, together with fragments of earthenware, and articles made of bone and horn.

The *Younger Stone Age* gives evidence that great progress had been made in many ways. Stone weapons and tools were made, as a rule, of flint, which was the best-known material for edged tools. They are nicely polished and graceful in form, bearing evidence of the taste and skill of the makers. Agriculture may be said to have begun, since both wheat and barley are known to have been cultivated. Nearly all the domestic animals were introduced, which can be seen from bones found in the graves from this period. The importation of flint from Denmark to the Scandinavian peninsula, of which there is evidence, seems to show that navigation, too, was in the process of development. Of special importance to the study of the Younger Stone Age are the many graves preserved from this epoch, a great number being found especially in southern Sweden. In Norway they are found in the south-eastern part. They may be divided into three groups: the dolmens, the passage or gallery graves, and the stone coffins. The dolmen consists of stone slabs reaching from the bottom of the grave to some distance above the ground, so placed as to form a circle, and a great stone slab is placed on top as a roof. The bottom of the grave is made of sand or gravel. These graves are made for a single body, which was usually buried in a sitting posture.

The gallery graves are constructed very much in the same way, but they are burial chambers of considerable size, supplied with an entrance passage. They are sometimes 6 metres (20 feet) long, 3.6 metres (12 feet) wide, and 2 metres (six feet) high. The stone coffins consist of stone slabs placed on edge, with other slabs placed over them for a cover.

The custom of constructing such permanent abodes for the dead rests, no doubt, on the belief that the spirits of the departed continued to exist after death, much in the same way as in this present life. The grave was to be a suitable habitation, supplied with such necessaries as they might need. Clothes, weapons, ornaments, even food and drink were placed in the grave with the dead body, and offerings, probably connected with the worship of the spirit of ancestors so common among early peoples, were, no doubt, performed on the flat stone forming the roof of the grave.

THE BRONZE AGE

The introduction of bronze, and the livelier intercourse with other countries, of which this is a proof, gave rise to a new culture in the Scandinavian North much higher than that which the Stone Age had produced. Weapons, ornaments, vessels, and utensils were now made with a taste in design and ornamentation sometimes worthy of the skilled artisans of Rome itself. Most of these articles were made at home, but the bronze had to be imported from the British Isles and the countries of central and southern Europe. This shows that ships of considerable size must have been built, and that the peoples of the North were able to navigate the sea, though they had not yet learned to use sails, which were first introduced in the Iron Age. This can be seen also from the rock tracings of this period. These strange records of the past are pictures chiselled on the flat surface of rocks, sometimes, also, on stone slabs in the graves, illustrating many phases of life. Among the many things represented in these pictures are boats, carrying sometimes as many as 30 men, but there is no indication of mast or sail. Horses can be seen drawing two-wheeled carts, spans of oxen hitched to four-wheeled wagons, farmers engaged in ploughing, warriors on horseback, etc. The full meaning of this system of picture writing has not been deciphered, but the pictures themselves throw considerable light on the life of this early period, and they are especially interesting as the earliest written records of the past in the North.

Besides bronze, ornaments of gold and many other articles were imported. Many of these articles of foreign make show that the Scandinavian countries already at this time must have been in communication with southern Europe. The earliest routes of intercourse seem to have followed the large rivers of southern Russia from the Black Sea into Poland, and thence along the Vistula to the shores of the Baltic Sea. The mode of burial was also changed. During the first centuries of this era the bodies of the dead, together with weapons and ornaments, were placed in coffins made of hollowed oak logs which were deposited in mounds. To this mode of burial we owe the fortunate circumstance that garments have been found in so remarkable a state of preservation that not only the material, but also the style, can be determined. The garments found are made of woollen cloth; in one instance of linen. The women wore cap, waist and skirt, very much of the same style as they still wear them in our time. The men's dress, besides cap and footwear, consisted chiefly of a cloak-shaped garment fastened about the waist with a belt. No trousers were yet worn.

It became customary quite early in the Bronze Age to burn the bodies of the dead, a custom which also marks a great change in the ideas regarding the life hereafter. It is believed that the body was burned in order that the soul might the more quickly be liberated from the fetters of the natural world, and begin its own separate existence; but the graves still contained weapons, ornaments, and other articles needed by the departed, which shows that, though the body was burned, the spirit was thought to continue its existence after death. Women were buried with the same elaborate care as the men, which indicates that already in this early period they were held in high esteem in Scandinavia, and that their position in society was one of dignity and honour.

THE IRON AGE

About the beginning of the fifth century BCE iron replaced bronze as the most important metal. Throughout the Bronze Age the peoples of the North had been in communication with the countries of southern Europe, and through this intercourse they became acquainted with iron, as they had learned to know bronze in the same way at a still earlier period. The Iron Age may be divided into several quite distinct periods. During the *pre-Roman period*, embracing the earlier centuries of the era from about 500 BCE to the birth of Christ, the influence of the Celtic peoples of Gaul and the Alpine region is especially noticeable, but this influence ceased when the Romans, by extending their sway over Gaul and Britain, came into direct contact with the Germanic world. From that time to the fall of the Roman Empire the superior Latin civilization exerted a preponderating influence on the development and culture in the North. This period has, therefore, been called the *Roman Iron Age*. The culture which developed under the influence of Roman civilization unfolded itself of a sudden with a certain gaudy splendour produced by the influx of Roman customs and ideas. Richly ornamented swords, coats of ring mail, metal helmets, spurs, elegantly mounted bridles and rich trappings for war horses give evidence of the splendour of war accoutrements which now came into use. Silver, lead, zinc and glass were introduced, and money of Roman coinage makes its appearance. A variety of articles for domestic use, such as elegantly designed vases and drinking horns of glass, metal mirrors, bronze statuettes, strainers, silver goblets, bronze vases, razors, shears, tweezers and costly ornaments of gold and silver, furnish an even stronger proof of the luxury which had been developed in the North long before the Viking Age.

The mode of burial remained much the same as it was in the later Bronze Age. The bodies of the dead, together with weapons and ornaments, were usually burned on a funeral pyre, and the ashes and other remains were deposited in bowl-shaped graves, over which sometimes a mound was thrown up, on which a runestone was placed, bearing the name of the dead. The swords and other articles found in these graves have been damaged by fire; often they have been purposely bent and twisted, so as to be rendered useless. Sometimes the body was not burned, but was buried with weapons and ornaments in grave-chambers made of stone slabs.

The contact of the North with the Roman world, though not a direct one, exerted a great influence. Trade was greatly stimulated; possibly also shipbuilding and navigation. The great number of Roman coins and other articles of Roman make brought to Scandinavia by traders show that a lively intercourse must have been maintained with the provinces of the Empire. Shipbuilding reached a high stage of development during this period. In 1863 two boats were unearthed in the Nydam bog, near Sundeved in Schleswig, together with 106 swords, 552 spear points, 70 shield bosses, coins, toilet articles and other objects; among other things, also, a shirt, or blouse, and a pair of trousers made of woollen cloth were found, which show that trousers were worn at this time. The collection seems to have been deposited by the victors after a battle as a sacrifice to the gods, and is thought to date from about 400 CE. One of the boats is of oak, the other of pine. The oak boat is about 24 metres (80 feet) long, and 3.3 metres

(11 feet) wide at the middle. It is made for 14 pairs of oars, and is riveted together with iron rivets. It has no mast. The prow and stern are both sharp and of equal height, so that it is difficult to tell which is the rear, and which is the front end of the vessel. It is of the same shape as the ships of the Suiones (Swedes) described by Tacitus. 'The states of the Suiones, situated in the ocean itself, are strong in fleets as well as in men and arms. Their ships differ from ours in this respect; that both ends present a front always ready for landing. They do not equip their ships with sails, nor do they join the oars in due order to the sides. The oar-age is loose, as on certain river boats, and can be changed from one side to the other as circumstances demand.'

The most striking evidence of the development of culture during this period is the introduction of the runic alphabet and the art of writing. The older runic alphabet consists of 24 characters, divided into three equal groups.

The first six characters form the word *futharc*, which is often used instead of the word *alphabet* to designate the system of runic letters. The resemblance between the runes and the letters of the Latin alphabet is, in several cases, quite apparent, and the Danish scholar L. F. A. Wimmer advanced the theory, which was for some time everywhere accepted, that the runes have been derived from the Latin alphabet, and that they first came into use in southern Germany. The change in the form of the Latin letters was occasioned by the fact that the runes were carved on wood, or cut in stone or metal, which made the use of the angle and straight line much more convenient than the curve or circle. Later the Norwegian scholar Sophus Bugge advanced the opinion that they originated among the

Goths, in the region north of the Black Sea, an idea which gained further support through the investigations of the Swedish archaeologist Bernhard Salin. He showed that the runes must have been brought to the North along the old routes of intercourse between the Black Sea and the Baltic, known to have existed even in the Bronze Age, as they first made their appearance in those regions. Professor [Otto] von Friesen, of Upsala University, has since shown that the runes have been derived from a system of Greek letters, the so-called cursive or running hand, which was much used in everyday life in the eastern part of the Empire. Of the 24 runes in the older runic alphabet, 15 are surely derived from this Greek alphabet, and five more are, presumably, traceable to the same source. Only four are derived from the Latin alphabet, with which the Goths may have become acquainted in the Latin colony of Dacia, north of the Danube.

Runic inscriptions have been found wherever Germanic peoples have dwelt, but they are especially numerous in the Scandinavian countries, and in Great Britain. The runic inscriptions on stone are by far the most important, and these are found principally in the Scandinavian countries. One hundred inscriptions in the older runic alphabet, from 300 to 700 CE, are found in Denmark, Norway and Sweden, some of which are of great length. The language is everywhere the same, showing that, as yet, no difference in speech existed in the three countries. Besides the Wulfila Bible translation, and a few loan-words in the Finnish and Lappish languages, these earliest runic inscriptions are the oldest remains in the Germanic tongue that have been preserved to us.

As a result of the closer contact of the Empire with the Germanic peoples of the North, the Romans became better acquainted with this part of the world hitherto so unknown. The enterprising Greek explorer Pytheas from Massilia, in southern Gaul, made voyages to Britain and northern Europe about 330 BCE. On one of these expeditions he also visited Thule and the Amber Coast. His own accounts of these voyages have been lost, but brief notices are given by the Greek geographer Strabo in his *Geographica*, and by Plinius the Elder in his *Historia Naturalis*. According to Pytheas, Thule was situated six days' sailing from Britain, and one day's sailing from the frozen, or half-frozen, ocean called *mare cronium*. He regards Thule as the most northern country, and relates that summer is a continuous day, and winter a continuous night, there for six months. 'The people live on hirse [a cereal crop also known as millet] and garden vegetables, as well as on wild fruit and roots. Those who have grain and honey make also a drink from these. When they have cut the grain, they bring it into large houses and thrash it there, because they have no bright sunshine, and thrashing floors in the open would be useless because of excessive rains' (Strabo, lib. IV, ch. V.) That Thule is identical with Norway can scarcely be doubted, but the description given of the people may apply to Britain and the North in general.

This was about the only knowledge which the world possessed of Scandinavia prior to the Christian era. In the year 40, or 44, CE, Pomponius Mela, a Roman geographer, wrote a book, *De Chorographia*, describing the countries of the then-known world, in which he also mentions Scandinavia. This is the first time the name is employed by Roman writers.

'In that bay which we have called Codanus, Scandinavia is prominent. It is still occupied by the Teutons, and surpasses the other islands in fertility and size.' (*Chorographia*, III, 54.)

Plinius the Elder (23–79 CE) also uses the name in his *Historia Naturalis*. He had served as cavalry officer in the German campaigns, and had visited the shores of the North Sea. He manifests a real interest in Scandinavia, which he believes to be an island, or a group of islands, in the northern sea. 'There the Mount Saervo, itself of great height, and not lower than the Riphaeic Mountains, forms a bay with the promontory of the Cimbri. This bay, which is called Codanus, is full of islands, the most noted of which is *Scatinavia*, of unknown size.' (Lib. IV., 96.)

'There are those who tell of other islands, Scandia, Dumnam, Bergi, Berice or Nerigon, the largest of all, whence one sails to Tyle. One day's sailing from Tyle lies the frozen ocean called Cronium by some.' (Lib. IV., 104.)

Tacitus, in his *Germania*, written 98 CE, distinguishes between the Suiones (Swedes) and their neighbours, the Sitones.

'Beyond the Suiones lies another ocean, sluggish, and almost without motion, which is thought to terminate and encompass the sphere of the earth, since the light of the setting sun continues so bright till it rises, that it makes the stars dim.' (*Germania*, 44, 45.)

In the second century CE, Claudius Ptolemy of Alexandria mentions Scandia and Thule.

'North of the Orcades lies Thule, of which the western part is in the latitude 63°, o., longitude 29°.' (*Geographia*, lib. II., ch. III.)

'East of the Cimbrian peninsula (the Danish peninsula) there are four islands called Scandiae; three indeed are small; the middle one is in the latitude 58°, longitude 41° 30'. The one which is largest and farthest to the east, near the mouth of the river Vistula, is properly called Scandia. Its western part is inhabited by the Chaideinoi, the eastern part by the Phanonai and the Phiraisoi, the southern part is occupied by the Gautai and the Dauchiones, and the middle part by the Lenonoi.' (*Geographia*, lib. II., ch. XII.)

These peoples are unknown, except the Gautai, or Gotar, here mentioned for the first time as the inhabitants of Scandinavia, and the Chaideinoi or Heiner, the inhabitants of Hedemarken, in eastern Norway.

Denmark and southern Sweden had up to this time been the most densely populated portions of the North, but throughout the Iron Age the population was growing rapidly, and the remoter parts of Norway and Sweden were cleared and settled. Norway, which had hitherto had the smallest population, made gains during this period which placed her on a more equal footing with the other two northern countries.

THE MIGRATIONS

From 400 CE, Rome was fighting her last desperate battles with the conquering hosts of Germanic warriors, and, like a bleeding gladiator, was fast tottering to her fall. The legions were withdrawn from Gaul and Britain for the defence of the Italian peninsula, but this served only to give the untiring victors new vantage ground. The weakened defences of the frontiers were forced, Gaul and Spain were overrun, Rome was sacked, the Empire was crumbling to pieces before the onset of this new race, destined to wrest the sceptre of empire from the withering hands of Rome that they might teach the world new lessons. The peoples of Germany were no longer unskilled barbarians, unacquainted with culture. Since the days of the Emperor Augustus they had followed the Roman eagles as soldiers of the legions, from the praetorian guard in Rome to the remotest provinces of the Empire. They now possessed great skill in the art of war; they had great leaders, excellent arms and an efficient military organization, as they had attained to a high degree of general culture, gained through long periods of development, and, finally, through direct contact with the Roman world. This accounts for their victory over Rome in this most notable contest for world power.

That the warriors from Scandinavia also took part in the expeditions against the Roman Empire can be seen from the great treasures of gold brought to the North during this period. At Tureholm, near Trosa, in Sweden, were found, in 1774, articles of gold weighing all together 11 kilograms (25 pounds); the actual metal value of which at the present time would be $7,214 [over $213,000 in 2023]. So many similar treasures have been found, that it is regarded as certain that they are the spoils of warlike expeditions against Rome, or part of the tribute paid the Germanic peoples by the emperors of the East Roman Empire during the fifth century. The first Germanic peoples who crossed the borders of the Roman Empire were the Cimbri and the Teutones. They came from the peninsula of Jutland, and appeared in the Roman province of Noricum in 113 BCE. Their combined fighting force is said to have numbered 300,000 men, and they repeatedly defeated the Roman armies sent against them. The terror in Rome was so great that the expression *terror cimbricus* became proverbial. In 104 BCE, Gaius Marius, the hero of the war against Jugurtha, was made consul and general. He took the field with a large and well-disciplined army. In 102 he met the Teutones in southern Gaul, and destroyed them in the battle of Aquae Sextiae. The next year he annihilated the Cimbri, who had penetrated into the Po valley in upper Italy. The size of the fighting forces of these great migrating hosts indicates that other tribes must have joined them on their southward march.

The Herules, a people who played a conspicuous part in the migrations, came from southern Scandinavia. Jordanes [a sixth century historian] says that they were driven from their homes by the Danes, and Procopius [of Caesarea, a prominent Greek scholar of the sixth century] states that when their king died they sent to their own royal race in Thule for a leader. Very early in the period they migrated southward into the region north of the Danube, where they founded a kingdom. A part of their force joined the army of Odovacer, and aided him in destroying the West Roman Empire. According to Procopius, their kingdom was destroyed by the Longobards, with whom they were waging war; some of them sought refuge in the East Roman Empire, and some returned to Scandinavia, taking up their abode near the Gautar, where they seem to have had their original home.

The Gautar and the Swedes are the first peoples in the Scandinavian North which passed out of mere tribal organization, and founded kingdoms of some strength and importance. The Gautar inhabited Gotaland, a region around the great lakes Venern and Vettern in Sweden. The Swedes founded the kingdom of Svitiod, which embraced the tribes and territories farther north, around Lake Malaren. They gradually enlarged their dominions until all Sweden was united under the rule of their kings. The Swedes were closely related to the Goths, among whom kingship had reached a much higher development than in western Germany, where the kings were still mere tribal chieftains and leaders of the armed host. Among the Goths the king was the ruler of his people – a national sovereign, who traced his lineage to the gods themselves. This institution of national kingship also obtained among the Swedes, and it is probable that they had adopted it from their Gothic kinsmen. The royal seat and centre of the kingdom was Upsala, the oldest and most famous sanctuary in Sweden. The king served also as priest in the great temple there, and this union of the priestly with the royal office must have tended to strengthen greatly the power and influence of the kings of Upsala. They were of the Scilfing family, a royal race which had ruled in Svitiod long before historic times, and were supposed to be the descendants of the god Frey, who, according to tradition, had built the temple at Upsala.

The Angles, Saxons and Jutes, who effected the conquest of England, came from the Cimbric peninsula. The Saxons were a German tribe dwelling north of the Elbe, in what is now Holstein. Ptolemy says that they lived 'on the neck of the Cimbric Chersonesus'. From the third century they are frequently mentioned by Roman historians as marauders in the North Sea.

North of the Saxons, in what is now Schleswig, dwelt the Angles. Their name is still preserved in *Angeln*, a district in southern Schleswig. They are mentioned by Ptolemy, and Tacitus speaks of them in connection with several other tribes, as worshipers of the goddess Nerthus. King Alfred says that northwest of the Saxons lies the land called Angle (Angeln), and Sillende (Seeland), and a part of the Danes. Bede, in his account of the conquest, says: 'From the Angles, that is, from the region which is now called "Angulus", and which is said to have remained from that day till now depopulated, lying between the boundaries of the Jutes and the Saxons, came the East Angles, the Mid Angles, the Mercians, and all the race of Northumbrians who dwell north of the river Humber.' They seem to have inhabited the greater part of Schleswig, possibly also some of the Danish islands. They must have migrated to Britain during the conquest, since Bede states that their country was depopulated from that day.

The Jutes are a more obscure people. They have given their name to Jutland, the northern part of the Cimbric peninsula, where they are thought to have dwelt as early as 100 CE, though they are not mentioned by Ptolemy. They are believed to be the Eudoses mentioned by Tacitus. To them belonged Hengist and Horsa, the chiefs of the Anglo-Saxon host which invaded Britain. The Angles and Saxons were related Low-German tribes, but the Jutes seem to have been of Danish origin.

The Danes inhabited southern Sweden and the Danish isles. The first account of them is given by Jordanes, who says that they came from Scandinavia, and that they drove away the Herules. Procopius states that a part of the Herules returning northward to their old homes came to the ocean; no doubt, the Baltic Sea. From there they wandered through the Danish territories, whence they returned to Thule. From about 500 CE, the Danes entered upon a period of remarkable development and greatness. Their kings, the Skjoldungs (Scyldings), dwelt at Leire in Seeland, where they built the royal hall *Heorot*, celebrated in the Old English poem 'Beowulf'. In 515 CE their king Hygelac made an expedition against the Hetware near the mouth of the Rhine, where he fell in battle. He is, no doubt, the *Chochilaicus* mentioned by Gregory of Tours and the 'Gesta Regum Francorum', who, on an invasion of the lower Rhineland, lost his life in a battle against the Frankish prince Theodebert in 515. In 565 CE, the Danes made another similar expedition westward. They fought many hard battles, especially with the Heathobeards dwelling south of the Baltic Sea. These landed on Seeland at one time, and advanced almost to Heorot, but they were defeated by King Hrothgar (Roar) and his nephew Hrothulf (Rolf Krake). Rolf Krake became the ideal king and semi-mythical hero of tradition, who is said to have been slain in his royal hall, together with his 12 champions, in a treacherous night attack. The Danes were at this time the most renowned people in the North, though the Swedes rivalled them in warlike achievements, as well as in wealth and power. The Swedish kings waged war with the Danes, and made expeditions into Estonia, and other regions east of the Baltic. Their royal family was the oldest in the North, and their kingdom, Svitiod, had risen into prominence before that of the Danes. No such united national kingdom had yet been founded in Norway as in Sweden and Denmark, but kings ruled here also, and the tribes had formed larger unions in different parts.

Jordanes speaks of the Norwegian king Rodulf, who, fleeing from his own country, went to Theoderic the Great in Italy and became his man. Rodulf seems to have ruled over a confederation of tribes in southern Norway.

The Old English poem 'Widsith', and more especially 'Beowulf', preserves many traces of historic events, and of social life in Denmark and southern Scandinavia in the sixth century. The detailed descriptions of arms and customs given in 'Beowulf', no doubt, reflect quite accurately many features of the life of the chieftains and their followers during the sixth and seventh centuries. Heorogar, Hrothgar and Halga are the sons of Healfdene, of the dynasty of the Scyldings (Skjoldungs).

Hrothulf, son of Halga, is the Rolf Krake so famous in Danish tradition. Hrothgar builds the hall Heorot at Leire in Seeland, a feature of the tradition which preserves the memory of the power of the Danish kings at that time. Beowulf, a nephew of King Hygelac, comes with a band of followers to help Hrothgar against the monster Grendel. After the military guards of the coast have permitted him to land, he proceeds to Heorot with his companions. They have shields, helmets, and coats of ring-mail, and are in every way well-armed and trained warriors. They are courteously received, and are entertained in the most hospitable manner.

'Then Wealhtheow, the queen, entered, the lady mindful of good manners. Adorned with golden ornaments she came to greet the guests. She first gave the drinking cup to the king of the Danes, and asked him to partake of their banquet. He gladly took the cup, and accepted the entertainment. She went all about, this high-minded lady from the country of the

Helmings, and gave gifts to young and old, till the opportunity came when the ring-adorned queen handed the mead cup to the prince of the Geatas, and she thanked God that her wish had been fulfilled, that at last she could expect from an earl help out of their difficulties.' ('Beowulf', 608–629.)

When Beowulf had succeeded in killing Grendel, there was great joy at Heorot, and many came from far and near to see what had happened. When the festivities at the hall were at their height, a scop, or skald, arose. Everyone became silent, and listened to what he might have to say. He sang of Beowulf's journey, and 'Every old song which he had heard of Sigemund, and of many an unknown heroic deed; about Wølsung's combats and distant journeys, about battles and malice, of which none of the children of men yet knew, save he and Fitela alone.' ('Beowulf', 872–880.)

Sigemund the Wølsung is the father of Siegfried, or Sigurd, the slayer of Fafnir, so well-known from the *Elder Edda*, the 'Vølsungasaga', and the 'Nibelungenlied', and Fitela is Sinfjotle, Sigurd's half-brother.

'Then the king himself, the giver of rings, stepped from his queen's apartment, rich in glory, with an excellent band of followers, and the queen walked with him into the festive hall with her train of maids.' ('Beowulf', 920–925.)

The cultural life of this period must not be judged by twentieth century standards, still there was among these early ancestors of ours, not only a very considerable civilization in the externals of life, but intellectual culture and a spirit of refinement were not wanting. They appreciated art and fine manners. They had lofty sentiments and noble virtues, less polished, but, probably, no less vigorous and constant than those which have graced society in later ages.

The migrations checked the peaceful intercourse which the Germanic peoples had hitherto maintained with the Roman Empire, and the necessity of supplying their wants through their own skill and industry, created by this change, made itself more strongly felt. The ideas and cultural elements which had been borrowed from the Romans could now be better assimilated, and the native mind began to put its own impress even on articles of luxury, which were now, to a great extent, produced at home. The gold bracteates [gold medal worn as jewellery] of this period bear evidence of this transition from Roman to native industry and art. These are ornaments and amulets of gold made in imitation of Roman coins. Besides the original image of the Roman emperor, they are often ornamented with runes, and sometimes with quite original designs representing Thor driving his goats, or Odin with his horse and ravens. The beautifully decorated helmets, swords, shields, buckles, necklaces and other articles made by native metal workers show these to have been veritable masters in their art. These articles are made with artistic skill and taste. Some are of pure gold, others of gold-plated bronze, or silver, with ornaments of filigree and inlaid jewels. Pictures on helmets show the style of dress worn both by men and women in this period. The men wore a coat reaching to the knees, and fastened about the waist with a belt. It was edged with fur, it had sleeves and was ornamented in various ways. Trousers were also worn. The lady wore a dress, sometimes ornamented in front with embroidered bands. She wore shawl and necklace, while her hair seems to have hung loose over the shoulders.

Different modes of burial prevailed during this period. The bodies of the dead were sometimes burned, and a mound was, as a rule, thrown up over the charred remains, and a runestone was erected on the mound. Sometimes the body, together with weapons and ornaments, was buried in a carefully constructed grave. Over the grave a mound might be constructed, or stones might be set up around it. The dead, both men and women, were often buried in boats. In 1880 a ship was found in a burial mound at Gokstad, near Sandefjord, in Norway, the blue clay of the mound having preserved it from decay. The vessel, which is made of oak planks, is 24 metres (80 feet) long, and 5 metres (16 feet) wide. It has a mast, and 16 pairs of oars. Around the ship was hung a row of shields coloured black and yellow alternately. A chieftain, no doubt the owner of the vessel, had been buried in it. A burial chamber is constructed in the stern, where the body was placed on a bed furnished with a feather mattress. The grave had been robbed of all ornaments of precious metals, but a complete supply of articles belonging to the outfit of a ship at that time was found. Among these articles were: several bedsteads, a sleigh, a bronze kettle and many kitchen utensils; also the bones of 12 horses, six dogs and some birds, which, evidently, had been sacrificed at the burial. The ship is supposed to date from about 900 CE.

In 1904, another ship was unearthed in a large mound at Oseberg, near Tunsberg, in southern Norway. Two women were buried in it; one of high birth – possibly a queen the other evidently a maid servant. The ship was packed with goods, both fore and aft. Several bedsteads, a sleigh, a four-wheeled wagon, the queen's shoes and her trunk containing toilet articles were among the objects found. Most of the articles, as, for example, the sleigh and the wagon, are decorated with wood carvings so exquisitely done that they are real treasures of beauty. The ship, which is now fully restored, is 20 metres (68 feet) long, and had been beautifully ornamented. It is more tastefully made than the Gokstad ship, and it is regarded as certain that it is the queen's own pleasure yacht. The find dates from about 800 CE Together, the articles present a picture of civilization most interesting and impressive. It is quite evident that the districts around the Baltic Sea, and, more particularly, the Scandinavian countries, possessed a culture superior in many ways to that of any other region of the continent north of the Alps. The population seems to have been denser here than elsewhere. Nowhere else are the graves from early periods so numerous as in this region, and nowhere are the relics of stone, bronze and other metal work so tastefully designed, or so skilfully made. When Tacitus says of the Estonians that they raise more grain than is otherwise customary among the Germans, it is only another bit of evidence of the superior culture then existing on the shores of the Baltic Sea.

THE PEOPLE

In 1677–98, the Swedish scholar Olof Rudbeck published a large work, *Atlantica s. Manheim vera Japheti Sedes et Patria*, in which he sought to prove that the Atlantis described by Plato was Sweden, the original home of the descendants of Japhet, i.e. the Europeans. The work was held in high esteem until more scientific methods were introduced in archaeological research. Since then, it has been regarded merely as a literary curiosity. The theory that Scandinavia was the original home of the Indo-European race was again revived by K. Penka, who treated the question in a scientific way in his work *Die Herkunft der Alier*, 1886. The theory that the Indo-Europeans migrated from India into Europe has of late years been discarded by many scholars, who hold that the original home of this family of peoples must be sought in northern Europe. Of recent years some scholars have come to regard the region of the Baltic Sea as the original home of this race. Noteworthy is the theory advanced by Matthaeus Much that Europe is the original home of the Indo-Europeans, since, in Denmark and the region of the western Baltic, relics have been found showing every stage of development from the earliest to the latest Stone Age, without break or interruption. This continuous development is not found in southern Europe, or in western Asia. The Indo-Europeans raised cattle, and tilled the soil in their original home, says Much, and the domestic animals which have been thought to come from Asia are, no doubt, native to Europe.

The attempted solutions of this difficult problem will, probably, never be much more than more or less plausible conjectures. A similar difficulty confronts us when we ask how long the Scandinavians have lived in the countries which they now inhabit. Archaeology shows a gradual and unbroken development from the Stone Age to later eras, with no interruption to indicate any invasion or sudden immigration of any new people. This would tend to prove that the Scandinavians have dwelt in their present home since the Younger Stone Age. Philology holds, on the other hand, that the peoples now living in the Scandinavian North have migrated into these regions at a much later period. The Norwegians are not a wholly unmixed people, any more than are other European nations today. A considerable foreign element has immigrated into Norway from various countries, at different periods in historic times, and far back of all history there may have been migrations and a consequent mixing of races about which we know little or nothing. The theory that there have been in Scandinavia since prehistoric times two ethnically distinct elements is as old as the 'Rigsmal' of the *Elder Edda*, which tells of the *thrall*, with his yellow skin and black hair, of the fair-faced and light-haired *karl*, or freeman, and of the *jarl*, with light hair, bright cheeks and eyes like a serpent. This idea of two distinct racial elements in the Norwegian people has been advanced by many leading scholars and anthropologists [...].

The theory of a migration from the east into Scandinavia was held even earlier by [Gerhard] Schøning, [Rudolf] Keyser and P. A. Munch. A. W. Brøgger remarks that the older and more commonly accepted form of this theory is not verified by his investigations. What can be shown from archaeological finds, thinks Brøgger, is that away back in the Stone Age there were two groups in Scandinavia, ethnically somewhat different. The south Scandinavian group, who at one time must have come from the south, had fixed homes, and were engaged in agriculture. The northern or arctic group inhabited the northern part of the peninsula, and must have come from the east, or north-east. They lived by hunting and fishing. From Sweden they penetrated farther to Trøndelagen, and spread along the coast of Norway from Jaederen to Finmarken. The south Scandinavian group advanced northward, and the northern group were either absorbed or driven out, and ceased to exist as a distinct element. How great the difference was between the two groups, and how far down in time distinct traces of the northern group existed, we do not know. Scientific research has not yet been able to throw full light on these problems, but in so far as it is possible to determine distinct racial traits in modern nations, we are justified in saying that the Scandinavians belong to the Germanic branch of the Indo-European race. Anthropological investigation shows that they have preserved more fully the characteristic Germanic traits than have any other people. Skeletons found in the graves from early periods show them to have been at all times a tall race, and all early accounts describe them as blue-eyed, with light hair and fair complexion. The song 'Rigsmal', of the *Elder Edda*, says of the lady whom the god Heimdall visits:

> *Her eyebrows were light,*
> *her bosom lighter,*
> *her neck whiter*
> *than the white snow.*

Of her son it says:

> *Light was his hair,*
> *bright were his cheeks,*
> *and sharp his eyes*
> *like the serpent's.*

[...] The extreme northern part of Norway is inhabited to a large extent by two peoples of Mongolian race, the Finns and the Kvaens. The Finns are small, the men averaging about five feet in height. Their face is broad, with prominent cheek bones. Their complexion is dark, their hair generally chestnut brown, the growth of beard scant. In the inland districts they live as nomads on their flocks of reindeer, with which they move about from the mountains to the seacoast and back again, as the seasons require. The greater number, however, live in permanent homes near the coast, where they are engaged in fishing. In 1891, the Finnish population in Norway numbered 20,780. Of these 2,912 spoke the Norwegian language, the rest still use their own Finnish tongue. The Bible has been translated into their language, and the government has, especially of late years, done much to Christianize and educate them.

The theory that the Finns once occupied the whole of Scandinavia, and that they were gradually forced northward when the Scandinavians entered the peninsula, can no longer be maintained. They seem to have immigrated from Asia at a time when the Scandinavians already dwelt in the peninsula, and they have never occupied a territory much larger than at the present time.

The Kvaens are a large and well-built people. Like the Finns, they are found mostly in the two northern provinces, Tromsø and Finmarken. Norway has at different times received immigrants from this Finno-Ugrian race. In the thirteenth century some Permians came from northern Russia into the Tromsø province, but no trace of them can be found at the present time. More important was the emigration from Finland about 1600 to the forest regions along the eastern borders of Norway. Most of the immigrants settled in Sweden, but some located on the Norwegian side of the border, and the tract has since been known as the Finn-forest. They have now been so far assimilated that only a few individuals speak the Finnish language.

The most important emigration from Finland to the northern provinces of Norway took place in the eighteenth century. It began during the great Northern War, 1700–20, when the Finns who lived in what was then Swedish territory were so sorely harassed by the Russian soldiery that many fled from their homes. The movement increased about the middle of the nineteenth century, but of late years it has ceased.

THE DAWN OF HISTORIC NORWAY

Many invaluable finds of relics of antiquity have helped to throw light on the life and customs of the Scandinavian peoples in pre-historic ages, but, valuable as this evidence is, it is circumstantial and indirect. No account was left by the people themselves of their life and institutions, or of the vicissitudes and struggles through which they passed. But about 800 CE the silence of the past is broken by the *skalds*, who in their songs celebrate the exploits and great qualities of chieftains and rulers, and recount many important historic events. As an historical source the skaldic songs are of the highest value. The skalds were, as a rule, members of the king's *hird*, or court, and followed him on his military expeditions. They were not only contemporary with the events which they describe, but were often eyewitnesses of, or even partakers in them.

Another important and, generally, quite reliable source for the early history of Scandinavia are the accounts given of the Norsemen by early writers in other European countries. In many lands old chroniclers have recorded, often with glowing colours, but usually with solemn brevity, the unwelcome visits of the bold warriors of the North. Fragmentary and often one-sided as such accounts necessarily are, they furnish many valuable data regarding the life and doings of the Vikings in foreign lands.

It was left, however, for the saga writers to give comprehensive and detailed accounts of the persons and events during the Viking Age. The *sagas* are narratives written in excellent prose style, and in many instances they are based on the songs of the skalds as a source. Though very similar in form and style, they differ widely in contents and character. Some resemble more closely the historical novel, others are still more imaginative productions, dealing with mythological and heroic elements, while some are history in a strict sense, where the author pursues his narrative with critical method, and with strict regard for truth and accuracy. With consummate skill the writer pictures the character and psychological traits of the persons in the narrative. Life and customs, thoughts, sentiments, social and political institutions, are described with never erring insight, and with nicely measured regard for detail and colouring. The events are narrated with simple straightforwardness, but the circumstances and motives giving rise to them, and the long train of results following them, often lend the story dramatic features cast in a calm and sombre epic mould. The sagas which deal with fabulous, or mythological, heroes and traditions are held by many to be a later growth in saga literature. Such are: the 'Vølsungasaga', the 'Hrolfssaga', the 'Ragnar Lodbrokssaga', the 'Friðþjofssaga' and others. The earlier sagas were written about distinguished men and their families, for the purpose of recounting their great achievements, and especially for the sake of perpetuating the knowledge of the family relationship so important in all early Germanic society. Many of these sagas furnish important historical material. Among these may be mentioned the 'Egilssaga', the 'Laxdølasaga', the 'Njalssaga', and the 'Gunlaugssaga'. Sagas were also written about the Norwegian kings, and about discoveries, and colonies founded in the western islands. 'Olafssaga Tryggvassonar', 'Olafssaga ins Helga', 'Sverrissaga'; 'Orkneyingasaga', narrating the history of the Orkney Islands; 'Landnamabok', dealing with the colonization of Iceland; 'Sigmund Brestissonssaga', containing the early history of the Faroe Islands; and the 'Saga of Eirik the Red', or 'Thorfinn Karlsevnes-saga' (found in the 'Hauksbok'), which tells about the discovery of America by the Norsemen, are among these.

Some authors undertook more ambitious works, and wrote in connected narrative the whole history of Norway from about 850 to their own time. Of such works may be mentioned: *Historia de Antiqnitate Regum Norwagiensium*, written in Latin by the monk Thjodrek (Theodricus Monachus), and *Historia Norwegiae*, also in Latin, by an unknown author; *Agrip af Noregs Konungasøgum*, *Morkinskinna*, *Fagrskinna* and, above all, Snorre Sturlason's masterly work, *Heimskringla*. Snorre was an historian of high rank. He is a writer of rare ability, and a scholar with historical and critical method. Most of the sagas were written in Iceland during the twelfth and thirteenth centuries. Some were written in Norway, partly by Icelanders, and partly, also, by native sagamen. As the sagas do not always describe contemporary events, but often deal with periods long past, it need cause no wonder that in these narratives the real historic occurrences are often hidden by a growth of fiction which only the most careful critical analysis can pare away. Where the saga writers describe the institutions, life and customs of their own time, they generally give a most vivid and realistic picture, but in the finer details of historic events it is often difficult to separate fact from fiction, a weakness common to all early historians.

The new period of development which began in the eighth century is heralded by many important changes which show that cultural life in the North had begun a new and more independent growth. The language, which hitherto had been but slightly differentiated from the Germanic tongue, now became a distinct Scandinavian dialect. The runic alphabet of 24 characters, common to all Germanic peoples, was replaced in the North by the younger runic alphabet of 16 characters about 850 CE. This system is developed from the older runic alphabet, and has been used exclusively in the Scandinavian countries.

THE AGE OF VIKING EXPEDITIONS

The Viking Age refers to a period in Scandinavian history from the late eighth to the early eleventh centuries when the Vikings, a seafaring people from what is now Norway, Denmark and Sweden, undertook a series of trade excursions and colonization attempts. The Vikings travelled widely and established settlements in Iceland, Greenland and parts of the British Isles; they also undertook raiding and trading missions throughout Europe, as far east as the Byzantine Empire and what is today Russia. This period of discovery and expansion is considered a pivotal moment in Scandinavian history and has had a lasting impact on the cultures and economies of Europe.

As you'll see in this section of our book, accounts of these fierce raiders differ widely, depending on whether they are written by the Vikings themselves or the victims of their pillaging. As the text of *Laxdæla saga* describes it, Höskuld Dala-Kollsson thought his farm was less well-stocked than he wanted. 'Then he buys a ship for a man from Hjalta. [...] He builds that ship and declares that he plans to leave, but [his wife] preserves the farm and their children'. On the other hand, the thirteenth-century *Chronicle of John of Wallingford*, written at roughly the same time as the saga by a monk at the Abbey of St. Albans in south-eastern England, takes a less matter-of-fact approach. John not only decries the general barbarism of the Norsemen and the destruction they brought, but also deplores their good grooming and frequent washing, whereby 'they laid siege to the virtue of the married women and persuaded the daughters even of the nobles to be their concubines'. Truly the Viking Age was rough all over.

THE OPENING OF THE SEAS

Along with the cultural and linguistic development mentioned in the previous chapter, began the Viking expeditions, which became of such far-reaching importance to the development of the North. The word Viking means warrior, not, as hitherto generally held, a dweller by a *vik*, or bay. The word was applied earlier, also, to other Germanic peoples. It is found in the Old English poem 'Widsith', and in South Germany it occurs as a man's given name. From now on it was used to designate the bold Scandinavian sea rovers. Their journeys across the sea into foreign lands, which hitherto had occurred rather sporadically, now took more definite shape. The Scandinavian peoples began a great forward movement eastward, southward and westward, which can only be regarded as a continuation of the great migrations. Just when the movement started cannot be definitely stated, neither is it possible to determine with accuracy when it terminated, but it is certain that it began prior to 800 CE, and that about 1050 CE it had spent its force. This period, called by archaeologists the *Younger Iron Age*, is known in history as the *Viking Age*.

Shipbuilding had reached a high stage of development in the North even prior to this era. The Norsemen had well-constructed sea-going vessels, fitted out with mast and sail. Their home environment pointed to the sea as the surest and quickest road to wealth and conquest. Hitherto it had been regarded as a barrier behind which the peoples could dwell secure, and hamlets and monasteries nestled in profound quiet along the unprotected shores. The Norsemen made it a highway from island to island, and from coast to coast. When their well-equipped fleets, tired of coasting along their own shores, turned their sharp prows westward in search of conquest and adventure, it marked, not only the beginning of the Viking Age, but the dawn of ocean navigation, and the development of naval warfare, which was gradually to produce the formidable navies and the interoceanic commerce of modern times.

THE EARLY VIKING EXPEDITIONS

The Viking expeditions began about 790 CE. The *Anglo-Saxon Chronicle* mentions the Vikings even earlier. For the year 787 it records the following:

> 'In this year King Breohtric married King Offa's daughter Eadburge. And in his days came the first three ships of the Northmen from 'Hereðalande'. [...] These were the first Danish ships which visited the land of the Anglian people.'

King Breohtric ruled from 787 till 800. The chronicle does not say that the ships came in 787, but in his day.

In 793 the Vikings plundered the monastery of Lindisfarne. They came from the North, that is, from Norway, or the islands north of Scotland. The next year they appeared in Northumbria, where they attacked the monastery of Jarrow, near the mouth of the Tyne, but this time they were driven away. We are also told that in 795 a fleet numbering more than 100 ships came to South Wales, but they were driven off by King Maredudd. The spirited resistance which they met with may have been the reason why no further attempts were made against England for many years. Instead, they turned their attention to Ireland, and to the islands along the coast, which proved to be an easier prey. In 795 the Norwegian Vikings appeared on the coast of Leinster, where they seized the island of Rachru, which they called Lambay, a name which it still bears. Two years later they took the island Inis-Padraig, which they gave the Norwegian name Holm-Patrick. The home of these Vikings is called 'Hirotha' by the Irish annalists, which is, no doubt, a corrupted form of Hereðaland (Hordaland), on the south-west coast of Norway. From year to year the ravages were renewed. The shrine of St. Columba in the island of Iona was plundered in 802, and again in 806. The treasures were carried away, and many of the monks were slain. The survivors fled to Ireland, bringing with them the bones of the saint. Lindisfarne and Iona were still regarded as the greatest sanctuaries in the western Christian Church, and the wanton destruction of these holy places filled the minds of the Christian nations of western Europe with an almost superstitious fear of this hitherto unknown enemy.

These early expeditions to the British Isles, which, evidently, came from the west coast of Norway, were undertaken for the sole purpose of plunder. The Shetland and Orkney Islands served as vantage points from which the marauders would sweep down on the unprotected coasts, plunder some town or monastery and depart with their booty as suddenly as they came. Seldom did the terror-stricken inhabitants offer any effective resistance.

THE VIKINGS IN IRELAND AND IN THE ISLANDS

The success which the Vikings met with encouraged them to renewed attempts. Year by year their fleets grew larger, and their attacks soon changed from mere piratic forays to well-organized expeditions aiming at conquest and colonization. The year after the sack of Iona they landed on the west coast of Ireland, and destroyed the monastery of Innishmurray. From 812 till 814 they appeared far inland in Munster, Ulster and Connaught, defeating the bands of the Irish kings, and plundering churches and monasteries. Their fleets soon swarmed around all the coasts of Ireland. In 826 they made the first permanent settlement in the county of Meath, and during the next decade they extended their marauding expeditions almost to the heart of the country. In 836 two fleets, numbering in all about 60 ships, sailed up the rivers Liffy and Boyne. Torgils or Turgeis, the great sea-king, was the leader. He became king of all the Norsemen in Ireland, and began a systematic conquest of the country. He built fortified strongholds, both inland and along the coasts, and founded the city of Dublin, which soon became the centre and seat of government of the Norwegian colonies in the island. Limerick, a second Norwegian city, was founded on the Shannon River, in the north of Ireland, where Viking colonies were springing up.

Turgeis evidently aimed at destroying Christianity in Ireland; monasteries were destroyed, and churches were plundered and turned into heathen temples. For a while it looked as if the Asa faith would triumph over the Cross, but in 845 the Viking king fell by chance into the hands of Maelsechlainn, high king of Erin, who put him to death. He was long remembered as the founder of the Viking dominion in Ireland. On these westward expeditions the Vikings had discovered the Faroe Islands, the Orkneys and the Shetland Islands prior to the year 800. These barren and inhospitable island groups had at the time a few Celtic inhabitants, but the Norsemen took full possession of them, and planted settlements there, and the population soon became wholly Norwegian. The Hebrides, too, were settled. From 820 to 830 the Vikings came in such numbers that the islands were called by Irish annalists 'Innse Gall' (i.e., the islands of the strangers). The new settlers accepted the Christian faith and culture of the native Celtic population in the Hebrides, but Norwegian customs and mode of life prevailed. The original inhabitants gradually adopted the ways of the conquerors, and Norwegian social organization became general throughout the islands.

THE VIKINGS IN FRANCE AND SPAIN

In 810-820 the Vikings began to visit the island of Noirmoutier, near the mouth of the Loire, on the west coast of France. That they came from Ireland, where the Norwegian Vikings were gathering in great numbers, seems the more certain, because the northern coasts of France were not disturbed at this time. In 843 a fleet of 67 ships came to the Loire directly from Norway, and a permanent colony was established on Noirmoutier. They called themselves Westfoldingi, i.e., men from Vestfold, in southern Norway. From this base of operations they ascended the Loire, and captured and sacked the city of Nantes. Returning to Noirmoutier with their booty, they made another expedition up the Garonne River in 844, under their leader Asgeir, attacking the cities of Toulouse (844), Bordeaux (848), Nantes and Tours (853). They also ascended the Adour, in Gascogne, as far as to Tarbes, but lost many men in battles with the mountaineers. Leaving southern France for a time, they made an attack on the coast of Spain. After an unsuccessful siege of Lisbon, they followed the coast to Cadiz, plundered the city, and ascended the Guadalquivir to Sevilla, in Andalusia. They besieged the city, and captured the suburbs, but they were unable to take the city itself. In Spain they fought many battles with the Saracens, whose prowess they soon learned to respect. From their settlements on the Loire the Norsemen made repeated expeditions into southern France. In 877 they took permanent possession of a region along the coast, and founded a colony which long maintained its independent existence. The colonies on the Loire acknowledged the supremacy of the Norwegian kings of Dublin, who were regarded as overlords of all the Norwegian colonies in the West.

In 859 a new Viking expedition was fitted out in western France for a voyage to Spain and the Mediterranean Sea, possibly, also, for the purpose of attacking Rome itself. The wealth and glory of the Eternal City must have presented special attractions to these bands of professional warriors, who sought in hazardous adventure both honour and pastime. Danish Vikings seem to have joined with the Norwegians from the Loire colonies in the enterprise, as the renowned Hasting, or Haastein, the son of Atle Jarl in Fjalafylke (Søndfjord), in western Norway, and Ivar Boneless, son of the famous Danish chieftain Ragnar Lodbrok, were the leaders of the expedition. Hasting is well known in the annals of western Europe, which describe him as the incarnation of all that was fierce and terrible in Viking character. Ivar, who later became the leader of the great Viking army which invaded England in 866, was one of the most renowned of Ragnar Lodbrok's sons.

The fleet sailed around Spain to the mouth of the Rhone River, in southern France, where they seized and fortified the island of Camargue. From here they made an attack on the coast of Italy, where they captured the city of Luna, mistaking it for Rome.

Through these expeditions the Norsemen came into contact with the Saracens in Spain, and communications were established between Dublin and southern Europe. In 844 the Norwegian king in Dublin sent an embassy to Emir Abderrhaman II of Spain, who, in return, sent the poet Alghazal as special envoy to the 'King of the Pagans' in Ireland. Alghazal has left an account of his mission, in which he speaks of the many conversations he had with the queen, whom he praises highly for her beauty and courtly manners. When he expressed anxiety lest their conversations should arouse the king's jealousy, the queen replied: 'It is not customary with us to be jealous. Our women stay with their husbands only as long as they please, and leave them whenever they choose.' 'The Vikings brought a large number of Moors as prisoners to Erin,' says the chronicle; 'these are the blue men in Erin [...] long indeed did these blue men remain in Erin.' Commercial relations were also established between Spain and the Norwegian colonies in Ireland, and merchants sailed from Dublin to Spain to buy silk, leather and costly cloth from the Arabs.

The geographical location of the Scandinavian countries determined, very largely, the routes taken by the Viking bands from each, as well as the localities to which their operations were chiefly confined. Those coming from Norway followed, as a rule, a northerly route, leading to Ireland, Scotland and the islands in the northern ocean. From Ireland this route led farther to the west coast of France, to Spain, and the coasts of the Mediterranean Sea, and there can be little doubt that the hosts who directed their warlike activities to these regions were, in the main, Norwegians, led by Norwegian chieftains.

The Danish Vikings usually followed a more southerly route, leading to Friesland, Flanders, England and the north coast of France. That Danish Vikings in early centuries took part in the great migrations is possible. The expedition of Chochilaicus (Hygelac) into the Rhine country in 515 has already been mentioned, but their powerful kinsmen, the Saxons, dwelling to the south of them, seem to have been an effective barrier against extensive operations in that direction, and no general movement is noticed before the beginning of the Viking Age. During the reign of Charlemagne, Viking fleets were seen to hover around the northern shores of the

Empire, but the energetic emperor, who discerned the danger, established military posts to guard the coasts. He even ordered fleets to be built, but the order was not carried out. His aggressive policy on the southern borders of Denmark aroused, however, the hostility of the Danes, and King Sigfred gave aid and shelter to those who had rebelled against Charles. In 810 a Danish fleet of 200 ships ravaged Friesland. Later the powerful King Godfred began war against the emperor, but he was killed by one of his own men in the midst of the campaign (811).

While Charles lived, no other general advance against the Empire was attempted, but when he died, the opportunity came. The strength of the Empire was soon lost through weak rulers and internal dissensions; maladministration and disorder prevailed, and the Vikings were quick to seize the opportunity. The attack began in 834, when a Danish fleet sailed to the Rhine, and ascended the river to the rich city of Dorstadt, which was seized and plundered. In rapid succession new attacks were made during the years following. In 837 the Vikings also captured the island of Walcheren. These events led the emperors Lewis the Pious and Lothair to grant Dorstadt, Walcheren and neighbouring districts to a Danish prince, Harald Klak, with the understanding that he should defend the coast of Friesland against the Vikings, but this only served to give them a new foothold. The Danes were soon masters of Friesland, whence they could fit out new expeditions into the wrecked Empire. The Frankish kings, who were unable to meet them on the field of battle, were forced to buy peace by paying a yearly tribute, which was often made oppressively high by the victorious Viking chieftains. In 845 an expedition led by Ragnar Lodbrok captured Rouen, advanced up the Seine, and fortified themselves on some islands in the river. King Charles the Bald hastened to Paris to defend the city, but he failed to bring with him a sufficient military force, and was obliged to seek refuge in the fortified monastery of St. Denis. Most of the inhabitants fled from the city, and the Vikings plundered the suburbs and penetrated far into the neighbouring districts, practically unmolested.

Again the old method of buying peace had to be resorted to. King Charles agreed to pay Ragnar 3,175 kilograms (7,000 pounds) of silver on condition that he should leave France, and that he should not again attack the country. Ragnar returned to Denmark, it seems, but new hosts soon appeared under new leaders. Following the large rivers, they penetrated far inland, and plundered large districts. Paris was again attacked in 857, and once more heavy taxes had to be levied to buy off the enemy. The leader of the Viking host now operating on the Seine was Bjørn Ironside, a son of Ragnar Lodbrok, whom King Charles the Bald sought in vain to drive from his fortified camp on the island of Oissel, above Rouen. Piratic expeditions were constantly undertaken into the neighbouring country, and in 861 Paris was again sacked. King Charles now offered the Norsemen on the Somme River 1,360 kilograms (3,000 pounds) of silver to attack the Viking camp on Oissel, and the attack was also made, but the two Viking hosts soon came to an understanding, we are told, and left France in the spring of 862.

The Viking inroads in France continued. In 885 a large army assembled on the Seine and laid siege to Paris, but they were, finally, persuaded to withdraw upon receiving a tribute of 300 kilograms (700 pounds) of silver. They were, however, allowed to advance, and plunder the rich districts of Burgundy. The great Viking army met with no real check till it was finally defeated by the German emperor, Arnulf, near Louvain, in 891.

THE VIKINGS IN ENGLAND

After their first visits to the coasts of England an interval of some 40 years passed, during which the Vikings made no further attempt to gain a foothold there. They pressed with vigour their conquests in Ireland and France, and England was given a respite, during which ample preparation might have been made to meet the coming storm. But internal strife between petty kingdoms, and ceaseless feuds among princes and other men of quality gradually wore down the strength of the Anglo-Saxons, and left them weak and disorganized. One thing had been achieved, however, in these 40 years, which became of far-reaching importance in the coming struggle. King Ecgbert of Wessex succeeded in uniting all the Anglo-Saxon kingdoms in 827, and could now rule as 'King of the English'. But of more immediate importance than this weak union, and Ecgbert's precarious supremacy, was the fact that the kingdom of Wessex now became the centre of English national life and development, and that a dynasty of kings of superior ability ascended the throne, and made this small kingdom a tower of strength which ultimately broke the force of the coming invasion.

In 834 the Vikings began their attack on England in earnest by ravaging the island of Sheppey, at the mouth of the Thames.

In 836 they returned to the coast of Wessex with 35 ships, and near Charmouth, in Dorsetshire, where King Ecgbert resided, a bloody battle was fought in which the Vikings were victorious. It is noteworthy that this attack occurred almost simultaneously with the plundering of Dorstadt, and the expeditions against the Frankish kingdom. It can scarcely be doubted that it was the same armed host which operated on both sides of the English Channel, and that the Vikings who now appeared in England were Danes.

In 838 a great fleet came to the land of the West Welsh, made an alliance with them, and attacked Wessex. King Ecgbert marched against the allies, and defeated them with great slaughter at Hengestesdune, near Plymouth, but this was his last exploit. He died the following year, and was succeeded by his son Ethelwulf, a pious and conscientious, but weak man, who was unable to cope successfully with the invaders. After Ecgbert's death the Vikings began more extensive operations in England. In 840 they made two successful raids on the coast of Wessex, and in the year following they entered the Wash, defeated and slew the ealdormen [alderman] of Lindesey and plundered his land. They then turned south to ravage the coasts of East Anglia and Kent. London and Rochester were attacked in 842 by a large fleet, and the following summer King Ethelwulf was defeated in the second battle of Charmouth, in Wessex. Northumbria, too, was attacked in 844, and King Redwulf was slain by the invaders.

Norwegian Vikings, too, seem to have taken part in these raids on the English coasts; but, as a rule, no distinction between Norwegians and Danes is made in the early English annals, and it is left for us to draw what conclusions we may from the general direction of the attacks. In 846 a Viking band attempted to land on the coast of Somersetshire, but they were defeated by Bishop Ealhstan and two ealdormen at the mouth of the Parret. The locality of the fight makes it probable that this band, at least, were Norsemen from the coast of Ireland. The *Three Fragments of Irish Annals* states that in the year 851 the Norsemen attacked Devonshire, while the Danes harried Kent and Surrey. This agrees in the main with the *Anglo-Saxon Chronicle*, which records for the same year the fact that the ealdorman Ceorl fought with heathen men in Devonshire, near Wicgeanbeorge, killed many of them, and gained the victory.

These raids on the coast seem to have been mere skirmishes preliminary to the more general advance which began in 851, when a fleet of 350 ships entered the Thames River. A force was landed, which captured Canterbury, while the fleet proceeded to London, which was stormed and plundered. The invading host began to spread over the inland districts, but King Ethelwulf and his son Ethelbald arrived with the whole military force of Wessex, and defeated the Vikings in the bloody battle of Aclea. This produced a brief lull in the invasion, but a new host appeared in 854, and, taking up quarters on Sheppey Island, in the Thames, they were now able for the first time to spend the winter in England.

Every summer the attacks were renewed, until, in 866, the great Viking army led by Ivar Boneless and Ubbe or Hubba, the sons of Ragnar Lodbrok, arrived and began a conquest which placed the greater part of England under Viking dominion before another decade had passed. This time the attack was directed against Northumbria, which was more torn by internal troubles than any other part of England. Wars between rival candidates for the throne had been waged there constantly for many years, and were still in progress when the Vikings arrived. They mixed merrily in the fight, and made themselves masters of the important city of York, a calamity so great that it even brought the two fighting rivals, Osbeorht and Aella, to their senses. They patched up their differences, united their forces, and made an assault upon York in an attempt to recapture the city. But they were both killed, their army was cut to pieces, and Northumbria submitted to the conquerors, 867.

In 868 the Viking chieftains advanced with their army to Nottingham, and wintered in Mercia. In 870 they entered East Anglia. King Edmund met them in the battle of Hoxne, but lost both his army and his life. The story is told that he was captured, and, being unwilling to pay tribute, and to submit to Ivar Boneless, he was tied to a tree and shot to death with arrows. This may be true, since he was worshiped as a saint not long after his death.

The Danes at York invited the Norwegian kings Ivar and Olaf of Dublin to join in the conquest of England. They accepted the invitation, harried northern England, and captured Dumbarton on the Clyde; but they soon had to return to Dublin to defend their own dominions against the Irish. In 870 a large army came from Denmark to join in the conquest. It was led by Halvdan (Halfdene), Hubba (Ubbe), Guthrum (Guttorm or Gorm), and many other kings and jarls. The next year they advanced through Mercia to attack Wessex, and pitched their camp at Reading, which they took care to fortify. A fierce campaign was now fought. The men of

Wessex, led by King Ethelred and his younger brother, Alfred, advanced to attack them, and a series of sharp engagements were fought which forced the Danes to retire to their fortified camp at Reading. An attempt to take the camp by assault proved unsuccessful, and the English were driven back with great slaughter. The Danes now emerged from their camp, but were again met by Ethelred and Alfred on the hills of Escesdun (Ashdown), where they were defeated, after a desperate battle in which the young Alfred especially distinguished himself. The Danes lost one of their kings, Begsceg, five jarls and many thousand men. The remaining king, Halvdan, shut himself up in the camp at Reading with the remnant of his army to await reinforcements.

In two weeks he was again able to take the field, fighting a successful engagement at Basing, and the battle of Bedwyn soon followed, in which the Danes were again victorious. King Ethelred died shortly after from wounds received in the battle, as it seems, and Alfred the Great succeeded to the throne of Wessex. As he had but a small army, and no navy, he was forced to buy peace from the victorious Vikings. They received a tribute, and withdrew from Wessex, and the kingdom was left unmolested for about four years. During this time Alfred began to organize a navy, which in future contests was to develop strength and efficiency in the hard school of sharp naval warfare with the powerful Viking admirals, who regarded the sea as their own undisputed domain.

The Viking army, after leaving London and subjugating Mercia, was divided into two parts, one under King Halvdan, and the other under Guthrum, Aasketil and Aamund. Halvdan raided Bernicia, Strathclyde and parts of Scotland, and settled permanently at York, in 875. The other part of the army camped in Mercia. All England was now in the hands of the invaders, save the kingdom of Wessex, south of the Thames.

During the 80 or 90 years which had passed since the first Viking bands visited the shores of England, great changes had taken place both in the extent and character of their operations in foreign countries. The early piratic attacks changed in time into well-planned expeditions undertaken by large fleets and armies bent on permanent conquest. Wars were waged which were often attended by wanton destruction of life and property, but the Vikings now fought for the purpose of gaining full dominion over territory in which they wished to live and rule. They were no longer a mere destructive force. The conquest once accomplished, they settled down to till the soil, to build cities and to develop the country. In the various pursuits of peace they often showed an energy, a practical insight and a talent for organization not exhibited by the native inhabitants. In many fields they exerted a stimulating influence which made future progress possible.

During the winter which King Halvdan spent in London after retiring from Wessex, he minted coins bearing sometimes his own name, sometimes that of the city. The designs were later used on English coins struck by Alfred the Great, and by Ceolwulf, king of Mercia. In 875 Halvdan took up his permanent abode in York. The *Anglo-Saxon Chronicle* states that he portioned out the lands of Northumbria, and that his followers henceforth continued to plow and to till them. Every Dane received his allotment of land, while the original inhabitants continued to exist as a dependent class. According to Viking custom York was strongly fortified, and became again the great city which it had been in the days of Roman dominion in Britain. This custom of walling in the cities, and of building fortified strongholds, which was so important, both in warfare and for the development of cities, was first introduced into England by the Vikings. The coining of money was also carried on here, and the crude copper coins heretofore used were soon replaced by coins of silver. Deira, the southern part of Northumbria, was organized into the Danish kingdom of York, while Bernicia, the northern part, was tributary to the kings of York, but formed no integral part of their kingdom.

ALFRED THE GREAT AND THE VIKINGS

After Alfred had entered into an agreement with the Vikings, Wessex enjoyed peace for some years, but in 875 the Viking host was again collected for a new attack on the kingdom. The invaders marched across Wessex to Wareham, on the south coast, where they constructed a fortified camp. Alfred met them here with a large force, and the two armies lay watching each other for some time. The Danes finally agreed to depart if they received a tribute, and a treaty was concluded, but a part of their force escaped from Wareham and marched to Exeter, which they seized and fortified. Alfred followed close on their heels, and besieged the town. The remainder of the force at Wareham soon evacuated their camp and put to sea to join their besieged companions, but their fleet was destroyed in a storm, and the detachment at Exeter, being hard pressed by Alfred, promised to leave Wessex. Alfred allowed them to depart, and they advanced into

Mercia, where they forced King Ceolwulf to give them a large part of his kingdom. This land was divided among many jarls; the five most important divisions being: Stamford, Lincoln, Derby, Nottingham and Leicester, which were later known as the 'Five Boroughs'. All the divisions formed together a loose confederacy embracing the eastern half of Mercia.

The great Viking army was still kept united under the command of King Guthrum (Guttorm). Aided by other forces operating in the Irish Sea, they again advanced to attack Wessex. An auxiliary squadron was led by Hubba (Ubbe), a brother of Halvdan and Ivar Boneless, and Guthrum began his campaign in the middle of January, 878. The unexpected attack at this season of the year caused the greatest panic. Many fled the country without thinking of resistance, and King Alfred with his military household was forced to take refuge on the island of Athelney, in the Parret River in Somerset. During the remaining months of the winter of 878 the Vikings were masters of all Wessex, but when spring came, the tide began to turn. Hubba fell in Devonshire in an attack on the English stronghold Cynuit, and his force was cut to pieces. Shortly after Easter, Alfred left Athelney, gathered all forces possible, and attacked the Danish army at Ethandun, gaining a complete victory. Guthrum submitted, and received baptism with 29 other leaders. The treaty concluded received its name from the royal manor of Wedmore, where the baptismal feast was celebrated. According to its stipulations, a region including Northumbria, East Anglia and all central England east of a line stretching from the mouth of the Thames River along the River Lea to Bedford, along the Ouse to Watling Street, and along Watling Street to Chester, was ceded to the Vikings. This region was henceforth known as the 'Danelag' (Danelaw). Guthrum seems to have carried out quite faithfully the agreement entered into. He left Wessex, and took possession of East Anglia and Essex, where he founded a kingdom similar to that established in York by King Halvdan. He took part in Viking expeditions to France, and even aided Danish Vikings operating on the coast of England, but he never again attacked Wessex. He died in 890.

After the treaty of Wedmore, in 878, Alfred's kingdom enjoyed comparative peace until 892, when the 'Great Army' undertook a new invasion of England. This permanently organized host of Danish Vikings had been operating in Brabant and Flanders, where it had been defeated by Emperor Arnulf, in 891. The names of the leaders of the 'Great Army' are not mentioned, but it was joined by a smaller detachment of 80 ships, evidently coming from the Norwegian colonies on the west coast of France led by the famous Viking chieftain Hasting. The war lasted for three years, but the Vikings could gain no permanent advantage over Alfred's well-organized armies. Alfred captured their fleet, and besieged them closely in their camps. Finally, worn out by fruitless fighting, the 'Great Army' broke up, and joined their countrymen in East Anglia and Northumbria, but a detachment sailed across the sea to the Seine. These must have been the Norsemen under Hasting, with whom Alfred seems to have concluded a treaty of peace. Alfred had broken up the great organized host of invasion, and had created an efficient fleet which was able to cope successfully with Viking detachments along the coast. Hasting left England in 897, and the peace was not again disturbed during the remaining four years of Alfred's reign.

King Halvdan of York had ruled his kingdom only one year (876–77), when he was expelled by his own people. His successor, Gudrød, died in 894, and Knut, who was then placed on the throne, had to share his authority with the Norwegian jarl, Sigurd, who had gained great power in northern Scotland. This shows that there were Norsemen, as well as Danes, in the Viking kingdom at York, an assumption which is borne out by the many names of Norwegian origin found in Northumbria. Snorre Sturluson says in the *Heimskringla* that Northumbria was mostly settled by Norsemen after the sons of Lodbrok had conquered the land. Norwegians and Danes must often have fought side by side, and, the conquest once completed, a period of immigration followed in which men and women from both countries flocked across the sea to settle in the new and inviting land which they had won. During the first stages of the struggle the invading armies were almost exclusively Danish, but the Norwegian element must have grown rapidly in importance, especially in the North, and their leaders soon gained the ascendancy in Northumbria.

NAMES APPLIED TO THE VIKINGS

Long before the beginning of the Viking Age the Gautar (Gotar), Swedes, and Danes seem to have been quite well known as distinct peoples, occupying clearly defined regions of the Scandinavian North. The names are used frequently both by early Old English authors and by Latin writers of the early centuries of the Christian era. But Norway, as a term applied to the western half of the Scandinavian peninsula, and Norsemen, or Norwegians, as a name used to designate all the inhabitants of this region, are terms which do not occur till in the Viking period. The notice in the *Anglo-Saxon Chronicle* for the year 787, already mentioned elsewhere, uses the name *Nordmanna*: 'On his dagum comon III scipu Norðmanna of Hereðalande.' King Alfred uses the name *Norðmenn* in his writings (880–900), and Olithere (Ottar), the Norwegian explorer, who stayed at his court, uses the names *Norðmannaland* and *Norðweg* for the whole of Norway. The Irish monk Decuil, who wrote in 825, states that the Irish monks on the Faroe Islands had to flee because of the *Latronum Normannorum*. It seems, then, that these names must have been quite commonly used about 800. Norway (Noregr, Norvegr, Norge) means the northern way, and Norsemen, men from the North. These names seem first to have been applied to the Norwegians and their country by their neighbours in southern Sweden and Denmark. On the continent the Vikings, both Danes and Norwegians, were, as a rule, called Northmen, or Norsemen, while in England and Scotland they were called Danes.

In Ireland they were called Gall (strangers) or Normanni (Norsemen). Later, when the Danes also began to harry the country, the Irish called the Norsemen Finn-Gall (fair strangers), and the Danes Dubh-Gall (dark strangers). The country whence the Norsemen came is called Lochlann (the land of the fjords) by the Irish annalists already in the ninth century. From this word a new name was in time formed for the Norwegian Vikings, namely Lochlannac or the people from Lochlann.

STRUGGLE BETWEEN NORSEMEN AND DANES IN IRELAND

The Norwegian Vikings overran Ireland with astonishing rapidity. Shortly after the close of the eighth century they were found in nearly every part of the island. Dr. [Heinrich] Zimmer says: 'If we read the annals of the period 795–950, we are compelled to ask if there were a cloister, a lake, a mountain, a valley, a brook on the island where the Vikings had not been, or where they had not dwelt in great numbers for a longer or shorter period.' Year by year colonists arrived with their families from Norway to take possession of districts where the army of conquest had gained more or less firm control. The Irish were warlike, and could often meet the invaders in overwhelming numbers, but they were unable to carry on a successful campaign of defence for want of systematic organization. It would have required the united strength of the whole country to withstand so formidable an invasion, but the obsolete Irish clan system stood in the way of centralization of power, and of effective cooperation in the common cause. The high king (Ard Righ) was indeed regarded as over-king of all Erin, but his exalted station was at the time an empty title which carried with it no real authority. Civil strife between hostile clans and petty princes was the normal condition throughout all Ireland. Many of the natives even abandoned Christianity and joined the Vikings, aiding them in the attacks upon their own country. They were called 'Gall-Gedhel' or 'Irish strangers'. The Irish people often fought with reckless bravery, and gained many a victory over the enemy, but their planless efforts could not stay the progress of the invaders. Not till complete subjugation or ultimate extermination stared them in the face did they think of seeking refuge where alone it can be found under such circumstances, in unselfish and systematic cooperation; and even then the lesson was but indifferently learned.

The Norsemen operated, on the whole, with skill and caution, employing tactics which we have observed in Viking expeditions elsewhere. With their fleets they entered the fjords and estuaries, where they constructed fortified camps, or founded cities, and built strong castles, as at Dublin. Sometimes they would establish their camps and naval stations on islands near the coast, where they could not be attacked by the Irish, who possessed no war vessels of any kind. From such a fortified base of operations they would ascend the rivers to the lakes of the interior, where they would build other strongholds at well-selected strategic points, from which they were able to control the neighbouring districts with a comparatively small force. Turgeis sent a part of his fleet up the Bann River into Loch Neagh, in the north-eastern part of Ireland, and with another part he ascended the Shannon River to Loch Ree, in the very heart of the island, where, according to the annals, he built a number of strongholds. Their firmest hold was on the coast region, where colonists and reinforcements could be received at any time. In the shelter of their camps at Strangford, Carlingford, Dublin, Wicklow, Limerick and other places, permanent Norwegian colonies sprang up which, in course of time, extruded themselves along the coast from the Boyne River to Cork, while more isolated areas were settled at Dundalk and Limerick. The numerous Norwegian names of islands, bays, headlands, cities and localities along the Irish coast, which in anglicized form have been preserved to the present time, attest to the thorough and permanent occupation of these parts by the Norsemen.

THE VIKING EXPEDITIONS EASTWARD

When the Scandinavians entered into communication with the peoples dwelling east of the Baltic Sea cannot be determined, but it is quite certain that such an intercourse existed from very early times, since even the oldest historic traditions mention expeditions made by Swedish kings to the countries across the Baltic. The first account of the old Yngling dynasty is given by the Norwegian skald Thjodolv af Hvin in his song 'Ynglingatal'. Among the old kings of Svitiod here mentioned is Vanlande, a great warrior who visited many foreign lands, and at one time spent the winter in Finland.

Agne, another king of the same dynasty, subjugated Finland, and brought with him home the daughter of the Finnish prince. Ingvar and his son Anund, two other kings of the Yngling family, made expeditions to Estonia, and brought great booty home. These traditions point to a connection between Scandinavia and the regions east of the Baltic in very early ages. This is further verified through the more reliable evidence of archaeological finds, which prove that the Scandinavians must have paid frequent visits to the eastern shores of the Baltic, that their civilization was transplanted to those regions, and that they must have founded settlements there in many places. These finds are especially numerous in Tavastland and Satakunda, in southern Finland, but they have also been made in many other places.

Of special interest is the account given by the Russian chronicler Nestor of the founding of the kingdom of Russia by the Swedes. Nestor was a monk in Kief in the latter part of the eleventh century. He tells the story as follows: 'In the year 6367 after the creation of the world (859 CE), the Varangians came across the sea and exacted tribute from the Tchouds and the Slavs, from the Merians, Vesses and Krivitches. In the year 6370 (862 CE) they (i.e., the Slavs) drove away the Varangians across the sea, paid them no tribute and began to rule themselves; but disorder prevailed. One tribe rose against the other, there was enmity between them, and they began to wage war on each other. Then they said to each other: "Let us get a prince who can rule over us, and who can judge rightly." And they went across the sea to the Varangians, to the Russians, for so the Varangians are called, while some are called Swedes, others Norsemen, others Angles, and Goths. And the Tchouds, the Slavs, the Krivitches and the Vesses said to the Russians: "Our land is large and fertile, but there is no order there; come, therefore, and rule over us." Three brothers were chosen, and they took with them all the Rus, and they came. And the oldest, Rurik, settled in Novgorod, and the second, Sineus, at Bieloe-Ozero, and the third at Izborsk; his name was Trouvor. From these Varangians the Russian kingdom received its name; that is the Novgorodians; these are the Novgorodian peoples of Varangian descent; before the Novgorodians were Slavs. After two years had passed, Sineus died, and also his brother Trouvor. Rurik then became ruler in their stead, and gave cities to his men; to one he gave Polotsk, to another Rostof, to a third Bieloe-Ozero. Into these places the Varangians had immigrated; the former inhabitants in Novgorod being Slavs, in Polotsk Krivitches, in Rostof Merians, in Bieloe-Ozero Vesses.'

The Frankish annals tell of an embassy sent by the Byzantine emperor, Theophilos, to the Frankish emperor, Louis the Pious. Along with this embassy came some men who said that they were from a people by the name of Ros, that they had been sent as messengers by their king to the emperor at Byzantium, and wished now, with Louis' aid, to return to their own country, because the route which they had followed to Constantinople led through the lands of strange and barbarous peoples, where it was very dangerous to travel. Upon closer investigation Louis found that they were Swedes.

That Rurik and his followers, the Varangians, or Russians, came from Scandinavia is seen also from the great number of names of unmistakable Scandinavian origin in early Russian history. The names of Rurik's successors, Oleg and Igor, are but slightly altered forms of the Scandinavian names Helge and Ivar, or Ingvar. The representatives sent by these rulers to conclude peace with the Byzantine emperor in 912 and 945 had Scandinavian names. As examples may be mentioned: Karl, Inegeld, Ivar, Vuefast, Uleb, Bern, Schigbern, Turbern, Grim, Kol, Sven, Gunnar, etc. As late as in the eleventh century the name Oleg was still used in the Russian dynasty.

In the beginning Novgorod or Holmgard was the chief city in the new Russian kingdom, but soon Kief grew into great importance, and became the real capital.

Great trade routes were opened along the Volga to Astrakhan, and along the Dnieper to the shores of the Black Sea. Here the Varangians met the Arab tradesmen, and a lively commercial intercourse sprang up, through which a great number of coins and other articles of value were brought to Scandinavia. Kief, which was situated on this main trade route, reached its highest splendour in the time of King Jaroslaf. He wished his capital to rival Constantinople, and Kief became famous as the 'city of four hundred churches'.

The Varangian prince Ivar of Novgorod concluded a treaty of commerce with the emperor of the Byzantine Empire, and traders and slave dealers carried on a steadily growing traffic along the Volga and the Dnieper to Novgorod and the shores of the Baltic Sea. Many names of towns and waterfalls along these routes still preserve the memory of the Scandinavian traders and travellers who sojourned in those regions in ages past. As an illustration may be mentioned Bjarkowitz, a Russian form of the Scandinavian Bjarkø, an island near the coast of Ingermanland, where a trading station was located. The kings of Sweden and Norway were related to the Russian princes through marriage, and often sent them troops when needed, or they sought refuge with them in times of trouble at home. A lively intercourse between Scandinavia and Russia, or Gardarike, as it was usually called in the North, continued till the death of Jaroslaf in 1045. The Slavs then gained the ascendancy, and Scandinavian influence in Russia came to an end. Through the Varangians these dark and far-off regions were brought into the daylight of history; colonies were founded, cities were built, commerce and government were established and this hitherto unknown domain was opened to the forces of civilization and progress. Russia became under Varangian rule a European kingdom, aspiring to rival in culture the nations most advanced in those times, something that cannot be said of Russia through many centuries after the Scandinavians had ceased to rule.

After having penetrated the wilds of Russia, and established permanent communication with the Black Sea, it was comparatively easy for the enterprising Vikings to push across that sea to Constantinople, or Myklegard (the great city), as they called it. Nestor says that a number of Varangians in the service of Vladimir the Great of Russia became dissatisfied and went to Constantinople. This is said to have happened about 980, but these were not the first Varangians in the Byzantine Empire. The emperor had already at that time an army of Scandinavian warriors who served, not only as his bodyguard, but were also used in active warfare in different parts of the Empire. Most famous of all the Scandinavians in Constantinople was Harald Sigurdsson, son of the Norwegian king, Sigurd Syr, and a half-brother of King Olaf Haraldsson (St. Olaf). He became chief of the Varangians in Constantinople, and took part in many campaigns in Syria, Armenia, Palestine, Sicily and Africa. He captured many fortified cities, and gathered immense treasures. Snorre says that there was a law, that when the Greek emperor died, the Varangians should have *polata-svaro* [robbery of the palace]. They were then allowed to go through all the royal palaces where the treasures were stored, and take what they could seize with their hands. Harald Sigurdsson had three times taken part in such a *polata-svaro* in Constantinople. He returned to Novgorod with great treasures, married King Jaroslaf's daughter, and became later king of Norway. As such he is known as Harald Haardraade.

An object which preserves in an interesting way the memory of the Vikings in the Byzantine Empire is the great marble lion from Piraeus, now standing at the entrance to the arsenal in Venice, where it was brought by the Venetians in 1687, after they had captured Athens. On this monument is found a delicately carved runic inscription in the snake-loop design so familiar from Scandinavian runestones. The characters are so nearly effaced that the inscription cannot be read, but it silently points to the days when Harald Sigurdsson and the Varangians served the Byzantine emperor in Constantinople and Jerusalem, and measured swords with the Saracens in Asia and Africa.

LIFE AND CULTURE OF THE VIKING AGE

Intellectual culture is a complex and delicate fabric into which the fibres of experience and the finer filaments of secret and mysterious influence are deftly woven. Social environment and native talent fashion the texture, but the threads have been brought from many climes, and every age has been laid under tribute. Wherever higher culture has been produced, a process of absorption of new elements, an accumulation of new experience, a borrowing and importation, have freely taken place. The stimulus produced by the new, with the attendant reaction of the native mind upon it, primarily determines all new cultural growth. The Greeks borrowed from the Orient, the Romans from the Greeks; from both came culture and Christianity to the rest of Europe. Even the far North had felt the thrill of this influence long before the Viking Age began, but the process of absorption of new elements had been slow, and the development uneventful. No sudden changes are noticeable till the migrations sweep over Europe, and roll high the billows of general tumult and upheaval.

The quickening effect of this great movement tore the peoples of the North from their ancient moorings, and as Vikings they burst forth, adding new terror to this dark and bloody period. In this first outburst of pent-up energy and unrestrained passions we see the worst instincts of a primitive race let loose in savage warfare which often throws the deepest shadow on the pages of Viking history. But justice even here constrains us to admit that it is but a shade deeper than a similar shadow which falls over the history of all human warfare. To consider minutely all the acts of vandalism and cruelty perpetrated by the Vikings would not even give us the satisfaction of having shown that their system of plunder and bloodshed differed essentially from that of the Roman generals, of the pious crusaders, the defenders of the faith, and most Christian princes of later, and more enlightened, ages. It must also be borne in mind that on these expeditions we meet the Vikings as warriors, and that the outrages often committed can furnish no adequate criterion for judging their life and culture in general.

The nature of the Viking campaigns furnishes an easy explanation of the panic which seems to have seized the inhabitants of the countries exposed to their attacks. A cruel fate usually befell the towns and cities they seized. Not only did they kill and plunder, and carry women off into slavery, but they spared no sanctuary, and nothing holy could stay their rapacious and destructive hands. When the battle was over, and the victory won, they would celebrate the event in drunken carousals in which the skulls of their fallen enemies often served as wine bowls, and other acts equally gruesome were committed, which might well strike Christian hearts with horror. Even human beings are known to have been sacrificed to the gods, and when a city was taken, children would be transfixed with spears, and 'given to Odin' amid wild outbursts of triumphant rejoicing. If we add that by means of their fleets they could depart at will, only to reappear at the most unexpected moments, that the inhabitants often felt powerless over against this dreaded enemy, we can understand the people's superstitious fear, the sad laments and exaggerated stories of the old writers, and the prayers offered up in the Christian churches: 'From the fury of the Northmen, Lord God, deliver us!'

Intellectually and culturally the whole period was one of general contraction and retrogression, in which ancient arts and civilization were forgotten, and ignorance and rude manners prevailed. Viewing the period thus, we may justly term it the Dark Ages. A tone of retrospection and sadness was prevalent among those who possessed learning and culture. They looked backward to the days of Greece and Rome as to a golden age that would never return. The sun had set, they thought; the world would never again become what it had been in ancient times; their only consolation was that after death there awaited the Christian a blissful life in heaven. But these dark centuries represent not only the downfall of the old, but also the birth of the new. Viewed from this side, we find the period to be an era of expansion and development in which old barriers were broken, and new opportunities were given to the peoples which had hitherto been regarded as dwelling outside the pale of civilization.

On their expeditions the Vikings had come into direct communication with nearly every part of the then known world. Their sphere of activity was thus immensely widened, and their ideas of the world were altered correspondingly. New ideas from the Christian faith, from Greco-Roman civilization, and from Irish poesy and learning poured into the North, and became the leaven which brought the half-slumbering energies of the Scandinavian peoples into full activity. A new culture was produced which soon placed the peoples of the North in the front rank of enlightened and progressive nations. Norway and her colony Iceland became the centre of literary activity in northern Europe during the Middle Ages, and Norse mythology was elaborated into a system which, though inferior to that of Greece in beauty, surpasses it in depth and grandeur. The Scandinavians became leaders in navigation, commerce, and discovery, and developed a system of laws and government which has left deep and lasting traces wherever permanent Viking settlements were founded.

The maritime enterprise and naval warfare attending the Viking expeditions gave a great stimulus to shipbuilding and navigation in the North. We have seen that even before this period the Scandinavians possessed great skill in shipbuilding, and could construct vessels of considerable size. In the Viking Age a great demand made itself felt for vessels suited for long voyages, and able to carry as large a number of warriors as possible. In the Mediterranean Sea they became acquainted with Greek and Roman ships, and every effort was now made to construct ships of large size, and of improved type.

The larger sea-going ships were of two kinds: merchant ships and war vessels. An early type of merchant ship was the *kjoll*, but during the greater part of the Viking Age the *knarre* and the *byrding* were common types. Later a larger-sized vessel, the *busse*, came into use, and still later the *kogge*, which soon developed into a war vessel. The merchant ships were quite broad and high in proportion to their length, with half-decks in the prow and stern. The goods were placed in the undecked middle part of the vessel. The ship had one mast and a four-cornered sail. The mast could be folded down, and would then rest on supports high enough so that a person could conveniently pass under it. The oar-shaped rudder was fixed to the right side of the vessel, near the stern. This side was, therefore, called the *steerboard*, while the left side, which was at the back of the helmsman, was called the *backboard*. Oars were used only in the front and rear ends of the vessel.

Of the warships the *askr* and the *elliði* were older types, which seem to have differed little from the ordinary merchant vessel. A later type was the *long ship*, so called, because it was long and narrow, with high prow and stern. This type seems to have come into use in the tenth century. These ships were beautifully painted in various colours, and were ornamented with wood carvings. Oars were used along the whole ship, and on both sides hung a row of shields painted black and yellow alternately. The prow was gilt and shaped like the head of a bird or animal; usually like that of a dragon. The sails were usually striped, red, blue and green, and were often made of costly material. The warships were divided into various classes according to their shape and size, and the service for which they were intended. The *skeið* was a narrow, swift sailing vessel. The *snekkja* was supplied with a sort of snout. The *drage* or dragon ship was larger than ordinary, with a prow like a dragon's head, and a stern often shaped like a dragon's tail. The *barði* was also a large ship, built for the special purpose of ramming and sinking the ships of the enemy. It had iron rams, both on prow and stern. The warships had a full deck, and second half decks in bow and stern. The forward half deck was called the *forstavnsdek*, and the rear half-deck *løftingen*. Another classification was made according to size by counting the number of row-benches on one side of the ship. In this classification the ships were known as 13-bench, 15-bench, 20-bench, 30-bench; etc., with 26, 30, 40 and 60 oars. The most common size was the 20-bench, with 40 oars, and a crew of 90 men. On the 30-bench there were two men to each oar, or 120 rowers, the crew consisting all together of about 260 men. King Olaf Tryggvasson's famous ship, the Long Serpent, is said to have had a crew of 300 men.

The scattered Viking bands, which operated in a more desultory way at the beginning of the period, were gradually united under aide leaders into fleets and armies of great size. *The Anglo-Saxon Chronicle* shows how the Viking fleets in England were growing:

Year 787 – In his (King Breohtric's) days came three ships of Northmen from Hereðaland.

Year 833 – In this year King Ecgbyrht fought with the crews of 35 ships at Carrum.

Year 840 – In this year King Ethelwulf fought at Carrum against the men of 35 ships.

Year 851 – In this year 350 ships came to the mouth of the Thames, and the men landed and took Canterbury and London by storm.

Year 877 – 120 ships were wrecked at Swanawic.

Year 893 – In this year the great army ... returned, ... and came to land at Limenemouth with 250 ships.

At this time the ships must have been of the older and smaller types; but if we assume that each ship had a crew of only 40 men, 350 vessels would bring an army of 14,000 warriors. Similar numbers of ships are mentioned by many other sources. The chroniclers describe in glowing colours the vast numbers of the invaders. They are compared to swarms of grasshoppers that cover the earth. The Viking ships, says an Arabian writer, fill the ocean like a flock of red birds. An Irish annalist says that the ocean rolls billows of strangers over all Erin. Fleet upon fleet is spewed out by the sea, so that there is not a spot in the island where their ships are not found.

Excepting the ships of the Saracens in Spain, and the small beginning made by King Alfred in England, the peoples of western Europe had as yet no fleets. These great naval armaments, therefore, gave the Vikings an advantage which largely explains the success which they achieved in their campaigns.

The size of the army was no less imposing than that of the fleet. At the siege of Paris in 885 the Vikings had 40,000 men, of which 30,000 probably constituted the actual fighting force, if we may believe the old sources. In the battle of Saucourt 9,000 Vikings are said to have fallen. But the success of the Vikings was due to their superior training and equipment rather than to the size of their armies, which in many cases seems to be exaggerated. Professor [Charles William Chadwick] Oman says: 'But no less important than the command of the sea was the superiority of the individual Viking in battle to the average member of the host that came out against him. The war bands of the invaders were the pick of the North, all volunteers, all trained warriors. In a Frankish or an English host the only troops that could safely be opposed to them, man to man, were the personal following of the kings and ealdormen of England — or the dukes and counts of the continent. And these were but a small fraction of the hasty levy that assembled, when news came that the Danes were ashore at Bremen or Boulogne, at Sandwich or Weymouth. The majority of the *hereban* of a Frankish county, or the *fyrd* of an English shire, was composed of farmers fresh from the plow, not of trained fighting men. Enormous superiority of numbers could alone compensate for the differences in military efficiency. If that superiority existed, the raider quietly retired to his ships, or to his fortified island base. If it did not, he fell upon the landsfolk and made a dreadful slaughter of them. How could it be expected that the ceorl, who came out to war with spear and target alone, should contend on equal terms with the Northmen equipped with steel cap and mail shirt, and well trained to form the shield wall for defence and the war wedge for attack? Working against the hastily arrayed masses of the landsfolk, the Viking host was like a good military machine beating upon an ill-compacted earthwork.'

The Viking army was a strong and permanent organization, with able commanders and officers. It had infantry and cavalry, spies, sappers and a well-organized commissariat. It had catapults and battering rams, and other machinery for the carrying on of sieges. Military tactics were well developed; there was strict discipline, and perfect obedience to authority.

CAUSES OF THE VIKING EXPEDITIONS

The Viking expeditions may have been due to a number of causes. In the Scandinavian countries, with their limited area of tillable soil, and their extensive seacoast, a seafaring life was necessitated from the start, which produced a hardy and energetic race, and fostered the spirit of daring and adventure which expresses itself in the whole movement. The size of the Viking armies indicates clearly that the population, in the North was increasing at a very rapid rate during this period, owing, no doubt, to polygamy, which, in one form or another, was extensively practiced. The number of those who found it necessary to follow war as a permanent occupation was growing. According to the old laws ('Frostathingslov' and 'Gulathingslov') all sons shared equally in the inheritance, but as both political power and social standing depended on wealth, and especially on the ownership of land, the aristocracy would not sell their estates, nor would they destroy them by dividing them into small parcels. The young men were partly encouraged, partly driven by necessity to seek their fortune on expeditions to foreign countries. Led by love of adventure, and encouraged by the prospects of wealth and fame, they flocked to the standards of the Viking chieftains in such numbers that the movement soon became a migration, and extensive campaigns were waged for conquest and colonization. The women and children usually accompanied the men, and were left in fortified camps while the army advanced to the attack. [...]

Before the arrival of the Norsemen, the Irish had no ships, only boats made of skin, frail craft in which, however, they had been able to reach the distant islands. They had no cities or commerce, and they coined no money. To facilitate trade, the Norsemen introduced in Ireland a system of weights and measures, and here, as in Britain, they began to coin money. The words *mark* and *penning* have been incorporated into the Irish language as *marc* and *pingind*. The growth of towns as centres of trade followed as a direct result of Viking settlement and the development of commerce. Waterford, Cork, Limerick and other cities founded by the Vikings became important trading places, while Dublin developed into one of the leading emporiums of commerce in northern Europe. Silks, and costly cloth of all kinds, leather, wines and other products from the South were imported to Dublin, whence they were again brought by merchants to Norway, Denmark, Sweden and Iceland. How rich and flourishing the Viking cities in Ireland were can be seen also from accounts of contemporary writers. In 941–42 King Muirchertach made a journey through all Ireland; he also visited Dublin, and nowhere did he receive such presents as there. In a song written by a contemporary poet his reception is described as follows:

> 'A supply of his full store was given
> to Muirchertach, son of Niall,
> of bacon, of good and perfect wheat;
> also was got a blood-debt of red gold.
>
> Joints (of meat), and fine cheese (were given)
> by the very good and very pure queen,
> and then was given, (a thing) to hear,
> a coloured mantle for each chieftain.'

After the battle of Glenmama, in the year 1000, King Brian captured Dublin. 'In this one place,' says the old writer, 'there were found the greatest treasures of gold, silver and findrun (a sort of white bronze), of precious stones, carbuncles, drinking horns and beautiful goblets.'

'The Norsemen brought with them to Ireland the ideas of cities, commerce and municipal life hitherto unknown,' says [historian] Aug. J. Thebaud. 'The introduction of these supposed a total change necessary in the customs of the natives, and stringent regulations to which the people could not but be radically opposed.... No more stringent rules could be devised, whether for municipal, rural or social regulations; and, as the Northmen are known to have been of a systematic mind, no stronger proof of this fact could be given.'

Also in the Scandinavian countries at home, and elsewhere along all the routes of trade, cities sprang into existence under the stimulating influence of Viking commerce. Rouen, in Normandy, became the most important trading centre in France, and merchant vessels from Norway and Iceland anchored in the Seine. In Norway the new commercial town of Tunsberg, on the Christianiafjord, soon outdistanced the older Skiringssal; and Konghelle, a new trading town, was founded in the south-eastern part. Haløre, probably located on the coast of Skåne, in Sweden, and Brannøerne, near the mouth of the Gota River, became important commercial centres.

A lively intercourse was also maintained between Ireland and the English seacoast towns across the Irish Sea, which had either been founded or developed by the Vikings. Several of these towns grew into prominence, such as Swansea, Tenby,

Chester and especially Bristol, which had become a great trading centre, and in course of time superseded Dublin and Waterford as the greatest commercial city on the shores of the Irish Sea. In the Midlands the towns of the 'Five Boroughs', Lincoln, Leicester, Nottingham, Stamford and Derby became cities of importance, and on the east coast of England, Grimsby and York grew into prominence. At the time of the *Domesday Book*, York was, next to London and Winchester, the largest city in England.

In speaking of the influence of the Vikings on the development of English commerce, Mr. W. [William] Cunningham [Scottish economic historian] says: 'The English were satisfied with rural life; they were little attracted by the towns which the Romans had built, and they did not devote themselves to commercial pursuits or to manufacturing articles for sale. The Danes, though so closely allied in race, appear to have been men of a different type. They were great as traders and also as seamen. We may learn how great their prowess was from the records of their voyages to Iceland, Greenland and America, from accounts of their expeditions to the White Sea and the Baltic, and from their commerce with such distant places as the Crimea and Arabia. Their settlements in this country were among the earliest of the English towns to exhibit signs of activity. Not only were the Danes traders; they were also skilled in metal work and other industrial pursuits. England has attained a character for her shipping and has won the supremacy of the world in manufacturing; it almost seems as if she were indebted, on those sides of life on which she is most successful, to the fresh energy and enterprise ingrafted by Danish settlers and conquerors. By the efforts of

Roman missionaries she had been brought into contact with the remains of Roman civilization, but by the infusion of the Danish element she was drawn into close connection with the most energetic of the Northern races.' Augustus J. Thebaud says: 'Endowed with all the characteristics of the Scandinavian race, deeply infused with the blood of the Danes and the Northmen, she (England) has all the indomitable energy, all the systematic grasp of mind and sternness of purpose joined to the wise spirit of compromise and conservatism of the men of the far North. She, of all nations, has inherited their great power of expansion at sea, possessing all the roving propensities of the old Vikings, and the spirit of trade, enterprise, and colonization of those old Phoenicians of the arctic circle.'

A similar influence was exerted by the Norsemen on the naval development of France. 'It is the great achievement of the Normans,' says [historian Georges Bernard] Depping, 'that they gave France a navy. There was no longer any navy in France, and she had ceased to be numbered among maritime nations. The Normans re-established the marine, and William the Conqueror succeeded in forming a fleet, the like of which France had not seen. The conquests made by the Normans in Sicily were due in part to their superiority in navigation.' It may be due to the same influence that Normandy furnishes more sailors and pilots than any other part of France, and that many of the leading French admirals have been Normans.

We have seen that the Vikings had early learned to build fortifications and stone towers of great strength, that, besides the fortified camps, and strongholds built for military purposes, they also surrounded their towns and cities, especially in the colonies, with walls and moats which virtually made them fortresses of great military importance. The building of castles was first developed in Normandy, and the *donjon* or square tower, so typical in medieval castles, is thought to be of Viking origin. In Ireland the Norsemen began to build fortified strongholds as early as 840. Cork was fortified in 866, and in a saga of the eleventh century Limerick is called 'the city with riveted stones'. Dublin, where stood the royal hall or castle, with its massive stone tower, was surrounded by walls and moats, and was called 'the strong fortress'. Waterford, too, had walls and moats, and a royal castle where the king used to dwell. An old stone tower is still found there called Reginald's Tower (Ragnvalds taarn) supposed to be the *donjon* of the old royal castle. It is known to have stood there in 1170, when the English captured Waterford. York and the cities of the 'Five Boroughs' in England were also well fortified.

The Roman towns in early Britain were destroyed by the Anglo-Saxons when they conquered the country. 'Of the fifty-six cities of Roman Britain,' says W. Cunningham, 'there is not one in regard to which it is perfectly clear that it held its ground as an organized centre of social life through the period of English conquest and English settlement.' Many of these old ruined cities were rebuilt by the Vikings, and many new ones were founded. These Viking cities were the first to show the signs of municipal and urban life, both in Great Britain and Ireland. They became centres, not only of trade, but also of industry, as the Danes and Norsemen also devoted themselves to industrial pursuits, and produced wares of their own make for the general market. The Vikings had a keen sense for legal justice, and maintained strict order in their towns. They developed a system of city laws of which traces are still found in English city government.

DRESS, HOUSES, FOOD AND DRINK

The many new wares brought to the North by enterprising Viking merchants increased the comforts of daily life, and created among the higher classes a taste for fine clothes, ornaments, and luxury in various forms which exerted a marked influence on cultural life in this period. From early ages the Norsemen had woven their own woollen cloth, but it was a coarse and common fabric which they had not learned to dye in striking or delicate colours; linen was also in common use. The new commerce brought rich supplies of costly fabrics from abroad: silk, satin, and fustian, a cotton cloth; scarlet, pell and purple were brought from Spain, France, Flanders, and England. Men of higher rank took great pride in wearing scarlet mantles embroidered with gold, and trimmed with costly furs. The skald Gunlaug Ormstunge, received such a mantle from King Sigtrygg, in Dublin, and Egil Skallagrimsson received 'a costly mantle' from King Ethelstan for composing a song in his honour. When Kjartan Olafsson from Iceland came to King Olaf Tryggvasson in Norway, he wore a scarlet mantle, and, when he left, the king gave him a complete dress of scarlet cloth. From Arinbjørn Herse, Egil Skallagrimsson received a silk cloak ornamented with gold buttons. The women exhibited the traditional feminine predilection for ornaments and fine dresses.

The song 'Rigsþula', in the *Elder Edda*, describes the lady visited by Rig (the god Heimdall) as follows:

> *The wife sat*
> *mindful of her arms,*

> *smoothed the veil,*
> *stretched straight the sleeves,*
> *made stiff the mantle.*
> *A brooch was on her bosom;*
> *long was the train*
> *on her silk-blue dress.*

> *The wife bore a son,*
> *and swaddled him in silk,*
> *sprinkled him with water,*
> *and called him jarl.*

When the Irish sacked Limerick in 868, they carried away the 'beautiful Viking women dressed in silk'.

The saga writers often dwell with pride on the elegant attire of the persons prominent in their narrative. 'Gunnar of Lidarende rode to the *thing* with all his men. When they came there, they were so well attired that there was nobody there so well dressed, and the people came out of the booths to look at them.... One day when Gunnar came from the *thing*, he saw a well-dressed woman approaching. When they met, she greeted Gunnar. He returned her greeting, and asked what her name was. She said that her name was Hallgerd, and that she was the daughter of Hoskuld Dalakollsson. She was rather forward in her speech, and asked him to tell her about his travels. This request he did not refuse, and they sat down and talked together. She was dressed in the following manner: She had a red skirt well ornamented, and over it she wore a scarlet cloak embroidered with gold. Her hair hung over her bosom, and it was both long and beautiful. Gunnar wore the scarlet clothes which King Harald Gormsson had given him, and on his arm he had the gold ring which he had received from Haakon Jarl.' The Norsemen were quick at imitation, and soon learned to dye their own homemade cloth in various colours. New fashions, too, were introduced from abroad, which becomes apparent from many foreign names of articles of dress which came into use at this time; such as, *sokkr*, *kyrtill* = coat, *kapa*, cloak, *mottul*, mantle, etc. The tailor makes the gentleman, says the proverb, and true as this seems to be, the Norsemen had fully learned to appreciate this side of culture. Neither did they forget to lay stress on fine manners and courtly bearing. Tall, blond, stately and self-conscious, they were manly and striking figures, and when in foreign lands they stepped before the kings and rulers in their finest attire, with gilt helmets and richly ornamented swords, they were not easily mistaken for barbarians.

In 'Ravnsmaal', a song by King Harald Haarfagre's hirdskald, Thorbjørn Hornklove, composed after the battle in Hafrsfjord (872), a raven and a valkyrie describe in a dialogue King Harald and his men.

Says the valkyrie:

> *About the skalds I wish to ask,*
> *those who follow King Harald,*
> *since you seem to know*
> *so much about brave men.*

The raven:

> *From their dress you may know,*
> *and from their rings of gold,*

that they are the king's friends;
red mantles they wear,
they have fine striped shields,
silver-decorated swords,
brynies of ring mail,
gold embroidered shoulder-straps,
and ornamented helmets
which Harald selected for them.

The description of the famous Norman warrior Robert Guiscard, given by Anna Comnena, the gifted daughter of Emperor Alexius, would fit just as well his Viking ancestors of a couple of generations earlier. She finds fault with his fierceness and his greed, but his manly qualities won her highest admiration, though he was her father's enemy:

'The Robert here mentioned was a Norman of quite humble extraction. He coveted power; in character he was cunning, in action quick and energetic. He eagerly desired to get possession of the wealth of the rich, and he carried out his wishes with irresistible energy, for in the pursuit of his aims he was resolute and inflexible. He was so tall that he carried his head above the largest men. He had ruddy cheeks, blond hair, broad shoulders and clear blue eyes, which seemed to flash fire. He was slender where he should be slender, and broad where he should be broad – in short, he was from top to toe as if moulded and turned, a perfectly beautiful man, as I have heard many declare. Homer says of Achilles that when he spoke it was as if a multitude of people were making noise, but they say that Robert could shout so fearfully that he could drive away thousands. It is natural that a man with such physical and intellectual qualities would not bend under the yoke, nor submit to anyone.'

The higher classes in Norway did not live in castles like the feudal aristocracy in France or Germany, but dwelt on their country estates, where they engaged in farming and cattle raising when they were not absent on Viking expeditions, or occupied in commercial pursuits. The farm labour was done by slaves, but even men of high station would put shield and sword aside and join in the work. We read in the sagas that Gunnar fra Lidarende was in the field sowing grain; that Thorbjørn Øxnarmegin was in the meadow making hay, and that King Sigurd Syr was superintending the harvest when his stepson, King Olaf Haraldsson, visited him. The life in the home was still one of patriarchal simplicity. The wife managed the household, looked after the work, and waited on her guests at the table. As a token of her dignity as head of the household she carried in her belt a bunch of keys. In the 'Rigsþula' she is called the *hangilukla*, or 'the lady with the dangling keys'. Besides the regular household duties, the women, even of the highest standing, spent much time in weaving fine linen, and in embroidering tapestries of beautiful design. The men spent much of their spare time at metal work, wood carving and the making of weapons, in which arts they possessed great skill. The houses were simple but well-built log structures. The principal house was the *skaale*, a long rectangular hall, often of great size. The gable over the main entrance was ornamented with carved dragonheads or deer horns. In the front end, in or near which the main entrance was located, were two smaller rooms, the *forstua* and the *kleve*, over which there was a loft. In the gables there were usually windows made of a thin membrane, as glass was not yet used for that purpose. On the side walls of the hall there were no doors or windows. If the hall was large, the roof rested on two rows of pillars. Along the middle of the hall was a fireplace, *arinn*, and above it in the roof was an opening, the *ljori*, through which the smoke escaped. Benches were placed along the side walls, and at the middle of one of these walls was placed the high-seat for the head of the family (hdsceti, ondvegi), with high carved pillars on each side, the *qndvegissulur*. Across from this seat, by the opposite wall, was a second and simpler high-seat for distinguished guests. Across the rear of the hall was placed a bench for the women, the *tverpall*, behind which were enclosed sleeping chambers. The benches along the walls were also used as beds at night by the men. At mealtime tables were placed in front of the benches on both sides along the hall, and when the meal was over, they were removed.

The walls were hung with shields, weapons, and woven tapestries. Sometimes they were ornamented with elaborate woodcarvings, like Olaf Paa's hall at Hjarðarholt in Iceland, described in the 'Laxdølasaga'. Of other houses the most important were the *dyngja*, or *skemma*, where the women spent most of their time, and where they did their weaving and needlework, and the svefnbur, where the lord of the household slept with his family. Usually there was also a *bur*, *jungfrubur*, where the young women stayed. The slaves had their own houses.

Great delight was taken in feasting and social entertainments, and the most generous hospitality was shown every wayfarer. It was regarded, not only as a sacred duty, but as a pleasure and a privilege to entertain strangers. Instances are mentioned in the 'Landnamabok' where the *skaale* was built across the road, so that no stranger could pass without entering the house. The husband and wife would then stand ready to invite the travellers, and to offer them food and drink. Says the 'Havamal', in the *Elder Edda*:

> 'Fire needs he
> who enters the house
> and is cold about the knees;
> food and clothes
> the man is in need of
> who has journeyed over the mountains.'

Festivals were held in connection with religious exercises, weddings, funerals, and other home events, and also in the winter, especially at Christmas time. The 'Saga of Olaf the Saint', in the *Heimskringla*, relates how Asbjørn Selsbane continued the old practice of his father of having three festivals every winter. To such festivals a number of guests were invited. Before they assembled, the tables were set up in the hall, and covered with beautifully embroidered linen tablecloths. Thin wafer-like bread served as plates. Ordinarily the men and women took their meals apart, but at festivals the women sat with the men at the table, occupying the inner end of the hall, to the left of the main high seat, while the men were seated at the outer end, toward the main entrance. Bowls of water and towels were passed around, so that the guests could wash their hands both before and after the meal. Wine and ale were served with the food, which was both abundant and well prepared. Again we must quote the 'Rigsþula', which describes how Rig (Heimdall) was entertained at the home of a man of higher social standing:

> Then took Moðir
> an embroidered tablecloth
> of white linen,
> and covered the table;
> took she then
> thin leaves
> of white wheat-bread
> and put on it.
>
> And she set
> filled dishes
> and silver-plated vessels
> on the table,
> and fine ham
> and roasted fowls;
> wine was in the can,
> they drank and talked
> till the day ended.

The women took pride in filling their chests with fine table linen, sheets, bed curtains and fine clothes, but they also devoted themselves to more intellectual pursuits. As the designs with which they adorned linen and tapestry generally represented events from history or tradition, they had to become acquainted with mythology and the lives and deeds of the heroes and great men of their people. The practice of medicine and surgery was left to them; they bandaged the wounded, and healed and nursed the sick. At times the woman would also be priestess, superintending the sacrifices and religious ceremonies, and, especially in early times, she might be *volva* or *seiðkona*, a woman who was believed to possess the power of witchcraft and prophecy, and a knowledge of the supernatural. Woman's position in society was, on the whole, one of great freedom and independence. Among the higher classes, at least, she was looked upon as man's equal. She might be his companion in battle and in the banquet hall; when she married, she received a dowry from her father, and a nuptial gift (*mundr*) from her bridegroom, which remained her own property throughout her married life. In the management of the household she had full authority. So great an influence did women exercise on the ebullient passions of the Norsemen that they appear as the easily discerned cause of bloody domestic feuds and dramatic historic events, like the fates themselves, breeding discord and bloodshed, or fostering peace and blessing by petty intrigues, by a nod or a smile.

The sagas have pictured most vividly a gallery of interesting women; some beautiful, jealous, plotting and revengeful, causing endless feuds, like Hallgerd, Gudrun Usvivsdotter, Freydis and Queen Gunhild some proud and ambitious, like Bergthora, Queen Aasta and Sigrid Storraade; some affectionate, mild and devoted, like Helga the Fair and Thorgerd Egilsdotter. We hear of domineering wives and hen-pecked husbands, like Aake and Grima, but also of women truly great, like Aud the Deepminded (Unnr), a lady of rare talents, who, as widow, became the acknowledged head of the family, and managed both her own affairs and those of her daughters and relatives so well under all difficulties that no one did anything of importance without seeking her advice and assistance. These heroic and self-assertive women of the Viking Age have a certain romantic charm, still woman had not yet been accorded her proper privilege in society or in the home. The most sacred relations were yet marred by harsh and corrupt primitive customs. Marriage was not based on mutual love and affection, but on wealth and social standing. It was a business affair, a contract concluded between the bridegroom and the bride's father and relatives. The bride's consent was necessary, it is true, but it was often a matter of form, rather than the result of natural inclination. Many a touching love affair is recorded in the sagas and elsewhere in Old Norse literature, but they usually represent the revolt of the human heart against harsh and selfish social laws. Love was regarded as a weakness, and a young woman was considered as being disgraced if a young man mentioned her name in a love song. The husband often had concubines besides his legally wedded wife. It also happened that men traded wives, or that a man gave his wife away to a friend if he did not like her. Divorce was common and easily obtained. There was nothing sacred in this most intimate and important relation into which human beings can enter.

In Viking culture we find the shadows and blemishes characteristic of pagan civilization at all times. The Norseman had a keen and well-developed mind, but his heart was as hard as the steel of his sword. He loved the battle and the stormy sea; he admired the strong, the brave, the cunning, the intellectual; for the old and feeble he had no interest, for the suffering no sympathy; the weak he despised. He sang of valour and of heroic deeds, not of love and beauty. The sagas of the rich and powerful have been written, the poor and unfortunate classes are passed over in silence. But in the Viking Age the lifegiving spirit of Christianity was breathed gently also upon the pagan North. Unconsciously at first the hard heartstrings were loosened, and the soul was stirred by a new life. Notes of love and sadness steal into their songs, words of affection and sorrow are chiselled on their tombstones, woman gradually rises to new dignity, and the rights of the heart gain recognition. Even religious life is deeply affected by this gentle influence. The Light of the World had cast its first faint glimmer upon the intellectual and moral life of the North — the Viking expeditions had begun to bear their greatest fruit.

RELIGION AND LITERATURE

Wherever the Vikings settled they established a well-developed social organization, infused new vigour into the peoples with whom they came in contact, and imparted to them ideas which germinated into new cultural growth. Along practical lines they were often much farther advanced than the nations which were subjected to their attacks. This was especially manifest in Ireland, where the people at the time of the Viking inroads yet lived under a tribal organization, amid most primitive economic and social conditions.

Not only did they lack a well-organized army, ships, commerce, cities, roads and bridges, but they paid little attention to agriculture, living for the most part on their herds and flocks, with which they moved from place to place. They were, as a rule, cruel and sensual; their warfare was savage, the position of woman was low and degrading, their houses were usually miserable huts. Yet this people possessed a remarkable intellectual culture, and became in this field the teachers and benefactors of their enemies, the Norsemen.

They had been Christians for many centuries before the Vikings began their conquests. Their missionaries were labouring, not only in Scotland and England, but had penetrated to the remote forest regions of Germany and France, to Switzerland and northern Italy. Even in the solitudes of the Faroe Islands and Iceland pious Irish monks had erected their hermitages. They had great scholars who diligently studied Greek and Latin authors, and profound philosophers like John Scotus Erigena. During the seventh, eighth and ninth centuries the Irish schools became celebrated all over Europe. Not only Greek and Latin, but philosophy, astronomy, mathematics and geography were studied. The Irish cloister schools became the refuge of those who loved intellectual culture in the Dark Ages, and scholars from many countries flocked to them. Alcuin, the great scholar at the court of Charles the Great, corresponded with one of the professors of the Irish school at Clonmacnois, whom he calls his dear master and teacher. Also in their own native tongue they produced a rich literature, both in prose and poetry. Heroic tradition flourished, sagas were written to commemorate the deeds of great chieftains, or to preserve the knowledge of the clan and of family relationship, and songs were composed by skalds in honour of their kings. They sang, too, of love and of the beauty of nature with a sweet tenderness strange in those days when such poetry was almost unknown. But both their poetry and their prose suffered from an overflow of fancy and feeling, uncontrolled by artistic taste. The wildest exaggerations abound, the characters are grotesque, superhuman and indistinctly drawn. There is an obscurity and lack of form which stand in the sharpest contrast to the brief, lucid style, and psychological character painting in the Norse sagas.

That the religious and literary life so highly developed among the Irish, their love of nature, their lyric sentimentality, and sympathetic and emotional character made a deep impression on the stern Norsemen is certain. They, who came to conquer, were in turn conquered by this new and gentle influence. Long before they were converted to Christianity, their lives and views were deeply affected by ideas acquired in the Christian countries which they visited, and especially through their sojourn in Ireland. It was largely due to this new stimulus that Norse skaldic poetry and the saga literature began to flourish in the Viking period, and that Norse mythology assumes at this time a distinctly new form in which we find embedded in the strata of pagan thought many unmistakable fragments of Christian ideas; as, the conceptions of creation, of righteousness, of good and evil, as well as views of the life hereafter, which can have their origin only in the realm of Christian faith and morality.

The skaldic poetry falls into two general groups: the skaldic songs, so called because they are written by skalds whose names and careers are known, and a body of old songs by unknown authors, called the *Elder Edda* or *Norren Fornkveði* The skalds were usually connected with a king's hird or court, and produced songs to extol the person and achievements of their patrons, on whose munificence they lived.

These songs, which contain much valuable information regarding persons and events of early Norwegian history, are usually composed in a most intricate verse form, the *drottkvett*, which abounds in word transpositions, allusions and metaphoric expressions (*kenningar*), which offer many difficulties to the modern reader. This verse seems to have been invented by Brage Boddason (Brage the Old), who lived in the first part of the ninth century and is the first Norwegian skald of whom we have any record. There were also skalds who did not stay at the courts, and who composed songs on more varied subjects. Egil Skallagrimsson, one of the great masters in skaldic song, and Ulv Uggason, the author of the 'Husdrapa', may be mentioned. Egil is well known from his songs 'Hofuðlausn' and 'Arinbjørnsdrapa', but especially for his great poem 'Sonatorrek', in which he laments the loss of his sons. Noteworthy are also Kormak's 'Mansongsvisur', love songs to the beautiful Steingerd. Many of the saga writers were also skalds, notably Snorre Sturluson and Sturla Thordsson. Snorre, the author of the *Heimskringla*, has also written the *Younger Edda*, a most important work intended as a book of instruction for young skalds. The work has preserved the names of a great number of skalds, together with fragments of their songs, and furnishes a key to the many difficulties in skaldic poesy. It gives a review of mythology (Gylfaginning) which a skald must necessarily know, it explains the poetical and metaphorical expressions (*heiti, kenningar*) used in skaldic poetry, and a poem written to King Haakon Haakonsson and Skule Jarl illustrates all the verse forms used by the skalds.

The *Elder Edda* consists of two series of songs, the mythological and the heroic, written by skalds whose names are not known. Besides the poems about Helge Hundingsbane and Helge Hiorvarðsson, the heroic songs deal with the great Nibelungen tradition, and constitute the first literary embodiment known of this great Germanic epic. The Eddie poems have preserved a much older form of this tradition than that found in the 'Nibelungenlied'. In the mythological poems we find clearly set forth in verse of classic simplicity and beauty the Norsemen's ideas of creation, the lives and character of their gods the destruction of the world, and of man's destiny after death. In the 'Havamal' we find outlined also their moral conceptions, and their view of life in general. The grandest of all these old songs is the 'Vgluspa' (the prophecy of the volva).

This volva can be none other than Urd, one of the three *norns*, or goddesses of fate (Urðr, Verðandi and Skuld). The gods are assembled in council at the Well of Urd. Odin calls the volva from the grave, and the great sibyl comes forth to reveal to the god of wisdom what even he does not know – the mysteries of creation, the destruction of the gods, the end of the world and the happy existence in the life to come. She commands silent attention, and tells the assembled gods that in the beginning there was neither sand, nor sea, nor cool billows; the earth did not exist, nor the heavens above; there was a yawning abyss, but nowhere grass, before the sons of Bur lifted up the dry land, they who created the beautiful earth. The sun shone from the south on the stones of the hall, and the earth was covered with green herbs. The sun, the moon and the stars did not know their proper courses, but the mighty gods held council, and gave them their right orbits, dividing time into night, morning, midday and evening.

The 'Gylfaginning' presents a more complete account of creation, giving in fuller detail a myth which is outlined also in the 'Vafþrudnismal'. Here we learn that in the beginning there were two regions, one of fire and heat, called 'Muspelheim', ruled over by Surt, who watches the borders of his realm with a glowing sword. When the end of the world comes, he will conquer the gods, and destroy the earth with fire. The other was a cold region, 'Niflheim', from which 12 rivers issue, called 'Elivagar'. Between these two regions is the great abyss 'Ginnungagap'. The masses of ice which had accumulated on the northern side of this abyss finally caught the spark of life from the heat issuing from Muspelheim, and a great man-shaped being, Yme, was produced, from whom the Jøtuns descended. The gods killed Yme, and from his body they created the earth, from his blood the ocean, from his bones the mountains and from his skull the heavens. From sparks from Muspelheim they made the sun, moon and the stars, and placed them on the heavens.

Again the gods assembled in council, says the volva, and created the dwarfs in the earth. From two trees, ash and elm, they created man and woman. Odin gave them the spirit, Hønir gave them reason, and Lodur colour and warmth of life. The gods were amusing themselves at the gaming tables, and there was no lack of gold until the three powerful maidens came from Jøtunheim. These maidens are the three *norns* or goddesses of fate, already mentioned. Strife had not yet begun; the gods were happy in this golden age, which lasted until the fates appeared to determine the destiny of gods and men. But the elements of discord had entered the world: gold, woman and witchcraft. The goddess Gullveig, who seems to be a personification of all three, was killed in Odin's hall, and this caused the first war, that between Esir and Vanir, the two tribes of gods, who now contended for supremacy. 'Odin threw his spear into the throng, this was the first combat in the world.' A peace was finally concluded, according to which the two tribes were united on equal terms.

The personification of evil itself is Loki and his children with the giantess Angrboda, the three monsters Hel, goddess of the underworld, the wolf Fenre, who at the end of the world will kill Odin, and the Miðgarðsormr, or Jørmungand, the world serpent, a personification of the ocean encircling the earth. The world, in which there is now continual strife, is represented under the symbol of a giant ash tree, the Yggdrasil, whose top reaches into the heavens, whose branches fill the world, and whose three roots extend into the three important spheres of existence outside the world of man. One root is where the Esir dwell. Under this root is the Well of Urd, where the gods assemble in council. Another root reaches to the home of the Jøtuns, or Rimthuser, under which is the Well of Mimir, the fountain of wisdom. The third root is in Xiflheim, and under it is the terrible well Hvergelme, by which is found the snake Niðhoggr, which, together with many others, continually gnaws at the roots of the world tree, and seeks to destroy it. Niðhoggr is the symbol of the destructive forces operating in the world.

> An ash tree I know,
> Yggdrasil l called,
> a tall tree
> sprinkled with water;

from it comes the dew
that falls in the valleys,
ever green it stands
by the fountain of Urd.

Much do they know
the three maidens
who come from the hall
which stands by the tree;
one is Urd,
the other Verdande,
Skuld is the third;
laws they make,
they determine life
and the fate of men.

The *norns* are not only in the world, but they are the real rulers of it; even the gods must submit to their decrees. They rule over life and death, and man's destiny; no one can escape the calamities which they have preordained. But they have not the absolute power attributed to the Fates in Greek and Roman mythology. They are also subject to an ultimate fate. They disappear at Ragnarok together with this present world.

Again the gods assembled, says the volva, to consider how evil had come into the world. Odin, who is interrogating her, tries to conceal his identity, but she recognizes him, and tells him the great secrets of his life. In Norse mythology Odin is the chief divinity and the father of many of the other gods, but it is evident that in earlier periods other gods have held the highest position. Ty, the god of war, seems to be the same divinity as the Greek Zeus, and has, no doubt, at one time been the principal god. Thor, the god of thunder and lightning, must also have ranked higher than Odin, but in Norse mythology he has become Odin's son. He is constantly fighting the wicked Jøtuns, at whom he hurls his hammer Mjølner (the thunderbolt). He is the farmer's special protector and benefactor. He shields them against the hostile forces of nature, and furthers husbandry and all peaceful pursuits. In Norway he was worshiped more extensively than any other god.

Odin seems originally to have been a storm god, but in later periods he becomes so prominent that he pushes the older divinities from their throne. Odin is an embodiment of the spirit of the Viking Age. Even in appearance he is a chieftain; tall, one-eyed, grey-bearded, attired in a blue mantle, carrying a shield and the spear Gungne, which never misses its mark. His life is rich in all sorts of adventures. He loves war, and is generally found in the midst of the battle. He is also the god of wisdom, and his desire for knowledge is almost a passion. His two ravens, Hugin and Munin, bring him daily notice of everything that happens in the world. No sacrifice is too great if thereby he can gain more knowledge. How did he lose his eye? It is a great secret, but the volva reveals it. He drank once from the Well of Mimir, the fountain of wisdom, and had to give one of his eyes as a forfeit. Odin is the personification of the heavens; his one eye is the sun, the other, which Mimir took, is the sun's reflection in the water. He also discovered the runes, but only by making another great sacrifice. The 'Havamal' gives the following account of it:

'I know that I hung on the windy tree nine nights together,
wounded by a spear, sacrificed to Odin, myself to myself, on the
tree which no one knows from what roots it springs. Neither with
food nor with drink was I refreshed. I looked carefully down and
raised up the runes; crying I raised them up, and fell then down.'

Even this great pain Odin is willing to undergo to discover
the runes, for through them he gains occult knowledge, and
becomes the god of sorcery, the wisest and most powerful
of all the gods. From his throne Lidskjalv he overlooks the
whole world. He is always thoughtful, and meditates on great
problems. Evil and good are equally interesting to him, for
both reveal some secret of life. He contemplates the mystery
of existence and the approaching end of things; he is never
glad, because he knows too much.

In Aasgaard the gods built a beautiful hall, Gladsheim, for
the gods, and another, Vingolv, for the goddesses, but greater
than any of these was Odin's own hall, Valhal. To this hall
the Valkyries bring the dead warriors who fall on the field of
battle, and they are feasted and entertained by Odin himself.
All who die a natural death are excluded. The heroes find
their pastime in fighting, and many fall every day, but they
rise again unharmed, and return to feast in Valhal as the best
of friends.

Another divinity who in the Viking period must have
undergone a great change, and who seems to reflect the new
spirit of that age, is Balder. The opinions of scholars with
regard to the Balder myth are hopelessly at variance. [Danish
folklorist and scholar] A. Olrik thinks that Balder is an old sun
god, that his death signifies the victory of darkness over light,

while H. Schuck thinks that he was not a real god till shortly before the advent of Christianity. According to [Danish historian] Saxo Grammaticus, he was a young and impetuous warrior who waged many combats with his rival Hother, by whom he is finally slain. He is a son of Odin, but lives on the earth. Sophus Bugge considers this to be the older form of the myth. In the 'Voluspa' and the 'Gylfaginning' he is pictured as the gentle god of innocence and righteousness, so bright that a light of glory surrounds him. He dwells in the hall Breidablik (the far shining hall), where nothing impure is found. He is wise, kind and eloquent, and so just that his decrees cannot be altered. His wife is Odin's granddaughter, the faithful Nanna; his son is Forsete, the god of justice and reconciliation.

While Balder lives, evil can gain no real control in the world, but bad dreams begin to trouble him, and as this portends some great misfortune to the Esir, Odin saddles his eight-legged horse, Sleipne, and rides to Niflheim to learn what evil is thus foreboded. He calls the volva from her grave, and asks her for whose reception they are making preparations in Hel's kingdom, and she answers that it is for Balder, who will soon die. This news causes great consternation among the Esir, and they assemble in council to discuss the matter. Frigg, Balder's mother, requires everything in the world to take an oath not to harm her son. The gods now feel secure, and in their joy that the danger is averted, they amuse themselves by throwing all sorts of things at Balder to show that nothing will hurt him. But Loki comes disguised to the assembly, and learns from Frigg that there is a tiny plant, the *mistilteinn*, which she has not required to take the oath, because it seemed too small. He pulls up the plant, brings it to the assembly, and asks the blind god Høð to throw it at Balder. Høð does so; the plant pierces him through, and he falls dead. The greatest misfortune has happened; Nanna's heart breaks of sorrow, and she is buried together with her husband, who is received by Hel in her kingdom. But there is a hope even in this great calamity. While Balder lies on the bier, Odin whispers something in his ear. This episode is mentioned in the 'Vafþrudnismal', where Odin asks the wise Vafþrudne:

> What did Odin
> whisper in his son's ear
> before he was laid on the funeral pyre?

> This is a riddle which even Vafþrudne
> cannot solve. He answers:

> No one knows
> What, in the beginning of time,
> thou didst whisper
> in thy son's ear.

No one knows; but it was, no doubt, a promise that he should not remain forever in Hel's realm, but that he should return when the world of strife had passed away, and the new life of peace and righteousness had begun.

In Norse mythology, as elsewhere in old religious systems, the ideas of the life hereafter are often vague, even contradictory. Mythology is a growth, a product of long periods of a people's intellectual development, in which old ideas have constantly been mixed with new conceptions. It represents a march of the human mind forward to new light, rather than a once for all perfected system. The Hel myth is an illustration. Hel, the name both of the goddess and of the realm over which she rules, is sometimes thought of as the home of all the departed, where even Balder goes after death. Hence the Norwegian expression *at slaa ihjel*, i.e. to kill, to deprive one of life so that he goes to Hel. But Hel is also thought of as the place for the wicked. Hel, the goddess, is white on one side and black on the other, and her hall is described as a frightful place. We have seen that from the earliest times the Norsemen believed in a life after death, which is shown by many burial customs. In course of time they began to construct large burial chambers where all the members of the family could be interred together. Professor H. Schuck thinks that these graves first engendered the idea of the lower world. He says: 'A primitive people does not think of death as annihilation, but rather as an entrance into new life. Only by premising such a belief can a number of antique burial customs be explained.... At first the dead person lived this new life in the grave itself, and these large family graves gave origin to the idea of the realm of the dead.' According to the oldest belief, then, all the dead came to this realm where Hel ruled. But it was a shadowy, joyless existence, and the feeling that heroes and good people deserved something better gave rise to new creations; to Valhal, Odin's hall; Folkvang and Sessrymne (Sessrymnir), where Freyja entertains one half of all the fallen heroes; Vingolv (Vingolf), where all heroes are entertained by the goddesses, and to the idea that all women who die unmarried go to the goddess Gefjon. Hel and her kingdom fell into disfavour, and were painted in ever darker colours.

Loki did not escape punishment. He was tied by the Esir in a rocky cavern where poisonous adders drop venom into his face, and there he will have to lie till Ragnarok, or the end of the world. But his faithful wife, Sigyn, stands always by him, and gathers the dripping venom in a cup. Only when she empties the cup does it drop into Loki's face, and then he writhes in pain so that the earth quakes. Hød, the slayer of Balder, is also punished. With the goddess Rind, Odin has the son Vaale, who kills Hød. But revenge cannot remedy the mischief done. Balder the Good has perished, and evil triumphs. In her hall Fensale Frigg weeps for her son; the end is approaching, Ragnarok, when gods and men must perish, and the present world will be destroyed.

Another divinity which, especially in Sweden, was worshiped more extensively than Odin himself, was Frey, the son of Njørd the god of the sea. He was the god of weather and of harvests, and was regarded as the giver of riches. He became so enamoured with the beautiful Jøtun maiden Gerd that he could neither eat nor sleep. One day he sat on Lidskjalv in Aasgaard and saw her far to the north, and so beautiful was she that she made sky and ocean resplendent with light. He sent his servant, Skirne (Skirnir), to woo her, but in order to win her he had to surrender his greatest treasure, his sword, and when Ragnarok comes, he will be slain by Surt, because he has no weapon with which to defend himself.

Heimdall, one of the oldest deifications of the heavens, is the sentinel of the gods, and lives at Bifrost, the celestial bridge over which gods and men ride to Valhal. Vidar, the silent one, is, next to Thor, the strongest of the gods. Ege (Egir) is the ocean god, and Brage the god of poesy and eloquence.

In Norse mythology there are twelve or thirteen principal gods, and an equal number of goddesses (asynjur). Frigg is Odin's wife and the queen of heaven, and dwells in Fensale, far to the west where the sun sets in the sea. Freyja, the beautiful goddess of love, lives in Folkvang, where the great hall Sessrymne is found. To her belongs one half of the warriors who fall on the battlefield, and she is accorded the right of first choice. Idun, Brage's wife, called the good goddess, keeps the apples from which the gods eat to preserve their youth. Thor's wife is the beautiful Siv (Sif), with hair of gold. Skade, Njørd's wife, was, like Gerd, of Jøtun race, and Snotra was the goddess of good sense and womanly graces.

Before Ragnarok evil passes all bounds. For three years there is perpetual strife. Brothers fight and kill each other, the ties of blood relationship are broken, morals are corrupted and one person has no compassion for the other. Then follow three years of constant winter, the Fimbulwinter (the great winter). Finally Yggdrasil trembles, Fenre breaks his fetters and the Midgardsorm comes out of the ocean. Surt, the fire demon, comes; Loki is free again and leads the sons of Muspell and other forces of destruction to the final battle with the gods on the plain Vigrid. Fenre kills Odin, but is in turn slain by the powerful Vidar. Thor and the Midgardsorm kill each other; Frey is slain by Surt; Ty fights against Hel's hound Garm, and both fall. Surt finally hurls fire over the earth; the sun grows dark, the earth sinks into the ocean, fire consumes all – the world of strife and bloodshed has disappeared.

Out of the ocean, says the volva, rises a new green earth, where grain fields grow without being sown, and where no evil exists. Here, on the Fields of Ida, the gods who have survived

Ragnarok reassemble. Balder, who has returned from Hel, is there; also Vidar, Hød, Hønir, and Thor's sons, Mode and Magne. A new race of men are also born.

Pursuing her story, the volva says:

> A hall I see
> on the heights of Gimle,
> brighter than the sun,
> and covered with gold;
> righteous men
> shall dwell there
> in endless happiness.

This hall is a perfect contrast to Valhal, where the heroes even after death amuse themselves by fighting and slaying each other; in Gimle the righteous live in peace and happiness. Gimle is the safe and secure home ornamented with precious stones. Sophus Bugge thinks that the Fields of Ida are in reality the Christian Garden of Eden, and that Gimle is the heavenly Jerusalem described in Revelation, xxi., 10–21:

'10. And he carried me away in the spirit to a great and high mountain, and shewed me that great city, the holy Jerusalem, descending out of heaven from God,

'11. Having the glory of God: and her light was like unto a stone most precious, even like a jasper stone, clear as crystal.

'21. And the twelve gates were twelve pearls; every several gate was of one pearl: and the street of the city was pure gold, as it were transparent glass.'

And, says the volva, bringing her narrative to a closing climax:

From above comes
to the great judgment
the powerful one,
the ruler of all.

This is the ruler of the new world whose name not even the volva knows. In Norse mythology the world is pictured as a scene of perpetual struggle between good and evil, a never-ending combat between the powers of life and the forces of destruction, and it is especially noteworthy that this struggle is a great tragedy in which the gods suffer complete overthrow. Balder was killed, Loki and Fenre broke their fetters; the struggle against evil has been unsuccessful on every point. Most of the leading gods themselves are destroyed by the forces of evil in the great final battle at Ragnarok. But evil, too, passes away with the world of strife in which it has existed. This thought of the overthrow and destruction of the greatest gods seems to be a new feature which could not very well have been developed until the faith in the old divinities was beginning to waver, and people began to feel that there was a heaven higher than Valhal and Vingolv, that true happiness was not to be found in strife, but in peace and righteousness, and that there was a god whom they did not yet know, who was more powerful than the Esir, and who, in the new world, would establish a reign of justice, peace, and happiness.

The 'Hyndluljoð' says:

Then comes another god
still mightier,

> *but his name*
> *I dare not mention;*
> *few can now*
> *see farther*
> *than to Odin's*
> *meeting with the wolf.*

The worship might be carried on privately in the home, where the head of the family would sacrifice to the gods, and bring offerings to their images, but it was usually conducted in temples, *huv*, or in simpler sanctuaries, *horg*, of which no description is given in the old writings. They seem to have been simple structures, stone altars, or the like, erected in the open, and dedicated especially to the worship of goddesses. In the 'Hyndluljoð' Freyja says:

> *Horg he built me,*
> *made of stone,*
> *now the stones have turned to glass;*
> *with fresh blood*
> *of oxen he sprinkled them.*
> *Ottar always believed in goddesses.*

R. Keyser and P. A. Munch are of the opinion that many of the stone circles found in Norway are remnants of this kind of sanctuaries. These circles, which are formed by placing great stones in an upright position, are often very large, and may have had an altar in the centre.

The temple consisted of two parts: the large assembly hall, or nave, and the shrine, a smaller room in the rear end of the building, corresponding to the choir of the Christian churches. The images of the gods were placed in a half-circle in the shrine. At the centre stood the altar (*stallr*), upon which lay a large gold ring (*baugr*), upon which all solemn oaths were sworn. The bowl containing the blood of the sacrificed animals (*hlautbolli*) was placed on the altar by the priest (*goði*), who, with a stick (*hlautteinn*), sprinkled it on the images of the gods, and on the persons present. The meat of the animals was boiled, and served to the assembled people in the large hall of the temple, where toasts were drunk to the gods for victory and good harvests. The sanctuary and the grounds belonging to it was called *ve*, a holy or sacred place, and anyone who violated its sanctity was called *varg i veum* (wolf in the sanctuary), and was outlawed. Three religious festivals were held each year: one at the beginning of winter (October 14), the *vinternatsblot*, or *haustblot*, to bid winter welcome; another at midwinter (January 14), *midvintersblot*, for peace and good harvest; and a third, *sommerblot*, held on the first day of summer (April 14), for victory on military expeditions.

The temples seem to have been quite numerous, but especially well known were the ones at Sigtuna and Upsala in Sweden, at Leire (Hleidra) in Denmark, and at Skiringssal in Norway. There was in the North no distinct class of priests. The priestly functions were exercised by the *herser* and the *jarls*, and even by the king himself. Women, too, might serve as priestesses. In Iceland the *gode* held about the same position as the *herse* in Norway. He was a chieftain, and the temple in which he served as priest was built on his estates.

EARLY SOCIAL CONDITIONS IN NORWAY

The first account of early Norwegian society is given by the 'Rigsþula', which describes the various social classes, and pictures conditions which resemble those of early Germanic society elsewhere. Rig (the god Heimdall) comes to a hut where he finds Aae and Edda, an old couple, grey-haired from work and hardship, sitting by the fire. Edda, who wore an old headgear, set before the visitor coarse bread and other simple food. Their son Thrall was stoop-shouldered and coarse-featured, with dark complexion and wrinkled skin. They evidently belonged to some foreign race, brought to Norway either as prisoners of war, or as slaves bought in the numerous slave markets. Thrall married without much ceremony the flat-nosed and sunburnt Thir. Their children were called Fiosnir (stable boy), Drumbr (the clumsy one), Ambatt (slave), Totrughypja (the ragged one), etc. When they grow up, they do all sorts of menial labour; they manure the fields, build fences and herd goats and swine. This is the slave class, which must have been quite numerous.

Rig proceeded on his way, and came to the home of Ave and Amma. The man was busy making parts for a wooden loom; he wore a tight-fitting shirt, his beard was in order, his locks hung over his forehead. The wife sat spinning, and was well dressed. Their son was called Karl. He was married to Snor with due ceremony, according to custom. He tamed oxen, made wagons, built houses and barns and drove the plow. Their children were Hal, Bonde, Hauld, Tegn, Bodde, etc. This is the farmer class, those who own land, and devote themselves to agriculture. The *karls* were the lowest class of landowning freemen, peasants. Below them were the freedmen and renters. The *haulds* (*storbondi*) were an aristocratic class of landowners, a gentry who held their land by inherited right and title, *odel*, and were said to be odel born. At the head of the *haulds* stood in each *herred*, or district, an hereditary chieftain, the *herse*, who was their leader in war, and commanded the local subdivision of the army. He exercised also priestly functions, and presided at the thing, or the assembly of the people.

Rig then came to a hall where Faðir and Moðir lived. The man was engaged in making bows and arrows. He belonged to the aristocracy. The wife decked the table with a fine linen tablecloth, placed silver vessels on it, and served wine, wheat bread, ham and roasted fowl. She was blonde, and was elegantly dressed.

> *Her brows were light,*
> *her bosom lighter,*
> *her neck whiter*
> *than the white snow.*

Their son was the golden-haired Jarl, who married the blonde and beautiful Erna, daughter of Herse. From them the king descends.

Over against their neighbours, the Swedes and Danes, the Norsemen felt themselves to be a distinct people from times which far antedate the beginning of authentic history, but they did not at first constitute a united nation. They consisted of a number of independent tribes, occupying quite well-defined districts. The names of many of these tribes are given by Jordanes, and Procopius says that 13 tribes live in

Scandinavia, the Gautar being the most numerous. The names of Egder, Ryger, Horder, Raumer, Heiner, etc., are still preserved in names of provinces and districts in Norway, like Agder, Rogaland, Hordaland, Romerike and Hedemarken. The tribe consisted of families to whom belonged the greater part of the land, and who, by virtue of wealth, influence and tradition, possessed all religious and political power. The title to the land was held by the head of the family, but the real ownership was vested in all the members jointly. It was called *odel*, and the principle seems to have prevailed that it could not pass out of the possession of the family. All the sons shared equally in the inheritance, but the old homestead was not divided, but was usually inherited by the oldest son. The younger sons received other portions of the estate, or they sold their interest and sought their fortune elsewhere.

The village system did not obtain in Norway, as among the Anglo-Saxons and Germans. Each family dwelt on its own separate estate. In Anglo-Saxon the word tun means town. In Norse it means the place on which the dwelling is located. The people were divided into *fylker*, and each *fylke* placed in the field an organized military force under its own commander. The *fylker* constituted the larger units of the army. A parallel to this system is found in the Anglo-Saxon tribal organization, and, especially, in the division of the tribes into smaller groups: East Saxons, South Saxons, West Saxons, North-folk and South-folk. The *fylke* had its own temple, and its own *thing*, or assembly of the people, where suits at law were tried and decided. The *fylke* was divided into *hereder*, which corresponds to the *hundreds* among the Anglo-Saxons, and the *centena* among the Franks. This seems to have been a district large enough to furnish a hundred warriors, which formed the unit of military organization. The *herse* was the hereditary tribal chieftain, while the jarls had about the same powers as petty kings, and ruled over larger districts. Before Harald Haarfagre's time most districts were governed by kings (*fylkeskonger*) who ruled over larger tribes, such as Ryger, Horder, Egder, Raumer, etc., but not till after the union of Norway did the king become distinctly superior to the jarls.

The movement towards a union of independent, but closely related tribes into a þjoð, or people, seems to have been well under way, both in Sweden and Denmark, already in the early centuries of the Christian era. Svitiod, the kingdom of the Swedes dwelling around Malaren, has already been mentioned, also Gautiod, the Gautar or Gøtar, inhabiting the districts farther south, about the great lakes Venern and Vettern. Denmark was united into one kingdom under the Skjoldung dynasty prior to 500 CE. In Norway, where deep fjords and snow-covered mountains made inland travel in early times difficult, and laid great obstacles in the way of closer intercourse between the different districts, national unity was effected later and with more difficulty. But from very early times the trend of social development towards ultimate union is clearly seen in the growing tendency to merge the isolated tribes into larger confederacies, and to adopt for these a uniform system of laws which were gradually made operative in larger districts.

The oldest confederacy was, probably, that of the Heiner dwelling in Hedemarken by the great lake Mjøsen, in the eastern part of Norway. They are mentioned in the Old English poem 'Widsith', and the runic inscription on the Rokstone in

Ostergotland, Sweden, states that, together with Horder and Ryger, they made a warlike expedition to Seeland in Denmark, under a common king. Their confederacy must have existed as early as at the time of the birth of Christ, and seems to have embraced, besides the Heiner, also Raumer, Ringer and Hader in Romerike, Ringerike, Hadeland and other districts. Together they constituted the Eidsivalag, i.e., the people united under a common law called the 'Eidsivathingslov'. The place of the common assembly, or *thing* (Eidsivathing) was Eidsvold, at the lower end of Lake Mjøsen. The name of the place of assembly brought about a change of the name 'Heiðsevislog' to Eidsivalag.

More powerful was the confederacy Trøndelagen, formed by eight *fylker* dwelling in old Prondheimr, the district around the Trondhjemsfjord. This region, which has been inhabited as long as records can trace the existence of Norsemen, is one of the best agricultural districts in Norway. The large areas of fertile soil, which form an undulating plain around this great fjord, explain sufficiently the fact that in very early times Trøndelagen was one of the wealthiest and most densely populated districts, and was regarded as the heart and centre of the country. Snorre calls it the 'centre of the country's strength'. The Trønders took little active part in the Viking expeditions. They regarded their own districts as the most desirable place to live in, and were too strongly attached to their own homes to be fond of adventure or emigration. Trøndelagen consisted of two parts: Indtrøndelagen, or the four inner *fylker*: Sparbuen, Verdalen, Eynafylke, and Skogn; and Uttrøndelagen, the four *fylker* situated towards the mouth of the fjord, Stjørdalen, Strinden, Guldalen, and Orkedalen.

Trøndelagen had two *things*: Ørething, on Bratøren, in the present city of Trondhjem, and Frostathing, on the peninsula Frosta, in Indtrøndelagen. Every farmer who had a manservant had to attend the Ørething, which assembled once a year. At the Frostathing 400 representatives met from the eight *fylker*, 40 from each *fylke* in Indtrøndelagen, and 60 from each *fylke* in Uttrøndelagen.

The Frostathing grew in importance, and gave its name to the body of laws called 'Frostathingslov', which was adopted by the whole northern part of Norway. Each *fylke* had its own temple and *fylkesthing*, and governed itself in all local matters. The *thing* was the assembly of the people in which the freemen met to decide matters of common interest. It was also a court of law. The *lagthings* or larger assemblies, like Ørething and Frostathing, tried all cases of greater importance; they were also appellate courts to which cases were brought from the lower courts. The president of the *lagthing* appointed a body of judges, the lagrette, usually 36 in number, chosen for one session, who served under oath, and had to interpret and apply the law in the cases that came up for trial. The decision prepared by the *lagrette* was submitted to the whole assembly for approval. The institution of *lagmand* was also found in Norway, though it was not so important as it became later in Iceland. At first the laws were not written, and the *lagmand* was one learned in the law, who could recite it to the assembly. It seems that in Norway several *lagmand* acted together in declaring the law. The place of assembly was one of peace and sanctity. 'Every man must go fasting into court, and no drink shall be brought to the thing, either for sale or otherwise,' says the 'Frostathingslov'. The place where the *lagrette* sat was regarded as a sanctuary, and was surrounded by ropes, *vebønd*, the sacred cords.

Duelling with swords was not infrequently resorted to in settling disputes. It was called *holmgang*, because the duels were generally fought on a holm, or small island. When blood was drawn, the affair was regarded as settled, and the losing party had to pay a sum previously stipulated. A duel between the skald Gunlaug and his rival Ravn led to its abolition in Iceland by the *Althing*, in 1006. In Norway it was abolished about 1012. After Christianity was introduced, the ordeal became a mode of trial occasionally resorted to. Its best-known form in Norway was the *jernbyrd*, which consisted in carrying a red-hot iron, or in walking barefooted over hot ploughshares. This mode of trial was abolished in 1247. In Trøndelagen, with its two *lagthings*, and dual arrangement in general, there were, besides the *fylkes-hov*, two great sanctuaries; one at Meren in Sparbuen, one of the most renowned heathen temples in Norway, and one at Lade in Uttrøndelagen, near the present city of Trondhjem. Before King Harald Haarfagre's time there were no kings in Trøndelagen. At the head of each *fylke* stood a chieftain, who was also priest and leader of the people at the *thing*. His office was hereditary, but whether he bore the title of *herse*, which was customary in Norway, or was called *gode*, like the chieftains in Iceland, is not known. The two *fylker* Nordmør and Romsdal, petty kingdoms from very ancient times, also belonged in a general way to the Frostathingslag. The people of Romsdal had their temple on the little island of Veey (the island of the sanctuary) in the Romsdalsfjord.

South of Romsdal lies Søndmør, a *fylke* which had its own king, and was the home of some of the most powerful families in the early history of Norway. Especially noteworthy is the great Arnmødling family, the descendants of King Arnvid who fell in the battle of Solskjel fighting against Harald Haarfagre. They resided on the island of Giske, near the present city of Aalesund, where a number of interesting archaeological finds have been made. The Søndmørings were great seamen, and took active part in the Viking expeditions.

North of Trøndelagen a large seacoast region fringed with thousands of islands stretches for many hundred miles towards the borders of Finmarken. This is Nordland, or, as it was called in earlier times, Haalogaland. The great cod and herring fisheries for which this region is still noted, made it in early days one of the most populous districts in Norway. Whale and walrus were caught here in large numbers, and the district was for centuries the centre of the rich fur trade of the North, until it was finally surpassed by Novgorod, in Russia, in the eleventh century. The powerful chieftains in Haalogaland carried on a lucrative fur trade with the Finns in Finmarken, on whom they also levied a tribute which brought them a large income. Ohthere says that the most precious thing for the chieftains in Haalogaland is the tribute paid them by the Finns. This consists of furs, feathers, whalebone, robes and ship ropes made from walrus hide. The people of Haalogaland were enterprising merchants and sailors. They went on trading expeditions to southern Norway, Denmark and the British Isles, and followed routes across the mountains to the Gulf of Bothnia. Many trading centres sprang up, like Vagar (Kabelvaag), and Tjotta, noted later as the seat of the great chieftain Haarek af Tjotta, still one of the largest country seats in northern Norway; also Sandness, and Bjarkey, later the home of the powerful Tore Hund. Wealth was accumulated, and literature and culture flourished. Three of the Edda songs, 'Vølundarkvioa', 'Hymiskvioa', and 'Grimnismal', are known to have been written in Haalogaland, and here lived also the great skald Eyvind Skaldaspiller. The jarls of this district were among the most powerful chieftains in Norway at that time; they had large fleets, and ruled over the whole region from Finmarken to the Trondhjemsfjord, including, also, the district at the mouth of the fjord.

In the southwestern part of Norway the three *fylker*, Firðafylke (Nordfjord and Søndfjord), Sygnafylke, or Sogn, and Hordaland (including Nordhordland, Søndhordland, Hardanger and Voss) were united in the Gulathingslag, a much looser confederacy than the Trøndelag. Firðafylke and Sogn are named after the fjords, while Hordaland bears the name of the Horder, one of the oldest known peoples in Norway. They are mentioned by Caesar, in the year 58 BCE, when, according to his account, 24,000 Harudes arrived, and joined Ariovistus. Hordaland was a very mountainous region, with numerous fjords, and but a small area of tillable soil, and the Horder became great seamen and Vikings from very early times. It has already been noted that the *Anglo-Saxon Chronicle* mentions them as the first Vikings in England, and from that time on, this region remained the centre of Viking activity in Norway. They extended their power over neighbouring tribes and districts, and Firðafylke and Sogn seem to have been new settlements founded by them. The Gulathing was held every spring. Twelve men were chosen from each of the three *fylker* as a *lagrette* by the chieftains who presided over the *thing*. In the mountain valleys farther inland the old organization, with petty kings and full tribal autonomy, still existed unmodified by any tendency towards union.

In southern Norway the Christianiafjord, known in earlier times as the Foldenfjord, extends for a distance of about 96 kilometres (60 miles) into a fertile and beautiful region called Viken. This district, which lies in close proximity to Sweden and Denmark, and faces the Skagerak and the Baltic Sea, was most favourably located for intercourse with other states. Rich soil, a fine climate, fisheries and trade made it an attractive and populous region. In early ages it became a harbour for foreign influence and new ideas, a centre of progress and development, in which was found all that was highest of art and culture in the North at that time. To the west of the fjord lay two *fylker*, Grenland (the land of the Grannii) and Vestfold; to the east Vingulmark, and southward from Svinesund to the Gota River stretched Ranrike, the land of the Ragnaricii, also called Alfheimr in the sagas, which in later times became a Swedish province. In the southern part of Vestfold, near the coast, lay the famous sanctuary Skiringssal, around which a town had grown up. Ohthere there says in his report to King Alfred the Great that he lived in Haalogaland, and that there is in southern Norway a town called Skiringssal (Sciringes heal), to which one can sail in a month by resting in the night, if the wind is favourable. As a commercial town it was soon outstripped by Tunsberg, not far away, on the west side of the Christianiafjord. In the neighbourhood of Tunsberg lay a number of sanctuaries, dedicated to various divinities, whose names are still traceable in Basberg (Baldersberg), Hassum (Haðsheimr), Horgen, and Oseberg (the land of the Esir), where the Oseberg ship was found.

The art and wealth exhibited in the grave chamber of the queen, or princess, buried in this ship furnish singular evidence of the culture and power of the princes of Vestfold in early ages. The kings of Denmark had won supremacy over this province. When this happened is not known, but in 813 the ruling native princes acknowledged the Danish king's overlordship, and Vestfold became a Danish province. But the powerful King Godfred of Denmark, who ventured to begin war even against Charlemagne, was killed by one of his own men in 810, and a period of confusion and strife between rival claimants to the throne was the result. During this period the Ynglings came into power in Vestfold, a family which was destined in time to rule over all Norway, and to unite it into one kingdom. They quickly seized the opportunity, and made Vestfold independent, but the Danish kings continued to claim it, even as late as in the reign of Valdemar the Victorious.

THE ICELANDIC SAGAS OF THE KINGS

The *kongesogor*, also called the 'King's Sagas', are a group of Old Norse sagas written in Iceland during the twelfth and thirteenth centuries. The sagas are mainly concerned with the acts of great men, describing the lives and reigns of Norwegian and Icelandic kings and their families. In doing so they provide a wealth of information about the social, political and cultural history of the time. These sagas were highly valued in medieval Iceland, both as historical records and as literary works. They remain important sources of information for historians and researchers today.

Among the best-known royal sagas – and included herein – are the collected histories of *Heimskringla* by Snorre Sturlason, a comprehensive chronicle of the Norwegian kings, and *Olafs saga Helga*, which tells the story of the life and deeds of St Olaf Tryggvasson, great-grandson of Harold the Fairhaired – a king so accomplished that he needed a separate saga to do his life justice. The name *Heimskringla* means 'The Circle of the World', and the work clearly encompasses the greatest monarchs in early Scandinavian history and their heroic deeds. It begins with no less an impressive figure than Odin, father of the Norse gods himself, a fitting point of origin for such an impressive bloodline, imbuing the dynasty with supreme power and authority. The lineage of this family, the House of Ynglings, begins with Halfdan the Swarthy in the ninth century and continues all the way to the reign of Magnus Erlingsson in the early 12th century.

To fill his manuscript, Snorre and his faithful scribes – of whom he employed no less than five at a time in his sprawling estate in western Iceland – drew on a variety of sources for his work. These included oral traditions, earlier sagas and poems and official records, combined to provide a comprehensive and detailed history of the Norwegian kings and their deeds. In addition to its historical value, *Heimskringla* is also considered a masterpiece of Old Norse literature, known for its vivid storytelling, sophisticated characterizations and vivid depictions of the Scandinavian world in its distant past.

HALFDAN THE SWARTHY

The Yngling race traced its ancestry from the god Frey. Snorre Sturluson, in his famous work, *The Sagas of the Kings of Norway*, mentions a long line of kings who were descended from Fjolne, a son of Frey, and reigned in Sweden having their residence in Upsala. Yngve was one of the god's surnames, and Yngling means a descendant of Yngve. One of the Ynglings, named Aun the Old, sacrificed every 10 years one of his sons to Odin, having been promised that for every son he sacrificed, 10 years should be added to his life. When he had thus slain seven sons, and was so old that he had to be fed like an infant, his people grew weary of him and saved the eighth son, whom he was about to sacrifice.

Ingjald Ill-Ruler, when he took the kingdom on the death of his father Anund, sixth in descent from Aun the Old, made a great funeral feast, to which he invited all the neighbouring kings. When he rose to drink the Brage goblet, he vowed that he would increase his kingdom by one half toward all the four corners of the heavens, or die in the attempt. As a preliminary step he set fire to the hall, burned his guests, and took possession of their lands. When he died, about the middle of the seventh century, he was so detested by his people that they would not accept his son, nor any of his race, as his successor. The son, whose name was Olaf, therefore gathered about him as many as would follow him, and emigrated to the great northern forests, where he felled the trees, gained much arable lands and thereby acquired the nickname The Woodcutter. He and his people became prosperous, and a great influx of the discontented from the neighbouring lands followed. In fact, so great was the number of immigrants that the country could not feed them, and they were threatened with famine. This they attributed, however, to the fact that Olaf was not in the favour of the gods, and they sacrificed him to Odin.

His son, Halfdan Whiteleg, was a great warrior. He conquered Raumarike in Norway and the great and fertile district called Vestfold, west of the fjord called Folden (now the Christiania Fjord). Here he founded a famous temple in Skiringssal, which soon became a flourishing trading station and a favourite residence of the Norwegian kings. The third in descent from him was the great Viking Godfrey the Hunter, who waged war against Charlemagne, and Godfrey's son was Halfdan the Swarthy.

Halfdan was but a year old in 810 when his father was killed. At the age of 18, he assumed the government of Agder, which he inherited from his maternal grandfather. By warfare and by marriage he also increased the great possessions he had received from his father, and, was, beyond dispute, the mightiest king in all Norway. It is told of him that he was a man of great intelligence, who loved justice and truth. He gave laws which he himself kept and compelled everyone else to keep. In order that no one should with impunity tread the law under foot, he fixed a scale of fines which offenders should pay in accordance with their birth and dignity. This code was the so-called Eidsiva-Law, which had great influence in politically uniting the southern districts of Norway which Halfdan had gathered under his sway.

About King Halfdan's second marriage a story is told, which, whether originally true or not, has obviously been the subject of legendary adornment. It runs as follows:

There was a king in Ringerike whose name was Sigurd Hjort. He was a large and strong man. He had a daughter named Ragnhild, who was very beautiful, and a son named Guttorm. While Sigurd Hjort was out hunting he was attacked by the *berserk* Hake and 30 men. He fought desperately, and slew 12 of his assailants, and cut off Hake's hand, but in the end he had to bite the dust. The berserk then rode to his house and carried away Ragnhild and Guttorm, besides much valuable property. He determined to marry Ragnhild and would have done so at once, if his wound had not grown constantly more painful. At Yuletide, when King Halfdan came to feast in Hedemark, he heard of the outrage and resolved to punish it. He sent one of his trusted warriors, named Haarek Gand, with 100 armed men to Hake's house; they arrived in the early morning before any one was awake. They set sentinels at all the doors, then broke into the sleeping-rooms and carried off Sigurd Hjort's children and the stolen goods. Then they set fire to the house and burned it up. Hake escaped, but seeing Ragnhild drive gayly away over the ice with King Halfdan's men, he threw himself upon his sword and perished. Halfdan the Swarthy became enamoured of Ragnhild, as soon as he saw her, and made her his wife.

While Queen Ragnhild was with child she dreamed marvellous dreams. Once she seemed to be standing in the garden, trying to take a thorn out of her chemise, but the thorn grew in her hand until it was like a long spindle – the one end of which struck root in the earth, while the other shot up into the air. Presently it looked like a big tree, and it grew bigger and bigger and taller and taller, until she stood in its shade and her eye could scarcely reach to the top of it. The lower part of the tree was red as blood; further up the trunk was green and fair, and the branches were radiantly white like snow. They were, however, of very unequal size, and it seemed to her that they spread out over the whole kingdom of Norway.

King Halfdan was much puzzled at hearing this dream, and perhaps a little jealous too. Why was it that his wife had such remarkable dreams, while he had none? He consulted a wise man as to the cause of this, and was by him advised to sleep in a pigsty; then he would be sure to have remarkable dreams. The king did as he had been told, and dreamed that his hair was growing very long and beautiful. It fell in bright locks about his head and shoulders, but the locks were of unequal length and colour; some seemed like little curly knots just sprouting from his scalp, while others hung down over his back, even unto the waist. But one lock there was that was brighter and more beautiful than all the rest.

The king related this dream to his sage friend, who interpreted it to mean that a mighty race of kings should spring from him, and that his descendants, though some of them should attain to great glory, should be unequal in fame. But one of them should be greater and more glorious than all the rest. The longest and brightest lock, says Snorre, was supposed to indicate Olaf the Saint.

When her time came, the queen bore a son who was named Harold. He grew rapidly in stature as in intelligence, and was much liked by all men. He was fond of manly sports and won admiration by his strength and his beauty. His mother loved him much, while his father often looked upon him with disfavour. Of his childhood many tales are told which cannot lay claim to credibility. Thus, it is said, that once, while King Halfdan was celebrating Yuletide on Hadeland, all the dishes and the ale suddenly disappeared from the table. The guests went home, and the king, full of wrath, remained sitting. In order to find out who had dared thus to trifle with his dignity, he seized a Finn, who was a sorcerer, and tormented him. The Finn appealed to Harold, who, contrary to his father's command, rescued him and followed him to the mountains. After a while, they came to a place where a chieftain was having a grand feast with his men. There they remained until spring, and when Harold was about to take his leave, his host said to him: 'Your father took it much to heart that I took some meat and beer away from him last winter; but for what you did to me I will reward you with glad tidings. Your father is now dead, and you will go home and inherit his kingdom. But some day you will be king of all Norway.'

When Harold returned home, he found that the chieftain had spoken the truth. His father had been drowned while driving across the ice on the Randsfjord (860). He was mourned by all his people; for there had been good crops during his reign, and he had been a wise ruler and much beloved. When it was rumoured that he was to be buried in Ringerike, the men of Hadeland and of Raumarike came and demanded that the corpse be given to them for burial. For they believed that the favour of the gods would rest upon the district where the king's barrow was. At last they agreed to divide the body into four parts. The men of Ringerike kept the trunk; the head was buried at Skiringssal in Vestfold; and the rest was divided between Hadeland and Hedemark. For a long time, sacrifices were made upon these barrows, and King Halfdan was worshipped as a god.

HAROLD THE FAIRHAIRED (860-930)

Harold was only 10 years old when his father died, and the kings whom Halfdan had conquered thought that the chance was now favourable for recovering what they had lost. But Harold's guardian Guttorm, his mother's brother, conducted the government with power and ability, and assisted his nephew in his efforts to put down his enemies. A long series of battles was fought in which Harold was usually victorious. It was but natural that the young king, flushed with success, should resolve to extend his domain. He knew that there was no king in Norway whose power and resources were equal to his own, and the determination to conquer the whole country may therefore have naturally ripened in his mind. Snorre, however, tells a different story, and as it is a very pretty one, it may be worth repeating.

There was a maid named Gyda, the daughter of King Erik of Hordaland; she was being fostered by a rich yeoman in Valders. When Harold heard of her beauty, he sent his men to her and asked her to become his mistress. The maid's eyes flashed with anger while she listened to this message, and throwing her head back proudly she answered: 'Tell your master that I will not sacrifice my maidenly honour for a king who has only a few counties to rule over. Strange it seems to me that there is no king here who can conquer all Norway, as King Erik has conquered Sweden and King Gorm Denmark.'

The messengers, amazed at her insolence, warned her to give a more conciliatory answer. King Harold was surely good enough for her, they thought; but she would not listen to them. When, at last, they took their leave, she followed them out and said:

'Give this message from me to King Harold. I will promise to become his wedded wife, on this condition, that he shall for my sake conquer all Norway, and rule over it as freely as King Erik rules over Sweden and King Gorm over Denmark. For only then can he be called the king of a people.'

When the messengers returned, they advised the king to break the girl's pride by sending them to take her by force. But the king answered: 'This maid has not spoken ill and does not deserve to be punished. On the contrary, she deserves much thanks for her words. She has put something into my mind, of which I wonder that it has not occurred to me before. But this I now solemnly vow, and call God to witness who made me and rules over all, that I will not cut or comb my hair until the day when I shall have conquered all Norway; or if I do not, I shall die in the attempt.'

Guttorm praised Harold for these words, saying, that he had spoken like a king.

In accordance with his promise, the young king now set about the task which he had undertaken. He went northward with an army and conquered Orkdale and Trondelag, the district about the Drontheim Fjord. In Naumdale, north of Drontheim, there were two kings named Herlaug and Rollaug. The former, when he heard of Harold's march of conquest, built a great barrow, into which he entered with 11 of his men and had it closed behind him. Rollaug, his brother, ordered his royal high-seat to be carried to the top of a hill, and an earl's seat to be placed below, at the foot of the hill. He seated himself in the royal seat, but when he saw Harold approaching, he rolled from the king's seat into the earl's seat, thereby declaring himself to be King Harold's vassal. Harold tied a sword about his waist, hung a shield about his neck, and made him Earl of Naumdale.

Wherever he went, Harold pursued the same policy. The old kings who acknowledged his overlordship he reinstated as his earls in their former dominions. Those who opposed him he killed or maimed. The earls were really governors or representatives of the king's authority. They administered justice in the king's name, and collected taxes, of which they were entitled to keep one-third on condition of entertaining 60 warriors, subject to the king's command. Each earl had under him four or more *hersir* (sub-vassals), who held in fief a royal estate, of an income of 20 marks, on condition of keeping 20 warriors ready to serve the king. It will be seen that the feudal principle was the basis of Harold's state. He deprived the peasants of their allodium, and declared all land to be the property of the king. The cultivators of the soil, from having been free proprietors, became the tenants of the king, and in so far as they were permitted to retain their inherited estates, derived this privilege no more from allodial but from feudal right.

It followed that the king could levy a tax on all land, and that every man who refused to pay the tax forfeited his title. Also a personal tax, which the peasants derisively called the nose-tax (because it was levied in every household according to the number of noses), is said to have been exacted by Harold, and to have caused much dissatisfaction. It is added that many of the former kings who accepted earldoms from him, found themselves in a better position, both financially and as to authority, than they had been before. And this is scarcely to be wondered at. Their royal title had conferred upon them no rights except such as their people voluntarily conceded to them, and their chief privilege amounted to a usage rather than a right to assume command in war, and conduct the public sacrifices. Still it was only in rare cases that they were willing to exchange this shadowy authority for the real power which Harold, by right of conquest, conferred upon them.

A still greater antagonism did the introduction of the feudal land tenure arouse among the free yeomanry, who in their fierce independence could not endure any relation of enforced obedience and subordination. Therefore rebellions against the royal authority, on a smaller or greater scale, were of constant occurrence during the first half of Harold's reign, and there are even indications that they continued much longer. Many of his provinces he had to conquer twice, and it was only the enormous odds in his favour, and the promptness and severity of his punishments, which at length forced the disloyal to accept his sway. It required an energy and resolution such as his to make a nation of all these scattered, predatory and often mutually hostile tribes; and his uniform and systematic policy, as well as his uncompromising sternness, in dealing with resistance, show that he was fully conscious of the magnitude of his task.

It would be tedious to enumerate the battles he fought and the victories he won. With every year that passed he approached nearer to his goal – to be the ruler of all Norway. Many of the mightiest men in the land who had hitherto held aloof now offered him their services, and were glad to accept honours at his hands. Among these were the earl Haakon Grjotgardsson of Haalogaland, and Ragnvald, late Earl of More, who was the father of Duke Rollo of Normandy, and through William the Conqueror the ancestor of the kings of England. Ragnvald was a brave and sagacious man, who assisted the king with counsel and with deeds, and became his most intimate friend and adviser.

Less readily did the men of the great Rafnista family accept Harold's overtures. Kveld-Ulf (Night-Wolf) pleaded old age, when the king sent messengers to him, requesting him to enter his service. This was the more disappointing to Harold, because he had counted on Kveld-Ulf's using the great influence which he wielded, in his favour. He sent messengers once more and offered Kveld-Ulf's son, Bald Grim, high dignities if he would become his vassal. But Bald Grim replied that he would accept no dignity which would raise him in rank above his father. Then the king's patience was exhausted, and he would have resorted to other arguments than verbal ones, if Kveld-Ulf's brother-in-law, Oelve Nuva, had not interceded in his behalf. Oelve finally obtained the old chieftain's consent to have his second son Thorolf enter the king's service if he saw fit. Thorolf was then out on a Viking cruise with Oelve's brother, Eyvind Lambe, but he was expected home in the autumn. On their return, both accepted Harold's offer and became his men. Thorolf particularly rose rapidly in the king's favour, on account of his intelligence, beauty and courtly manners. The old Kveld-Ulf, however, looked with suspicion upon their friendship, and hinted that he expected that nothing good would come of it.

The kings of Sweden had from of old had claims on that part of Norway which is called Viken. Also Vermeland, which since the days of Olaf the Woodcutter had belonged to the Ynglings, was declared to be an integral part of Sweden, and the Swedish king, Erik Eimundsson, seized the opportunity, while Harold was occupied with his conquests in the north, to invade the latter province, besides Ranrike and portions of Vingulmark. When these tidings reached Harold, he hastened southward, fined and punished those of the peasants who had promised allegiance to his enemy, and finally went northward to Vermeland where, by a singular coincidence, he met the Swedish king at a great feast given by the mighty yeoman Aake. Probably to avoid bloodshed, the two kings and their warriors were entertained in separate buildings; but while Harold and his men were lodged in the new mansion and made to eat and drink out of new horns and precious dishes, Erik's party were made to enjoy their cheer in an old building, and their horns and dishes, though artfully wrought, were not new. When the time came for leaving, Aake brought his son to Harold and begged him to take him into his service. At this Erik grew very wroth and rode away. Aake hastened to accompany him; and when asked why he had made such a difference in the entertainment, he replied that it was because Erik was old, while Harold was young.

'Thou must indeed remember that thou art my man,' said King Erik.

'When thou sayest that I am thy man,' answered the yeoman, 'then I may say with equal right that thou art my man.'

This answer so angered the king that he drew his sword and killed Aake. Harold, when he heard of his death, pursued his slayer but did not succeed in overtaking him.

The princes and chieftains who had opposed Harold had, so far, accomplished nothing but their own ruin. Those who still retained their lands concluded that separately they could never hope to prevail against him, and they therefore united and met the conqueror in 872 with a great fleet in the Hafrs-Fjord. The war-horns were blown, and King Harold's ship was foremost, wherever the fight was hottest. In its prow stood Thorolf, the son of Kveld-Ulf, who fought with splendid bravery, and the brothers Oelve Nuva and Eyvind Lambe. The issue seemed long doubtful, and many of the king's best men were slain; spears and stones rained down in showers, and the arrows flew hissing through the air. At last, Harold's *berserks*, seized with a wild fury, stormed forward and boarded the enemies' ships. The carnage was terrible, and one by one the chieftains fell or fled. King Harold here won (as the sagas relate) one of the greatest battles that was ever fought in Norway; and there was from this day no longer any formidable opposition to him. Among the many who were wounded at Hafrs-Fjord was Thorolf, and in fact all who had stood before the mast in the king's ship, except the *berserks*. The skald Thorbjorn Hornklove made a song about the victory, fragments of which are still extant.

At a feast which shortly after the battle was given in his honour, Harold's hair was cut by Ragnvald, the Earl of More, and all marvelled at its beauty. While he had formerly been called Harold Lufa, i.e., the Frowsy headed, he was now named Harold the Fairhaired. Having now accomplished what he had set out to do, he married Gyda. The romance is, however, spoiled by the fact that he had some years before married Aasa, the daughter of the earl, Haakon Grjotgardsson, and had by her three sons – Halfdan the White, Halfdan the Swarthy and Sigfrid. The sons Gyda bore him were named Guttorm, Haarek and Gudrod.

In his relations with men Harold was no more faithful than in his relations with women. He was a man of indomitable will and courage, sagacious and far-seeing, shunning no means for the accomplishment of his ends. He could not, however, endure the characteristics in others which he valued in himself. When his jealousy was once aroused, it was not easily again allayed. As is the manner of tyrants, he was apt to humiliate those the most whom he had most exalted, and his suspicion often fell upon those who least deserved it. The first victim of his jealousy was Thorolf, the son of Kveld-Ulf, who, after the battle of Hafrs-Fjord, had stood especially high in his favour.

Thorolf had by a wealthy marriage and by inheritance accumulated a large fortune and lived in princely style. His liberality and winning exterior made him hosts of friends, and his thrift and ability procured him the means to practise a magnificent hospitality. The king had made him his *sysselmand*, or bailiff, in Haalogaland, and Thorolf particularly distinguished himself by the energy and shrewdness which he displayed in collecting the tax from the Finns, who, as a rule, were not anxious to make contributions to the royal treasury. During a journey which Harold made through Haalogaland, Thorolf made a feast for him, the splendour of which had never been equalled in those parts of the country. There were in all 800 guests – 500 of whom Thorolf had invited, while 300 were the attendants of the king. To the astonishment of his host, Harold sat, dark and silent, in the high-seat, and seemed ill-pleased with the efforts that were made to entertain him. Toward the end of the feast he repressed his ill-humour, however, and when his host at parting presented him with a large dragon-ship with complete equipment, he seemed much pleased.

Nevertheless, it was not long before he deprived him of his office as royal bailiff, then espoused the cause of his enemies, and used all sorts of contemptible slanders as a pretext for attacking him on his estate, Sandness, and burning his house. When Thorolf broke out through the burning wall, he was received with a hailstorm of spears. Seeing the king he rushed toward him, with drawn sword, and cut down his banner-bearer; then, when his foe was almost within reach of his sword, fell, crying: 'By three steps only I failed.' It was said that Harold himself gave him his death-wound, and he later avowed himself as his slayer to the old Kveld-Ulf. When he saw his former friend lying dead at his feet, he looked sadly at him; and when a man passed him who was busy bandaging a slight wound, he said: 'That wound Thorolf did not give thee; for differently did weapons bite in his hands. It is a great pity that such men must perish.'

When Kveld-Ulf heard of his son's death, his grief was so great that he had to go to bed. But when he heard that it was the king who had slain him, and that he had fallen prone at his slayer's feet, he got up and was well content. For when a dying man fell on his face, it was a sign that he would be avenged. In the meanwhile, being far from powerful enough to attack Harold openly, the old man gathered all his family and his goods and set out for Iceland; but lingered long along the coast of Norway, in the hope of finding someone of Harold's race upon whom he could wreak vengeance. In this he was successful. The two sons of Guttorm, Harold's uncle and former guardian, were sailing northward with two of the king's men. These Bald Grim and Kveld-Ulf attacked, killed the king's cousins, and captured the ship. Then, wild with exultation, Bald Grim mounted the prow and sang:

> Now is the Hersir's vengeance
> On the king fulfilled.
> Wolf and eagle tread on
> Yngling's children.
> Seaward swept flew Halvard's

> *Lacerated corpse,*
> *And the eagle's beak*
> *Tears Snarfare's wounds.*

From that time forth, there was a blood-feud between the Yngling race and Kveld-Ulf's descendants, and the famous saga of Egil, Bald Grim's son, tells of a long chain of bloody deeds which all had their origin in the king's treachery to Thorolf.

Kveld-Ulf and Bald Grim were not the only chieftains who sought refuge abroad from Harold's oppression. After the battle of Hafrs-Fjord, when the king proceeded with uncompromising rigor to enforce the feudal system, several thousand men, many of whom belonged to the noblest families of the land, crossed the sea, and found new homes in the Orkneys and the Hebrides, whence again many found their way to Iceland. A great number also sailed direct for the latter country, and the so-called *Landnama* book (the *Domesday Book* of Iceland) has preserved the names, and, at times, bits of the history of the most important original settlers.

Much as we may sympathize with the indomitable spirit which made these men sacrifice home and country for a principle, there is also another view of the case which has to be considered. Harold the Fairhaired was founding a state, which would support a higher civilization than could possibly be developed among a loose agglomeration of semi-hostile tribes. The idea of a national unity, which was the inspiration of his work, required the enforcement of an organic system which to the independent chieftains must have appeared extremely oppressive. The payment of taxes, which to the citizen of the modern state is not apt to appear humiliating, seemed to the Norse chieftains unworthy of a freeman. When Harold commanded them to refrain from robbing and plundering expeditions within the confines of his kingdom, they felt outraged, and could see no reason why they should submit to such unwarrantable curtailment of time-honoured privileges. One of them, Rolf, or Rollo, son of the king's friend, Ragnvald, Earl of More, defied the order, made *strand-hug* in Viken, and was declared an outlaw. Neither his father's influence, nor his mother's prayers, could save him. Just on account of his high birth, Harold was determined to make an example of him.

Rollo is known in the Norse sagas as Rolf the Walker, because he was so tall and heavy that no horse could carry him. With a large number of followers he sailed southward to France, and after having harried the country for several years, made in 912 a compromise with King Charles the Simple, by which he was to accept Christianity and receive a large province in fief for himself and his descendants. This province was named Normandy, and has played a large role in the history of the world.

It is told of Rollo that when he was requested to kiss the king's foot in token of fealty, he answered: 'I will never bend my knee before any man; nor will I kiss any one's foot.' After much persuasion, however, he permitted one of his men to perform the act of homage for him. His proxy stalked sullenly forward, and pausing before the king, who was on horseback, seized his foot and lifted it to his lips. By this manoeuvre, the king came to make a somersault, at which there was great laughter among the Norsemen. Rollo did literally, like the poor boy in the fairy tale, marry the princess and get half the kingdom. For, it is told, that Charles gave him for a bride his daughter Gisla, who, however, died childless. He ruled his duchy with a rod of iron; and he must have learned a useful lesson from King Harold, for it is said that he restrained robbery with a firm hand, and hanged the robbers. So great was the public security in his day, that the peasants could leave their ploughs and tools in the field over night without fear of losing them. Rollo's son was William Longsword, who was the father of Richard the Fearless, who had a son of his own name. This latter Richard, surnamed the Good, had a son named Rollo, or Robert the Magnificent, who was the father of William the Conqueror.

The emigration of the discontented yeomen and chieftains removed the last obstacle to the organization of Harold's feudal state. According to an approximately accurate calculation, about 800 heads of families went with their households to Iceland, to the Scottish isles and to Jemteland, leaving behind them estates which were promptly confiscated by the king. Those who endeavoured to sell their lands met with small success; for to buy the property of emigrants was considered as an act hostile to the king. Great wealth was thus accumulated in Harold's hands, and the means of rewarding his friends at the expense of his enemies were at his disposal.

The emigrants were, therefore, doubly instrumental in cementing the state which they had endeavoured to destroy. A large number of officials were needed to superintend the great landed estates, and Harold chose these from his immediate dependents. The so-called Aarmaend were merely superintendents or stewards, who took charge of the crown lands, and forwarded to the king his share of the income. They were often thralls or freedmen, and were looked down upon by the yeomanry as their inferiors. The earls, on the other hand, who belonged to the old tribal aristocracy, held their land in fief, and were, in a limited sense, proprietors, though their sons could not, by any absolute right, claim to inherit them. It was, however, the custom to continue such estates from father to son. The third class of property was the land which the yeomanry had formerly held by allodial right, and which they now held with as much security and right of inheritance, as the king's nominal tenants. As long as they paid their taxes, it was of course in the king's interest to leave them unmolested.

It was natural that with his great wealth Harold should keep a court of exceptional splendour. He was fond of song and story and always kept skalds about him who sang his praise and glorified his deeds. He could be generous when the occasion demanded, and would then scatter his gold with royal liberality. But in little things he was reputed to be mean; and it was a common complaint among his courtiers that they did not get enough to eat. Some legends recounted by Snorre show that with all his stern inflexibility toward men, he was easily deceived by women. Thus, it is related that once, while he was at a Yuletide feast, in Guldbrandsdale, a Finn came to him and persuaded him to accompany him to his tent. There he showed the king a girl named Snefrid, whose beauty made a great impression upon him. He chatted with her for a while; then drank a goblet of mead which the Finn brought him. No sooner had he swallowed the liquid than he became so enamoured of Snefrid that he refused to leave her, and demanded that she should that very day become his wife. He loved her with such abandonment and passion that he neglected the government and lived only for her.

She bore him five sons in rapid succession, and then died. Harold's grief knew no bounds. He refused to have her buried, but sat staring at her beautiful corpse, night and day. For, oddly enough, it is told that Snefrid's beauty remained unchanged after death, and there was no sign of decay. All the king's men feared that he had lost his reason, and one of them finally persuaded him, on some pretext, to have the corpse moved. But the very instant it was touched, the most hideous change occurred. The flesh turned blue, and a terrible stench filled the room. The king then recovered his reason, and ordered the body to be burned. But when it was placed on the pyre, snakes, adders, toads and horrible creeping things teemed in and about it, so that no one could endure the sight of it. Then Harold comprehended that he had been the victim of sorcery; and he grew so angry that he chased away from him the children Snefrid had borne him. And yet, strangely enough, it was this branch which endured the longest, and from which a long line of kings descended. The names of Snefrid's sons were Sigurd Rise (Giant), Gudrod Ljome, Halfdan Haalegg (Longlegs) and Ragnvald Rettilbeine.

The only one of King Harold's wives who was of royal birth was Ragnhild, the daughter of King Erik the Younger in South Jutland. She replied, when he first sent messengers to woo her, that she would not marry the mightiest king in all the world, if she had to put up with one-thirtieth part of his affection. To a second message she replied that she would marry King Harold if he would put away all his other wives. This he consented to do, and made Ragnhild his queen. She lived, however, only three years after her marriage; and Harold then took back several of his former wives and mistresses. Ragnhild had left him one son, Erik, whom he loved the most of all his children.

Marriage was entirely a civil contract during the days of Germanic paganism and was in no wise associated with religion or religious ceremonies. It was an easy thing for a husband to obtain a divorce from his wife, but it was customary to go through with this formality before marrying a second. Open polygamy, as practised by Harold, was contrary to custom and must have been regarded with reprobation by the people. For all that, Harold was, during the latter part of his reign, a popular ruler and well beloved both by yeomanry and chieftains.

As his children grew up, Harold began to reap some of the disadvantages of his scattered family relations. His sons, having different mothers, and having been fostered by yeomen in different parts of the country, could scarcely be strongly conscious of their kinship. They were jealous of each other, and particularly jealous of the mighty earls who sat like little kings upon their estates ruling over land and people. It was to give vent to this feeling that Halfdan Longlegs and Gudrod Ljome, without any warning, attacked Ragnvald, the Earl of More, and burned him up with 60 of his men. When Harold heard of this dastardly deed, he gathered an army and resolved to punish his sons. Gudrod, who had taken possession of the earldom after Ragnvald, surrendered without fighting, while Halfdan Longlegs sailed with three ships for the Orkneys, where he chased away Turf-Einar, the son of the Earl of More, and made himself king of the islands. Turf-Einar returned, however, surprised Halfdan, and put him to death in a barbarous manner. Although Halfdan had been a rebel against the king's authority, and Turf-Einar in slaying him had avenged his own father, Harold had no choice but to wreak vengeance upon the slayer of his son. He accordingly sailed with a fleet for the Orkneys, opened negotiations with Turf-Einar, and accepted as 'blood-atonement' 60 marks in gold. Whether it was on the same occasion that he made a cruise to Scotland, harrying the coast, is perhaps, doubtful. His chief purpose, as on a previous cruise in the same waters, was to break up the various nests of Vikings, who from this convenient retreat made frequent attacks upon the coast of Norway during the summer months.

A fertile cause of disagreement among Harold's sons was their jealousy of Erik, whom their father conspicuously favoured. When he was 12 years old, Erik was given five ships to command, and with a choice crew went on Viking cruises. Much did the old king delight in hearing the tales of his prowess, and the daring enterprises in which he had played a part. The ominous surname 'Blod-Oexe' (Blood-Axe), which the lad acquired by his deeds in battle, only endeared him the more to his father. It was his love of this favourite son which induced him in his 50th year (900) to commit an act, whereby he virtually undid the great work of his life and brought misery upon unborn generations.

He called a *thing* or general assembly of the people, probably at Eidsvold, and made all his sons kings, on condition that they should, after his death, acknowledge Erik as their overlord. To each he gave a province to govern, permitting him to keep one-third of the revenues for himself, leaving one-third for the earls, and sending one-third to the sovereign. The royal title should be inherited by all his direct descendants in the male line, legitimate or illegitimate birth making no difference. To the sons of his daughters he gave earldoms. In this disastrous act of Harold, making no distinction between legitimate and illegitimate children, lies the germ of the civil wars and terrible internecine conflicts which ravaged the kingdom he had established and exhausted its powers, until for 400 years it sank out of sight, and its name seemed to have been blotted out from among the nations. It seems incredible that the wisdom and energy which had built up a great state could be coupled with the unwisdom and the weakness which in the end broke it down again. Harold evidently looked upon the royal office as a piece of personal property which he had by his sword acquired, and which all his male descendants had an equal right to inherit. At the same time he must, after the experience he had had with his sons, have known them too well to suppose that they would peacefully acquiesce in his decision, living together in fraternal unity.

If he cherished any illusion, Erik lost no time in dispelling it. He first killed Ragnvald Rettilbeine, the son of Snefrid, because he was said to be a sorcerer. Next he attacked his brother Bjorn the Merchant (Farmand) because he declined to pay him tribute, killed him and plundered his house. Halfdan the Swarthy (Svarte) in Drontheim resolved to avenge this outrage, concluding that none of Harold's sons were safe, as long as Erik was permitted, with impunity, to take the law into his own hands. While Erik was feasting at the farm, Selven, Halfdan surrounded the house and set fire to it. Erik succeeded in escaping with four men, and he hastened southward to complain to his father. King Harold, it is told, was greatly incensed, collected his fleet and sailed to Drontheim, where Halfdan, though with an inferior force, stood ready to meet him. The battle was about to begin, when the skald, Guttorm

Sindre, reminded the two kings of a promise they had made him. Once he had sung a song in their honour, and as he refused all the gifts they offered him, they both swore that whatever he should ask of them, they would fulfil. 'Now,' he said, 'I have come to claim the guerdon of my song.'

Hard as it was, they could not break their royal promise. Peace was made, and father and son separated. Halfdan was permitted to keep his province, but had to vow solemnly that he would henceforth make no hostile demonstration against Erik. For all that the hatred between the two lasted, though curbed for a while by the fear of the king.

When Harold was nearly 70 years old, he took for his mistress Thora of Moster, who on account of her great height was surnamed Moster-stang (Moster-pole). She bore him a son who was named Haakon. Much dissatisfaction was there among the king's other sons when this latecomer made his appearance, and he would probably not have grown to manhood, if an incident had not occurred which removed him beyond their reach. The story told by Snorre in this connection is full of interest, but sounds incredible. Once, it is told, messengers arrived from King Ethelstan in England, bringing a precious sword to King Harold, who accepted it and returned thanks.

'Now,' said the messengers, 'thou hast taken the sword, as our king wished, and thou art therefore his sword-taker or vassal.'

Harold was angry at having been thus tricked, but did not molest the messengers. The next year, however, he sent his young son Haakon with an embassy to Ethelstan. They found the king in London, and were well received by him. The spokesman of the embassy then placed the boy, Haakon, on Ethelstan's knee, saying, 'King Harold begs thee to foster this child of his servant-maid.'

Ethelstan angrily drew his sword, as if he would kill the child; but the spokesman said: 'Now that thou hast once put him upon thy knee, thou mayst murder him, if it please thee; but thereby hast thou not slain all King Harold's sons.'

To foster another man's child was in Norway regarded as an acknowledgment of inferiority; and Harold had thus repaid Ethelstan in his own coin. There are, however, several circumstances which make the story suspicious. In the first place Ethelstan and his ancestors had had too severe an experience of Norsemen and Danes to wish to challenge the mightiest of them by a wanton insult; and again, it is more credible that Harold sent his youngest son out of the country for his own safety, than in order to play an undignified trick upon a foreign king. At all events, Haakon was treated with the greatest kindness by the English king, and won his affection.

When Harold the Fairhaired was 80 years old, he felt no longer able to bear the burden of the government. He therefore led Erik to his royal high-seat, and abdicated in his favour. Three years later he died (933), after having ruled over Norway for 73 years.

ERIK BLOOD-AXE (930-35)

While Harold's despotism had been civilizing and, on the whole, beneficent, that of Erik Blood-Axe was disorganizing and destructive. With him the old turbulent

Viking spirit ascended the throne. Power meant with him the means of gratifying every savage impulse. Brave he was, delighting in battle; cruel and pitiless; and yet not without a certain sense of fairness and occasional impulses of generosity. In person he was handsome, of stately presence, but haughty and taciturn. Unhappily he married a woman who weakened all that was good in him and strengthened all that was bad. Queen Gunhild possessed a baneful influence over him during his entire life. She was cruel, avaricious and treacherous, and was popularly credited with all the ill deeds which her husband committed. There are strange legends about her, attributing to witchcraft the power she had over everyone who came in contact with her. According to Snorre, Erik met her in Finmark, whither she had been sent by her parents to learn sorcery. For the Finns were in those days credited with a deep knowledge of the black art. The two sorcerers with whom she was staying were both determined to marry her, and like the princess in the fairy tale, she concealed Prince Erik in her tent, and begged him to rid her of her troublesome suitors. This, in spite of many difficulties, Erik did, carried Gunhild away to his ships, and made her his wife.

She was, it is said, small of stature, insinuating and of extraordinary beauty; but she was the evil genius of her husband, egging him on to deeds of treachery and violence which made him detested by his people. It was in great part the disfavour with which she was regarded which raised rebels against Erik's authority in various parts of the country and brought popular support to his brothers in their endeavour to cast off his yoke. In spite of his father's efforts, Erik's sovereignty had not been universally recognized, and no sooner was King Harold dead than Halfdan the Swarthy declared himself to be sovereign in Trondelag and Olaf in Viken. A few years after that, however, Halfdan died suddenly, and the rumour said that he had been poisoned by Queen Gunhild. The men of Trondelag then chose his brother Sigfrid for their king, and Erik found his kingdom gradually shrinking both from the north and the south. Being prepared for an attack from Erik, Sigfrid and Olaf determined to join their forces, and to complete all arrangements, the former went to visit the latter in Tunsberg. When Erik heard of this, he went in haste to the town with a large number of men, and surprised and killed both his brothers. Olaf's son Tryggve escaped, however, and was kept in concealment, as long as Erik was master in the land.

Erik had now killed four of his brothers, if not five, and it was the common opinion that Gunhild would not rest until she had exterminated all the race of Harold the Fairhaired outside of her husband's line.

While Erik was a youth, he had made the acquaintance of an Icelander named Thorolf, the son of Skallagrim (Bald Grim) and nephew of Thorolf Kveld-Ulf's son, whom King Harold had treacherously slain. This Thorolf, like his uncle and namesake, was a tall and handsome man, of fine presence and winning manners. He had made Erik a present of a ship, very beautifully built and decorated, and had thereby gained his friendship. In return Erik had obtained from his father permission for Thorolf to remain unmolested in the country. The handsome Icelander made many friends in Norway, among whom two mighty men named Thore Herse and Bjorn the Yeoman. When he returned to Iceland he brought with him, as a gift from the king to his father, an axe with a handle of precious workmanship. But Bald Grim, though he received his son well, treated King Erik's gift with contempt, and finally, when Thorolf again made a cruise to Norway, he sang an insulting verse and begged to have it reported to Erik. The axe he also wished to have returned. Thorolf, who was determined not to revive the ancient feud, threw the axe into the ocean, and conveyed his father's thanks and greeting to the king. If he had had his way, the blood feud would have been at an end. But he had a younger brother named Egil, who insisted upon bearing him company, and he soon fanned the dying embers into flame.

Egil was the very incarnation of the old untameable Norse spirit, the turbulent and indomitable individualism, which is incapable of considering any but personal aims, and of submitting to any kind of discipline. Like his father, Bald Grim, he was large of stature, swarthy and ill-favoured, and displayed in his childhood a fierce and revengeful spirit, but also a rare gift of song, which, no less than his foolhardy deeds, brought him fame during his long and adventurous career.

The two brothers arrived safely in Norway and became the guests of Thore Herse, between whose son Arinbjorn and Egil a warm friendship sprung up. While Thorolf went to be married to Aasgerd, the daughter of Bjorn the Yeoman, Egil was forced by a severe illness to remain at home. When he became convalescent, he accompanied one of Thore's overseers to a royal steward named Baard, and met there King Erik and Queen Gunhild. Baard, in his zeal to please the king, neglected the Icelander, and when the latter became unruly, at a hint from the queen, mixed soporific herbs in his beer.

Egil's suspicion was aroused, however, and he poured out the beer and killed Baard. Then he ran for his life, swam out to an island in the fjord, and when the island was searched, killed some of those who had been sent to find him; whereupon he made his escape in their boat. Although King Erik was very angry, he accepted the atonement in money which Thore Herse offered for Baard's death, and was persuaded to allow Egil to remain in the land. Queen Gunhild was much incensed at his forgiving spirit, and asked if he counted the slaying of Baard as naught; to which the king replied: 'For ever thou art egging me on to violence; but my word, once given, I cannot break.'

As no persuasions availed, Gunhild made up her mind to use someone else as the instrument of her retaliation. It is told that she had been fond of Baard, whom Egil had slain; but as he was a man of low birth, it was scarcely this personal fondness, but rather a sense of outraged dignity which impelled her to persevere in her plans of vengeance. At a great sacrificial feast, at the temple of Gaule, she made her brother, Eyvind Skreyja, promise to kill one of Bald Grim's sons; but as no chance presented itself, he slew instead one of Thorolf's men; in return for which he was outlawed by Erik, as a *vargr í veum* – i.e., wolf in the sanctuary. The two brothers now went on Viking cruises, took service under Ethelstan, in England, and fought under his standard a great battle, in which Thorolf fell. Egil now married his widow, Aasgerd, and returned with her to Iceland. He had then been abroad for 12 years.

Hardly had he settled down, however, when he learned that his father-in-law, Bjorn the Yeoman, was dead, and that one of Gunhild's favourites named Berg-Anund, had taken possession of his property. He therefore lost no time in returning to Norway, and with his friend Arinbjorn's aid pleaded his case at the *Gulathing*, in the presence of the king and queen. But the *thing* broke up in disorder, and Egil had to sail back to Iceland without having accomplished his purpose. Considerations of prudence had, however, no weight with him, and before long he started for the third time for Norway, surprised Berg-Anund, and killed not only him, but the king's son Ragnvald, who was his guest. In order to add insult to injury, he mounted a cliff, and raised what was called a shame-pole, or pole of dishonour, to Gunhild and the king. On the top of the pole he put the head of a dead horse, while he called out in a loud voice: 'This dishonour do I turn against all the land-spirits that inhabit this land, so that they may all stray on wildering ways, and none of them may chance or hit upon his home, until they shall have chased King Erik and Gunhild from the land.'

Thereupon he cut these words, in runes, into the pole, and sailed back to Iceland. It seemed, too, as if the curse took effect. For when Erik had been four years upon the throne, his youngest brother, Haakon, landed in Trondelag, and the following year was made king. The news ran like wildfire through the country, and was everywhere received with jubilation. Erik made a desperate effort to raise an army, but the people turned away from him, and he was obliged to flee with his wife and children, and a few followers. Among those who remained faithful to him was Egil's friend, Arinbjorn. He now sailed about as a Viking, harrying the coasts of Scotland and England, and finally accepted a portion of Northumberland in fief from King Ethelstan, on condition of defending the country against Norse and Danish Vikings. It was also stipulated that he should be baptized and accept Christianity. Although the different sagas which deal with Erik's later life give somewhat conflicting accounts, it is obvious that he was no more popular in England than he had been in Norway. It appears that he was once, or probably twice, expelled from Northumberland, but again returned. By a most singular chance, a tempest here drove his mortal enemy right into his clutches.

Egil, it is told, was restless and discontented at home; and the common belief was that Gunhild by sorcery had stolen his peace of mind. He wandered uneasily along the strand and looked out for sails, and took no pleasure in his wife and children. Finally, when he could stay at home no longer, he equipped a ship and sailed southward to England. He was shipwrecked at the mouth of the Humber, lost his ship, but saved himself and his 30 warriors. From people whom he met, he learned that Erik Blood-Axe ruled over the country; and knowing that there was slight chance of escape, he rode boldly into York and sought his friend Arinbjorn. Together they went to Erik, who inquired of Egil how he could be so foolish, as to expect anything but death at his hands. Gunhild, when she saw him, demanded impatiently, that he should be killed on the spot. She had thirsted so long for his blood; she could not endure a moment's delay in her hotly desired vengeance. Erik, however, granted the Icelander a respite until the next morning; Arinbjorn begged him, as a last bid for life, to spend the night in composing a song in honour of Erik. This Egil promised; and Arinbjorn had food and drink brought to him and bade him do his best. Being naturally anxious, he went to his friend in the night and asked him how the song was progressing. Egil replied that he had not been able to compose a line, because there was a swallow sitting in the window whose incessant screaming disturbed him, and he could not chase it away. Arinbjorn darted out into the hall, and caught a glimpse of a woman, who ran at the sight of him. At that very instant, too, the swallow disappeared. To prevent her from returning, Arinbjorn seated himself outside of Egil's door and kept watch through the night. For he knew that the swallow was none other than the queen, who by sorcery had assumed the guise of the bird.

The next morning Egil had finished his song and committed it to memory. Arinbjorn now armed all his men, and went with Egil and his warriors to the king's house. He reminded Erik of his fidelity to him, when others had forsaken him, and asked, as a reward for his services, that his friend's life be spared. Gunhild begged him to be silent; and the king made no response. Then Arinbjorn stepped forward and declared that Egil should not die, until he and his last man were dead.

'At that price,' answered the king, 'I would not willingly buy Egil's death, although, he has amply deserved whatever I may do to him.'

Suddenly, when the king had spoken, Egil began to recite with a clear, strong voice, and instantly there was silence in the hall. This is a portion of his song:

> Westward I sailed o'er the sea.
>> Vidrar himself gave me
>> The ichor of his breast,
>> And with joy I roamed.
>> As the ice-floes broke,

Forth I launched the oak;
For my mind's hull
Of thy praise was full.

For thy fame, O king,
Made me fain to sing;
And to England's shore,
Odin's mead I bore.
Lo, in Erik's praise,
Loud my voice I raise.
May my song resound
The wide earth around.

List to me, my king,
Well remembering
What I sing to thee
Now, unquailingly.
For the world knows well
How men round thee fell;
Glad has Odin seen
The field where thou hast been.

Burst the shield and bayed
Deep the battle-blade.
At its ruddy draught
The Valkyrias laughed.
Lo, the sword-stream swayed
Like a wild cascade.
O'er the fields away
Rang the steel's strong lay.

Men with eager feet
Sprang their foe to meet;
None thy band knew save
Heroes true and brave.
For in heart and frame
Bright burned valor's flame;
'Neath their thund'ring tread
Shook the earth with dread.

'Mid the weapons' clank
Men in death-throes sank:
From the heaps of slain
Rose thy fame amain.

Erik sat immovable while Egil sang, watching his face narrowly. When the song was at an end, the king said: 'The song is excellent, and I have now considered what I will do for Arinbjorn's sake. Thou, Egil, shalt depart hence unharmed; because I will not do the dastardly deed to kill a man who gave himself voluntarily into my power. But from the moment thou leavest this hall, thou shalt never come before my eyes again, nor before the eyes of my sons. Nor is this to be regarded as a reconciliation between thee and me or my sons and kinsmen.' Thus Egil bought his head by his song, and the song is therefore called 'Hofudlausn', or 'The Ransom of the Head'.

Egil then took his leave, visited Ethelstan once more; went to Norway and had many adventures, before he returned to Iceland, where he died between 990 and 995. He was then over 90 years old. Another of his poems, called 'Sonartorek', 'The Loss of the Son', is the most beautiful poem in the Icelandic language.

Erik Blood-Axe remained in England and suffered many vicissitudes of fate, until he fell in battle in 950 or 954. He is repeatedly mentioned by the English chroniclers under the name of Erik Haroldson. After his death Gunhild had a *draapa* composed in his honour, an interesting fragment of which is still extant. She then went to Denmark with her sons, and was well received by the Danish king, Harold Bluetooth (Blaatand), the son of Gorm the Old.

HAAKON THE GOOD (935-61)

Haakon, though he was outwardly his father's image, did not resemble him in spirit. He was of a conciliatory nature, amiable and endowed with a charm of manner which won him all hearts. It is said that his foster father had given him the counsel at parting never to sit glum at the festal board, and it is obvious that he took the lesson to heart. When he landed in Trondelag, people flocked about him, and he won the chieftains for his cause by friendliness and promises which he afterwards conscientiously kept. He took part in the games of the young, and in the serious discussions of the old, excelled in all manly sports, and won admiration no less by his beauty than by his intelligence and generous disposition. The rumour of his arrival spread like fire in withered grass, and people said that old King Harold had come back once more to his people, gentler and more generous than before, but no less mighty and beautiful.

The first chieftain whose influence Haakon sought to enlist in his behalf was the powerful Sigurd, Earl of Hlade, who had been the friend and protector of his mother, and the guardian of his infancy. The earl received him well, and promised to support his claims to the kingdom. With this view he called, in Haakon's name, a great meeting of the peasants in Trondelag, and made a speech in which he denounced the cruelty of Erik Blood-Axe and declared his allegiance to Haakon. When the earl had finished, Haakon arose and offered, in case the peasants would make him their king, to restore to them their allodium, of which his father had deprived them. This announcement was received with great rejoicing; and from all parts of the plain came cries of homage and approval. Amid joyful tumult Haakon was made king, and immediately started southward with a large train of warriors. Wherever he went, the people flocked about him and offered him allegiance. The Oplands followed the example of Trondelag, and in Viken both chieftains and peasants eagerly espoused his cause. As already related, Erik made a desperate attempt to gather an army, and, failing in this, fled with his family and a few faithful followers to the Orkneys, and thence to England.

It was consistent with Haakon's conciliatory disposition that he did not molest or depose his nephews, Gudrod Bjornsson and Tryggve Olafsson, but confirmed them as kings in Viken. It appears, however, that, nominally at least, they recognized his overlordship. Other sons and grandsons of Harold the Fairhaired he met with the same friendliness, giving to each what he considered to be his due. As soon as peace was thus established, and there was no one left to dispute his power, Haakon devoted himself energetically to the improvement of the internal administration of his kingdom. He divided the country into *Thing-Unions*, or judicial districts, and by the aid of wise and experienced men greatly improved the laws. One famous code, called the Gulathings-law, has particularly shed lustre upon his name, and the enlargement and improvement of the Frostathings-law is also, by some of the sagas, attributed to him. The only radical change which he introduced was the breaking up of his father's feudal state, by the restoration of the allodium to the peasants. But this one change necessitated many others. When the king relinquished his right to tax the land, he thereby deprived himself of the ability to keep an army, and had to consign, in part, to the peasants themselves the defence of their respective districts.

It was naturally the seacoast which was most exposed to attack; and in the absence of all but the most primitive means of communication it became possible for an enemy to ravage long stretches of land, before the intelligence of his presence reached the king. In order to remedy this, Haakon ordered *varder* or signal fires to be lighted, at fixed intervals, all along the coast at the approach of an enemy; but he partly counteracted the good effect of the reform by the severe punishment with which he threatened those who, without adequate cause, lighted the *varder*. In order to obtain the means to defend the coast, he divided it into marine districts, each of which was bound, on demand, to place a fully manned and equipped ship of war at the disposal of the king. This was, of course, but another form of taxation, but was less distasteful to the peasants, because its purpose and necessity were obvious, and no degrading dependence was implied, since the people had again become the free possessors of the soil. Nevertheless there are indications that the personal tax, derisively called the nose-tax, which had been introduced by Harold, was continued, at least for a while, by Haakon; as it is expressly stated that his first ships of war were built by the income of the nose-tax.

Having arranged the military and judicial affairs of his kingdom, Haakon turned his attention to a matter which he had long had at heart. He had been christened in his childhood in England, and was an earnest votary of the Christian religion. But, coming, as he did, to the kingdom of his father, not as a conqueror, but as a candidate for the people's favour, he did not venture at once to attack the national faith. His friend, Earl Sigurd of Hlade, was a fanatical adherent of the Asa-faith, and Haakon might have counted on his enmity rather than his support, if he had exhibited an ill-considered zeal for the displacement of the old by a new religion. Haakon, therefore, temporized, and it was not until the 15th or 16th year of his reign (950–51), when his unbonded popularity seemed to warrant any venture, that he took a decisive step on behalf of Christianity. He sent to England for a bishop and a number of priests, and published a decree, forbidding the people to sacrifice to the old gods, and demanding of them that they should accept the faith in Christ. He called upon the peasants to meet him at Drontheim, where he repeated his demand. But the peasants refused to declare themselves; and begged the king to have the matter legally settled at the *Frosta-thing*. Here there was a great concourse of people; and when the assembly had been called to order, Haakon rose and in an earnest and dignified speech begged the peasants to forsake the old heathen gods who were but wood and stone, and to believe in the one living God and be baptized in His name. An ominous murmur ran through the crowd at these words, and the peasant Aasbjorn of Medalhus arose and answered in these words:

'When thou, King Haakon, didst call thy first assembly here in Drontheim, and we took thee for our king, we believed that heaven itself had descended upon us; but now we do not know whether it was liberty we gained, or whether thou wishest to make us thralls once more, by thy strange demand that we shall forsake the faith which our fathers and all their forefathers have had before us [...]. They were sturdier men than we are; and yet their faith has done well enough for us. We have learned to love thee well, and we have allowed thee to share with us the administration of law and justice. Now, we peasants have firmly determined and unanimously agreed to keep the laws which thou didst propose here at the *Frosta-thing*, and to which we gave our assent. We all wish to follow thee, and to have thee for our king, as long as a single one of us peasants is alive – if only thou, king, wilt show moderation, and not demand of us things in which we cannot follow thee, and which it would be unseemly for us to do. But if thou hast this matter so deeply at heart that thou wilt try thy might and strength against ours, then we have resolved to part from thee and take another chieftain who will aid us in freely exercising the religion which pleases us. Choose now, O king, between these two conditions, before the assembly has dispersed.'

Loud shouts of approval greeted this speech; and it was, for a while, impossible for anyone to make himself heard. At last, when the tempest had subsided, Earl Sigurd of Hlade, probably after consultation with Haakon, rose and said that the king would yield to the wishes of the peasants and would not part with their friendship. Encouraged by this first concession, the peasants now demanded that the king should participate in their sacrifices and preside at the sacrificial feast. Much against his will, Haakon was again induced to yield, but tried to pacify his conscience by making the sign of the cross over the horn consecrated to Odin. During the following year he was also compelled to eat horse flesh at the Yuletide sacrifice, and to omit the sign of the cross when drinking the toasts of the heathen gods. Full of wrath he departed, intimating that he would soon come back with an army large enough to punish the Tronders for the humiliation they had put upon him. There is little doubt that he would have carried out this threat, if external enemies had not directed his energies in another direction.

The sons of Erik Blood-Axe had, after their father's death, sought refuge with King Harold Bluetooth in Denmark. The two elder, Gamle and Guttorm, had roamed about as Vikings, ravaged the coasts of Norway and the lands about the Baltic, while the third son, Harold, was adopted by his namesake, the Danish king, and received his education at his court. They were all valiant warriors, but were much governed by their shrewd and cruel mother, Gunhild. They naturally cherished no goodwill toward their uncle Haakon, who had dispossessed them of their kingdom; and while they were not yet strong enough to wage regular war, they seized every opportunity to annoy and harass him.

They fought many battles with Tryggve Olafsson, who, as king in Viken, was charged with the defence of the southern coast, and were sometimes victorious and sometimes vanquished. In the year 952, when Tryggve was absent, Haakon took occasion to deliver an effective blow at the

Danish Vikings who were infesting this part of the country (though the sons of Erik were not this time among them), pursued them southward, and harassed the coasts of Jutland and the Danish isles. It appears, however, that this mode of retaliation did not permanently discourage the Vikings, and as long as Harold Bluetooth showed open hostility against Norway, by espousing the cause of Gunhild and her sons, it is quite natural that the warlike zeal and rapacity of the Danes should be directed against the neighbouring kingdom. It is obvious, too, that Haakon, by his attack upon Danish soil, gave a more personal character to the animosity which the Danish king entertained toward him, and Gunhild lost no time in profiting by this change of feeling.

From this time forth her sons appear no longer as warlike adventurers, bent upon private vengeance, but as commanders of fleets and armies, and formidable pretenders to the Norwegian throne. In 953 they defeated Tryggve Olafsson at Sotoness, and compelled him to abandon his ships and save himself by flight. When the news of this disaster reached Haakon, he hastily made peace with the Tronders who had forced him to sacrifice, and called upon Earl Sigurd to aid him with all the ships and men at his command. Earl Sigurd promptly obeyed and sailed southward to meet the king. At Agvaldsness they overtook the sons of Gunhild and vanquished them in a hotly contested battle. Haakon slew with his own hand his nephew Guttorm Eriksson, and cut down his standard. The surviving brothers fled with the remnants of their army to Denmark, and kept the peace for two years. But in 955 they returned once more with a largely increased force and surprised King Haakon at Fraedo in Nordmore. The signal fires had not been lighted, and no intelligence of the presence of the enemy had reached the king until it was too late. He asked his men whether they preferred to stay and fight or avoid battle, until they had gathered a sufficient force. To this an old peasant named Egil Uldsaerk (Woolsark) made answer: 'I have been in many battles with thy father, King Harold. Sometimes he fought with a stronger and sometimes with a weaker foe. But he was always victorious. Never have I heard him ask counsel of his friends as to whether he should run; nor will we give thee such counsel. For we think that we have in thee a brave chieftain, and trusty aid shalt thou receive from us.'

When the king praised these words and declared himself ready to fight, Egil cried out joyously: 'In this long season of peace I have been afraid that I should die of old age on the straw of my bed – I who never asked anything better than to follow my chieftain and die in battle! Now, at last, I shall have my wish fulfilled.'

As soon as the sons of Erik had landed, the battle commenced. They had six men for every one of King Haakon's. Seeing that the odds were so heavily against his lord, Egil Woolsark took 10 standard-bearers aside and stole up a slope of land in the rear of Gamle Eriksson's battle array. He made them march with long intervals, so that only the tops of their standards could be seen above the slope, and not the men themselves. The Danes, spying the waving banners, supposed that a fresh force was coming to cut them off from their ships, and they raised a great cry and fled. It was in vain that Gamle, who had discovered the stratagem, shouted with a loud voice commanding them to stay. Panic had seized them, and their commander himself was swept away with the hurrying mass, until he reached the beach, where he made a final stand. Here Egil Woolsark attacked him and received his death-wound after a desperate conflict. Haakon too rushed in upon Gamle, who defended himself bravely, but having received terrible wounds, threw himself into the ocean and was drowned. The other brothers swam to their ships and returned to Denmark.

This victory secured peace to Norway for six years. Haakon had thus an opportunity to resume his efforts to Christianize the country. But his experience of the peasants' temper had apparently discouraged him. Personally he remained a Christian, and induced many of his friends to forsake the heathen faith. He lacked, however, the uncompromising vigour and the burning zeal of a martyr and propagandist. He preferred gentle to harsh measures, and shrank from antagonizing those who had been faithful to him in time of need. It is probable, too, that the counsel of his friend, Earl Sigurd, tended to cool his ardour, by emphasizing the political phase of the religious question. The result of this conciliatory policy, in connection with the good crops which prevailed during his reign, was to make King Haakon universally beloved. It is doubtful if a king has ever sat upon the throne of Norway who has been closer to the hearts of the people. Therefore, as an expression of their affection for him, they named him Haakon the Good.

In the 26th year of his reign (961) Haakon was summering with his men-at-arms on his estate Fitje in Hordaland. A large number of guests were with him, among whom the skald Eyvind Skaldespilder (Skald-Spoiler), who was on his mother's side a great-grandson of Harold the Fairhaired. The king was seated at the breakfast table, when the sentinels saw a large fleet of ships sailing in through the fjord. They called the skald Eyvind aside, and begged him to decide whether those were not hostile ships. Eyvind sprang into the hall where the king was sitting, and sang a verse, announcing the approach of the sons of Erik. Haakon arose and looked at the ships. Then he turned to his men and said: 'Here many ships are coming against us, and our force is but small. It is plainly to be seen that we shall have to fight against heavier odds than ever before; for the sons of Gunhild come with a larger force today than on previous occasions. Loath I am to bring my best men into too great a danger; and loath I am, too, to flee, unless wise men decide that it would be foolhardy to await the foe.'

Eyvind Skald-Spoiler replied in verse that it would ill befit a man like King Haakon to flee from the sons of Gunhild. 'Manly speech is that, and in accordance with my mind,' answered the king; and when the other warriors with one accord clamoured for battle, he put on his armour, buckled his sword about his loins and seized spear and shield. On his head he wore a golden helmet which flashed in the sun. Beautiful he was to behold, with his mild and noble countenance, and his bright hair streaming down over his shoulders. Upon the fields without he arranged his men in battle array, and raised his standards. The sons of Erik disembarked with a large army, commanded by the third of the brothers, Harold, and his two uncles, Eyvind Skreyja and Alf Askman. The battle which now commenced was wild and bloody. The army of the sons of Gunhild was six times as numerous as that of King Haakon. But Haakon, knowing his Norsemen well, did not lose heart. Wherever the fight was hottest, there flashed his golden helmet. He joked with Eyvind, the skald, when he passed him, and improvised a verse in reply to the one with which he was greeted. The fiercer the conflict grew, the higher rose the king's spirits.

At last, when the heat oppressed him, he flung away his armour and stormed forward at the head of his men. The supply of spears and arrows soon ran short, and the hostile ranks clashed together and fought, hand to hand, with their swords. The shining helmet made the king very conspicuous, and Eyvind Skald-Spoiler noticed that it served as a target for the Danish spears. He therefore took a hood and pulled it over the helmet. Eyvind Skreyja, who was just rushing forward to meet the king, thereby lost sight of him, and he cried out: 'What has become of the king of the Norsemen? Does he hide himself, or is he afraid? No more do I see the golden helmet?' 'Keep on as thou art steering, if thou wishest to find the king of the Norsemen,' shouted Haakon, and throwing away his shield, seized his sword with both hands, and sprang forward where all could see him. Eyvind Skreyja bounded forward with uplifted sword, but one of the king's men caught the blow upon his shield, and in the same instant Haakor cleft Eyvind's head and neck down to the shoulders. The example of their king fired the Norsemen's courage, while the fall of their greatest champion brought confusion to the Danes. The former charged with renewed fury, while the latter were pressed down to the beach, and leaped into the ocean; many were killed or drowned, but a few, including Harold Eriksson, saved themselves by swimming, and were picked up by the ships. While pursuing the fleeing foe, Haakon was hit in his right arm by a peculiarly shaped arrow, and all efforts to staunch the blood proved in vain. It was said that Gunhild had bewitched this arrow and given it to her chamberlain, with the charge that he should shoot it off against King Haakon. As night approached, the king grew weaker and weaker, and fainted repeatedly. One of his friends offered to take his body over to England, when he was dead, so that he might be buried in Christian soil. But Haakon replied: 'I am not worthy of it. I have lived like a heathen, and therefore it is meet that I should be buried like a heathen.'

Thus died Haakon the Good and, as the saga says, was mourned alike by friends and foes. His last act before dying was to send a ship after the sons of Gunhild, and beg them to come back and take the kingdom; for he had himself no sons, and his only daughter, Thora, could not, according to the law, succeed to the throne.

Eyvind Skald-Spoiler made a song in King Haakon's honor, called 'Haakonarmaal', in which he praised his virtues and described his reception in Valhalla.

HAROLD GRAYFELL AND HIS BROTHERS (961-70)

The sons of Gunhild lost no time in taking possession of the kingdom of their fathers. It was not, however, the entire Norway to which they succeeded, but only the middle districts. In Viken, Tryggve Olafsson and Gudrod Bjornsson, both grandsons of Harold the Fairhaired, ruled as independent kings, and in Trondelag Earl Sigurd, of Hlade, refused to acknowledge the supremacy of the race of Erik Blood-Axe. Undoubtedly the brothers were only biding their time until they should be strong enough to punish these contemptuous rebels; but so bitter was the feeling against them, even in the provinces which they nominally ruled, that they had all they could do in maintaining their authority within the narrow limits which had from the beginning been assigned to them. One of the chief causes of their unpopularity was their dependence upon the Danish king, by whose aid they had gained the kingdom, and to whom they apparently stood in a relation of vassalage. As a consequence of this, they took no pains to gain the favour of the Norwegian people, but surrounded themselves with a great throng of Danish warriors who constituted their court and the main-stay of their strength. Very unfortunate, too, was the influence which their mother Gunhild exercised over them. Scarcely had she returned to Norway, when she resumed her baneful activity, egging her sons on to cruel and treacherous deeds, by which they forfeited the people's respect and undermined their own power. Misfortune had not taught her caution, nor had age softened the fierce malignity of her temper.

The oldest surviving brother, Harold, surnamed Graafeld (Grayfell) resembled, in appearance his father, Erik Blood-Axe. He was haughty, avaricious and revengeful; tall of stature, finely built and of lordly presence, but for all that a weak and vacillating character. He lacked entirely that kindliness and *bonhomie* which had made his uncle Haakon the Good beloved of all the people. Of the other brothers we have no definite knowledge; they seem, however, all to have inherited their share of the traits which made their parents odious. Two of them, Gudrod and Sigurd Sleva, proved themselves worthy sons of the malicious Gunhild. The others are usually spoken of collectively, and their names are variously given.

It may have been the sense of his unpopularity which induced Harold Grayfell to make overtures to the former courtiers of King Haakon. Several of them, it appears, entered his service, but felt themselves ill at ease among the foreign warriors who enjoyed his favour and confidence. Jealousies and petty bickerings were the order of the day; every allusion to King Haakon's virtues gave offence, and when the song of Eyvind Skald-Spoiler, praising his former lord, reached the king's ears, he exclaimed angrily: 'You love King Haakon yet, and it is best that you follow him and become his men.'

The men then departed, not suddenly, but one by one, and made the names of the sons of Gunhild still more detested throughout the land. Eyvind Skald-Spoiler in a noble verse refused to be King Harold's court poet, and after his departure made a song in which he compared Haakon with Harold, much to the latter's disadvantage. There was in that year (962) a great dearth of food in the land; crops and fisheries failed, and the cattle had to be fed with leaf buds instead of grass. In some districts snow fell in the middle of summer. The people who believed that the gods had sent these evil times because of their anger at the kings, gave vent to their discontent in loud murmuring. Harold Grayfell and his brothers, it appears, had been baptized in their youth in England and were nominally Christians. They refrained from sacrificing, and broke down and destroyed many heathen temples. But they made no effort to enlighten the people regarding the new religion; and probably considered questions of faith as being of small moment. Surrounded, as they were, by enemies on all sides, their first ambition was naturally to re-conquer the kingdom which Harold the Fairhaired had bequeathed to their father.

It became, therefore, a political necessity to break the power of Earl Sigurd of Hlade, as well as of Tryggve Olafsson and Gudrod Bjornsson in Viken. To do this in open warfare was out of the question; and Gunhild, therefore, persuaded her sons to resort to treachery.

By flattery and promises, Harold bribed Grjotgard Haakonsson, a younger brother of Earl Sigurd, to send him word when a favourable opportunity should present itself for killing the earl. At the same time the king sent messengers with gifts and friendly assurances to the intended victim, but failed for a while to lead him into any trap. At last, when these repeated protestations of friendship had, perhaps, made him relax his vigilance, Harold Grayfell and his brother Erling, having received notice from Grjotgard, surprised the earl in the night, while he was away from home, and burned him and all his retinue. By this deed, however, they raised up against themselves an enemy who proved more dangerous to them than the one they had slain. Earl Sigurd's son, Haakon, was 25 years old, when his father died, and a man splendidly equipped in body and mind. He was a great warrior, handsome in person, sagacious, resolute and friendly and affable in his demeanour. His family was, in some respect, as good as any king's; for he belonged to the old tribal aristocracy which had maintained its authority in Trondelag from the earliest Germanic times. When he was born, King Haakon the Good, who happened just then to be his father's guest, had poured water upon his head and given him his own name.

When the intelligence of Earl Sigurd's death reached him, Haakon called the Tronders together, and a great multitude responded to his summons. They clamoured for vengeance upon the treacherous sons of Gunhild, confirmed Haakon in the dignity which his father had possessed, and declared themselves ready to follow him. With a great fleet he sailed out of the Drontheim fiord; but the sons of Gunhild fled southward and did not venture to give battle. The Tronders, having given their allegiance to Earl Haakon, refused to pay taxes to Harold Grayfell, who, after some indecisive fights, was compelled virtually to recognize his rival's independence. Haakon, however, was well aware what such a concession must have cost the haughty king, and he knew, too, that his independence would last only so long as he was able to defend it. With a view to strengthening his position, he therefore formed an alliance with the two kings in Viken, which only had the effect of speedily bringing down upon the latter the vengeance of Gunhild's sons. Harold Grayfell and his brother Gudrod made a pretence of quarrelling, and feigned a furious hostility to each other. A Viking cruise which they were about to undertake together was accordingly deferred, and Gudrod, complaining of his brother's conduct, sent a friendly message to Tryggve Olafsson, begging him to accompany him on his cruise. Tryggve accepted the invitation, and on arriving at the appointed place of meeting was foully murdered with all his men.

King Gudrod Bjornsson (the son of Bjorn the Merchant) was about the same time surprised at a banquet by Harold Grayfell, and slain after a desperate resistance. After these exploits, Harold and Gudrod re-united and took possession of Viken. They hastened to King Tryggve's dwelling in the hope of exterminating his whole race. But Tryggve's widow, Aastrid, anticipating their intention, had fled with her foster father,

Thorolf Luse-skjegg (Lousy-Beard), and a few attendants. She was then with child, and on a little islet in the Rand's fiord, where she was hiding, she bore her son Olaf Tryggvesson.

Wherever she went Gunhild's spies pursued her. Hearing that she had borne a son, the wily queen spared no effort to get her in her power. During the entire summer Aastrid was compelled to remain on the solitary islet, venturing out only in the night, and hiding among the underbrush in the daytime. When toward autumn the nights began to grow darker, she went ashore with her attendants, travelling only when the darkness protected them. After many hardships she reached her father Erik Ofrestad's estate in the Oplands; but even here the wily Gunhild left her no peace. A man named Haakon was despatched with 30 armed attendants to search for her and her child; but Erik of Ofrestad got news of their mission in time to send his daughter and grandson away. Disguised as beggars, Aastrid and Thoralf Lousy-Beard travelled on foot from farm to farm, and came toward evening to the house of a man named Bjorn. They asked for food and shelter, but were rudely driven away by the inhospitable peasant. At a neighbouring farm, however, they were kindly received by a peasant named Thorstein.

Gunhild's emissaries, having searched in vain at Ofrestad, got on the track of the fugitives, and learned at the house of Bjorn that a handsome woman in poor attire, bearing a babe in her arms, had applied for shelter early in the evening. This conversation one of Thorstein's servants happened to overhear, and on arriving home, related it to his master. Thorstein immediately, with loud chiding and pretended wrath, roused the supposed beggars from their sleep, and drove them out into the night. This he did in order to deceive the servants and other listeners. But when Aastrid and Thoralf were well under way, he told them that Gunhild's hired assassins had arrived at the neighbouring farm, and that his only desire was to save them. He also gave them a trusted attendant who could show them the best hiding places in the forest. At the shores of a lake they concealed themselves among the tall bulrushes.

Thorstein, in the meanwhile, sent their pursuers in the opposite direction, and led them a dance through forest and field in a vain search for the fugitives. The next night, when Haakon and his men had given up the search, he sent food and clothes to Aastrid, and furnished her with an escort to Sweden, where she found a place of refuge with a friend of her father's named Haakon the Old. Gunhild, however, was not to be discouraged. She sent two embassies to King Erik of Sweden, demanding the surrender of Olaf Tryggvesson, and received each time permission to capture the child, without interference on the part of the king. But Haakon the Old was a mighty man, and determined to defend his guests. The threats of Gunhild's ambassador did not frighten him. While the latter was speaking, a half-witted thrall, named Buste, seized a dung-fork, and rushed at him, threatening to strike. The ambassador, fearing to be soiled, took to his heels, and was pursued by the thrall. How the queen received him on his return is not recorded.

Of the internal enemies of Gunhild's sons, Earl Haakon of Hlade now alone remained; and it was not an unnatural desire on their part to reduce him to subjection. Anticipating, as usual, their action, the earl was on the look-out for them; but having ascertained the size of their fleets, he saw the hopelessness of his cause, and forthwith sailed to Denmark, where he was well received by King Harold Bluetooth (964). It will thus be seen that the friendship between Harold Grayfell and the Danish king had not endured the strain of diverging interests. The former, as soon as he felt secure in his power, refused to recognize the latter's claim to Viken, and paid him no taxes. Harold Bluetooth, therefore, allied himself with Earl Haakon, the bitterest enemy of the sons of Gunhild, hoping, by his aid, to regain his lost dominion. What particularly encouraged him in this expectation was the continued dearth which prevailed in Norway, and the resulting unpopularity of the kings which, with every year, grew more pronounced. It was of no avail that Harold Grayfell almost every summer went on Viking cruises, gaining a great fame as a warrior and bringing home rich treasures. The people hated him only less than they hated his mother Gunhild.

An exploit of his brother Sigurd Sleva aroused a demonstration of wrath which came near culminating in open rebellion. Sigurd Sleva had paid a visit to a mighty yeoman named Klypp Thorsson, and had, in the absence of the master of the house, been hospitably received by his beautiful wife Aaluf. He had become enamoured of his hostess, and had grievously insulted her. Klypp, on his return, learned what had occurred; and swore to avenge the shame which had been brought upon him by Gunhild's son. When Harold Grayfell and Sigurd, in the autumn of 964, held a *thing* at Vors, they were attacked by the enraged peasants, and had to save themselves by flight. Klypp, with a number of his friends, pursued Sigurd, slew him with his own hand, and was himself slain by one of Sigurd's men.

Earl Haakon, who, from his Danish retreat, watched the events in Norway, heard these tidings with satisfaction. The sudden check which his ambition had received had made him ill, and for some time he appeared listless, refusing to eat and drink, or to communicate with anybody. But when his plans of vengeance were matured, he rose from his bed, strode forth with his old vigour, and proceeded to weave a complicated net of intrigues. Harold Bluetooth had at that time a difficulty with his nephew Gold-Harold, who demanded a share in the government; and, having confidence in the sagacity of the earl, he asked his advice. The earl saw here his opportunity, and had no scruple in availing himself of it. He dissuaded the king from killing his nephew, because such a deed would arouse indignation and alienate the great party in Denmark, who desired to see Gold-Harold on the throne. Far better would it be if he employed Gold-Harold to punish Harold Grayfell and his brothers, and in the end reward him with the throne of Norway. Thereby the king would increase his own power, and convert a dangerous rival into a friend and ally. This advice seemed good to Harold Bluetooth, and after some persuasion he found courage to act upon it. He sent a friendly message to his foster son, Harold Grayfell, inviting him to come and take possession of his old fief in Denmark, the income of which he might, indeed, need during the hard times that prevailed in Norway. Harold Grayfell, after some vacillation, accepted this invitation, and sailed to Denmark with three ships and 240 men; but no sooner had he set foot upon Danish soil than he was attacked by Gold-Harold, who slew him and nearly all his men.

This was the first act in the drama which Earl Haakon had planned. The second contained a surprise. The earl went to Harold Bluetooth, and represented to him that his nephew, as king of Norway, would become a more dangerous rival than he had been before; and frankly offered to kill him, if the king would promise not to avenge his death. Furthermore, he demanded, as his reward, the kingdom of Norway in fief, under the overlordship of the king All this seemed very tempting to Harold Bluetooth; and like all weak and vicious men, he made objections only for the purpose of having them overcome. In the end he gave his consent; and Gold-Harold was immediately attacked and killed by Earl Haakon. With a large army the two conspirators now sailed for Norway, and won the whole country without striking a blow. So great was the hatred of Gunhild and her sons, that not a man drew his sword in their defence.

The two surviving brothers, Gudrod and Ragnfred, made a pretence of resistance, rallying a few followers about them; but did not venture to give battle. Seeing the hopelessness of their cause, they fled with their mother to the Orkneys (965). Ragnfred, however, returned the following year with a considerable fleet, largely made up of Vikings who had gathered about him, and fought an indecisive battle with Earl Haakon. He even succeeded in reconquering four of the north-western shires. For nearly a year Haakon made no effort to expel him. It was not until the spring of 967, that he felt himself strong enough to appeal to arms once more; and this time Ragnfred and his brother Gudrod, who in the meantime had joined him, were defeated at Dingeness, and driven into exile.

According to the most reliable accounts, they went to Scotland, but continued for several years to harass the coast of Norway by sudden attacks. They were, however, no longer sufficiently formidable to cause the earl any serious inconvenience, although he was not slow to seize upon their attacks as a pretext for discontinuing the payment of the tax which he had pledged to the Danish king. Gunhild died, in all probability, either in Scotland or the Orkneys, although one of the sagas relates, that she was enticed to Denmark by Harold Bluetooth, under promise of marriage, and at his command drowned in a swamp.

EARL HAAKON (970–95)

By his daring intrigue Earl Haakon had attained the goal of his desires. He had avenged his father's death, humiliated his enemies and gained a power far beyond that of any of his ancestors. With a nature like his, however, no goal is final. The ease with which he had managed Harold Bluetooth and his nephew – using them as tools for his own ends – had, no doubt, inspired him with a supreme confidence in his ability, and a corresponding contempt of those whose shrewdness was inferior to his own. The purpose therefore soon matured in his mind to repudiate his obligations to the Danish king, and make himself the independent ruler of Norway. The opportunity for carrying this purpose into effect soon presented itself.

The Emperor Otto I of Germany, who claimed sovereignty over Denmark, died in 973, and was succeeded by his young son, Otto II. Harold Bluetooth, who had always resented the emperor's claim, even though he was forced to recognize it, made extensive preparations for a campaign against Otto II, and sent messengers to his vassal, Earl Haakon, commanding him to come to his aid with all the forces at his disposal. Earl Haakon, whatever his inclinations may have been, did not deem it advisable to disobey, and in the spring of the year 975 sailed southward with a large fleet and army. He did duty for a while in defending the wall of Dannevirke, and actually beat the emperor in a great battle. Then, feeling that his task had been accomplished, he boarded his ships and prepared to sail homeward. The emperor, however, hearing that Dannevirke was deserted by its defenders, returned for a second attack, and forced his way into Jutland.

Whether Harold Bluetooth fought with him does not appear. We only know that he accepted a humiliating peace, reaffirming his vassalage, and, according to a creditable source, promising to introduce the Christian religion, both in his own kingdom and in Norway. It is probable that both Harold and his son, Sweyn Forkbeard, had been baptized before, but continued in their hearts to be devoted to the Asa faith. It was scarcely zeal for Christianity, but fear of the emperor, which induced Harold to send for Earl Haakon and force him to accept baptism and to promise to convert his countrymen to the new religion. It is strange that a man as shrewd as Haakon, after his recent desertion of Dannevirke, should have obeyed this summons. In all likelihood the victorious battle which he had fought gave him confidence in his power to justify himself; and there may also have been circumstances connected with the affair which changed its aspect to contemporaries. It is not inconceivable, however, that he really wished for a plausible pretext for rebellion, and deliberately took his chances.

With a shipload of priests Haakon departed from this fateful meeting with the Danish king. But no sooner was he out of Harold's sight, than he put his priests ashore, and began to harry on both sides of the Sound. On the rocky cliffs of Gautland he made a grand sacrificial feast, to counteract the effect of his recent baptism, and stood watching for a response from the old gods, that they looked upon him with favour, and would give him success in the war he was about to undertake. Then two ravens came and followed his ships, 'clucking' loudly. The ravens were the birds of Odin, and Haakon saw in their flight a happy augury. A warlike fury seems now to have possessed him. With a recklessness which in so prudent a man is inconceivable (except under high religious excitement), he burned his ships, landed with his army on the coast of Sweden and marched northward, ravaging the land with fire and sword. A broad track of blood and desolation followed his destructive progress. Even in the Norwegian province Viken, which Harold Bluetooth had given to Sweyn Forkbeard, he continued his devastations in pure wantonness, as if to advertise his defiance of the Danish king and all that belonged to him. From Viken he took his way overland to Drontheim, where he henceforth lived as an independent sovereign, though for some reason he refrained from assuming the royal title.

It was probably some time before Harold Bluetooth could raise an army strong enough to pursue the earl and defeat him in his own stronghold. There is some doubt, however, whether his campaign to Norway, for the purpose of punishing his rebellious vassal, took place in 976 or two or three years later.

Following Haakon's example, he laid the land waste, killing and burning everything in his path. In Laerdal in Sogn, he left only five houses unburned. When, however, Earl Haakon sailed southward to meet him with a numerous fleet, the king suddenly lost his courage, set sail, and made for home. It is said that Harold Bluetooth had on that occasion no less than 1,200 ships.

Earl Haakon had now peace for some years. He had, as soon as he had conquered the sons of Gunhild, married the beautiful Thora, daughter of the powerful chieftain Skage Skoftesson: and had by her two sons, Sweyn and Heming, and a daughter, Bergljot. Considerably older than these children, was the earl's illegitimate son, Erik, who, according to one account, was born when his father was but 15 years old. There is, however, good reason for questioning this statement. Erik was a stubborn and turbulent youth, who could not be induced to respect the authority of his father. When he was 10 or 11 years old, he got into a dispute with Haakon's brother-in-law Tiding-Skofte, about the right to anchor his ship next to the earl's. Tiding-Skofte, who was a great favourite of the earl's, had been especially granted this privilege and was inclined to insist upon it. To avenge this insult Erik watched his chance and slew him a year later. He thereby incurred the hostility of his father, and fled to Viken, where Sweyn Forkbeard gave him a cordial reception.

It was scarcely to be expected that Harold Bluetooth should quietly accept the humiliation which Earl Haakon had put upon him. He was, indeed, getting too old himself to measure strength again with his powerful antagonist; and he therefore delegated the task of punishing him to his friends and allies.

Among the latter were the celebrated JomsVikings, who lived at Jomsborg, on the island of Wollin, at the mouth of the river Oder. These Vikings were a well-disciplined company of pirates, who made war their exclusive business, living by rapine and plunder. They were bound by very strict laws to obey their chief, to spurn death and danger, to aid each other and to endure pain uncomplainingly. Like the Italian condottieri, they were willing to serve any master with whom their chief could make satisfactory arrangements. For women they professed contempt, and no woman was permitted to enter their burgh. These formidable marauders Harold Bluetooth endeavoured to stir up against his rebellious vassal.

At a funeral feast which their chief, Earl Sigvalde, made in honour of his father, a great throng of warriors were present; the ale and mead flowed abundantly, and there was much good cheer in the hall. When Earl Sigvalde rose to drink the toast to Brage, he vowed that before three winters were past he would kill Earl Haakon or expel him from his realm, or himself die in the attempt. The other Vikings, not wishing to be outdone by their chief, made vows scarcely less daring; and the enthusiasm rose to such a pitch that no achievement seemed beyond their strength. When they woke up the next morning, the affair wore a slightly different aspect; but having once promised, they could not retreat. So they made a virtue of necessity, and prepared in haste for the attack.

The rumour of their vows had, however, preceded them, and reached Erik, the son of Earl Haakon. Disregarding his father's hostility, he hurried northward to Drontheim with all the men he could gather, and placed them at the disposal of the earl. The JomsVikings, in the meanwhile, occupied themselves in plundering the coasts of Norway, sailing slowly northward with a well-manned fleet of 60 ships. The number of their warriors was between 7,000 and 8,000. They met Earl Haakon and his sons Erik, Sweyn, Sigurd and Erling at Hjorungavaag in Sondmore. The earl had 180 ships, the majority of which were inferior in size and equipment to those of his enemies; and according to a probable calculation, his force amounted to 10,000 or 11,000 men. So many men and ships had scarcely ever before been seen together in the North, and the sagas relate that the fight in Hjorungavaag (986) was the greatest battle that has ever been fought in Norway.

As Earl Haakon saw the first of the JomsVikings sailing up the sound, he disposed his own ships in battle array. He gave his oldest son Erik command of the right wing, placed Sweyn on the left, and himself commanded the centre. Opposite to Sweyn were the ships of the famous JomsViking Vagn Aakesson, whose impetuosity and daring had made him dreaded far and wide. The young Earl Sweyn was no match for such an antagonist, and after a gallant resistance he began to retreat. His brother Erik, seeing the imminent danger, rowed around to his wing, drove Vagn back, and forced his brother to resume his position. Then he hastened back to his own wing, and came just in time to check the progress of Bue the Big (Digre), who commanded the corresponding wing of the JomsVikings.

The battle now grew furious, and the carnage on both sides was tremendous. The spears and arrows fell in rattling showers about Earl Haakon, as he stood in the prow of his ship, and so many hit him that his shirt of mail was torn into strips, and he was forced to throw it away. The ships of the Vikings were higher than those of the Norsemen, and the advantage which this afforded the former told at first heavily against the latter. Then, it is told, Earl Haakon suddenly disappeared, and the legend relates that he took his youngest son Erling, went ashore with him, and sacrificed him to the gods for victory. Instantly the skies grew black, and a violent hailstorm beat down, pelting the faces of the JomsVikings and almost blinding them. Every grain of hail, says the saga, weighed two ounces. Some even declared that they saw the maidens of Odin, the Valkyrias, Thorgerd and Irp, standing in the prow of Earl Haakon's ship, sending forth a deadlier hail of unerring arrows. The JomsVikings fought half blindly, fell on the slippery decks in a slush of blood and melting hail, but in spite of the twilight and confusion yet held their own. Then suddenly their chief, Earl Sigvalde, turned and fled. Vagn Aakesson, who saw him, cried out in a frenzy of rage: 'Why dost thou flee, thou evil hound, and leave thy men in the lurch? That shame shall cling to thee all thy days.' Earl Sigvalde made no reply; and it was well for him that he did not; for in the same instant a spear was hurled forth from Vagn's hand, transfixing the man at the helm. A moment before Vagn had seen his chieftain there, and it was for him the spear was intended.

Confusion now became general; and all Earl Sigvalde's men, seeing that his standard was gone, fell out of line and fled. At last only Vagn Aakesson and Bue the Big were left. Earl Haakon pulled up alongside the ship of the latter and a combat ensued, which, in wildness and fury, has scarcely a parallel in the records of the sagas. Two great champions of the JomsVikings, Haavard the Hewer (Huggende) and Aslak Rock-skull (Holmskalle), vaulted over the gunwale of the earl's ship and made tremendous havoc, until an Icelander seized an anvil which was used for sharpening the weapons and dashed it against Aslak's head, splitting his skull. Haavard had both his feet cut off, but fought on furiously, standing on his knees. The spears whizzed about the earl's ears and the arrows flew past him with their angry twang. His men fell and the JomsVikings were pressing forward. Then, in the nick of time, came his son Erik, and, with a throng of his men, boarded the galley of Bue the Big.

In their first onset Bue received a terrible cut across the nose. 'Now,' he cried, 'I fear the Danish maidens will no more kiss me.' Then, seeing that resistance was vain, he seized two chests full of gold and shouted: 'Overboard all Bue's men,' and leaped into the sea. Vagn Aakesson's galley was likewise boarded, and there was a repetition of former scenes of carnage. When all but 30 of his men were dead he at last surrendered. The captives were brought ashore and ordered to sit down in a row upon a long log. Their feet were tied together with a rope, while their hands remained free. One of Earl Erik's men, Thorkell Leira, whom Vagn at that memorable funeral feast had promised to kill, was granted the privilege to reciprocate the intended favour toward Vagn. With his axe uplifted he rushed at the captives, and, beginning at one end of the log, struck off one head after another. He meant to keep Vagn until the last, in order to increase his agony. But Vagn sat chatting merrily with his men; and there was much joking and laughter.

'We have often disputed,' said one, 'as to whether a man knows of anything when his head is off. That we can now test, for if I am conscious, after having lost my head, I will stick my knife into the earth.'

When his turn came all sat watching with interest. But his knife fell from his nerveless grasp, and there was no trace of consciousness. One of the Vikings on the log seemed particularly in excellent spirits. He laughed and sang, as he saw the bloody heads of his comrades rolling about his feet. Just at that moment Earl Erik approached and asked him if he would like to live.

'That depends,' answered the Viking, 'upon who it is who offers me life.'

'He offers who has the power to do it,' said the earl; 'Earl Erik himself.'

'Then I gladly accept,' the Viking replied.

The next in order, as the executioner walked up to him, made an equivocal pun, which, however, pleased Earl Erik so well that he set him free. Eighteen had now been beheaded and two pardoned. The 21st was a very young man with long, beautiful hair and a handsome countenance. As Thorkell Leira paused before him he twisted his hair into a coil and begged him not to soil it with his blood. In order to humour him, Thorkell told one of the bystanders to take hold of the coil while he struck off the head. The man consented; but just as the axe was descending, the JomsViking pulled his head violently back, and the obliging assistant had both his hands cut off.

'Some of the JomsVikings are alive yet,' he cried, as he raised his head laughing.

Earl Erik, who had witnessed this scene, asked him his name.

'I am said to be a son of Bue,' he answered.

'Very likely is that,' said the earl; 'do you wish to live?'

'What other choice have I?' asked the young Viking.

When Thorkell Leira observed that Earl Erik was in a forgiving mood, he grew very wroth. Fearing that he might be thwarted in his vengeance on Vagn Aakesson, he sprang past the remaining men and, with his axe raised above his head, rushed toward his enemy. One of the men on the log, however, seeing his chief's danger, flung himself forward so that Thorkell stumbled over his body and dropped his axe. Instantly Vagn was on his feet, seized the axe and dealt Thorkell such a blow that the axe went through the neck, and the blade was buried in the earth. Thus Vagn Aakesson was the only one of the JomsVikings who accomplished what he had vowed to do. Earl Erik, full of admiration of his feat, now had his bonds removed and gave him his liberty. The other prisoners who were yet alive were also set free at the earl's command.

Not far from the spot where this occurred sat Earl Haakon with many of his chieftains. Suddenly the loud twang of a bowstring was heard, and in the same instant Gissur the White, from Valders, who sat next to the earl and was more magnificently dressed than he, fell dead, pierced by an arrow. Many men hastened down to the ship whence the arrow had come, and found Haavard the Hewer, who, half dazed with loss of blood, stood on his knees with his bow in his hands. 'Tell me, lads,' he said, 'did any one fall over there at the tree?'

He was told that Gissur the White had fallen.

'Then I was not so much in luck as I had hoped,' he remarked; 'for that arrow was meant for the earl.'

It was plain that the favourable result of this great battle was due chiefly to the intrepidity and circumspection of Earl Erik. His father would perhaps have recognized this fact, if the son had not apparently superseded his authority in sparing the life of so important a man as Vagn Aakesson without consultation with the commander-in-chief. He did not, however, venture to disregard Earl Erik's pardon, but loudly expressed his discontent, and parted from his son in anger. Vagn followed his rescuer southward, and became his familiar friend and companion.

Earl Haakon's power was now so well confirmed that no one ventured to dispute his supremacy. Crops and fisheries were good. The people enjoyed many years of peace and contentment. The earls of the Orkneys paid Haakon tribute, as if he had been a king, and a king he was in everything except the name. His family had always been associated with the ancient temple and earldom of Hlade; and it was a matter of pride with him to retain his ancestral dignity. This is significant when we consider how he was in all things a man of the old dispensation. At a time when heathenism was slowly crumbling away, and the faith in the old gods was losing its hold upon the upper classes, Haakon was a devout and sincere heathen.

The continual intercourse of Norway with England and the lands of the South had half imperceptibly weakened the old superstitions and made the legends of Odin and Thor appear to many like nursery tales which grown-up men could scarcely be expected to believe. Repudiation of all supernaturalism and a proud reliance upon his own good sword was at this time characteristic of the Norse Viking, who prided himself upon his knowledge of the world and his deeds in distant lands. For all that the Asa faith as later events will prove, had yet a sufficient number of sincere believers to make the progress of the new faith slow and sanguinary. Nevertheless so atrocious an act as the sacrifice of one's own child could not have failed to arouse indignation even among the worshippers of Odin and Thor. Such horrors were tolerated far back in the gloom of primeval antiquity, but must have been felt in the tenth century as a hideous anachronism. How much Earl Haakon's heathen fanaticism contributed to his downfall is difficult to determine. The sacrifice of Erling during the battle with the JomsVikings, though it was generally regarded as a fact, was not the original cause of the rebellion which cost the earl his throne and his life. The vices by which he forfeited his early popularity were of a kind which assert their sway over men, irrespective of religions.

In the year 995 Earl Haakon was travelling in Gauldale, collecting taxes. His son Erlend, of whom he was very fond, lay with some ships out in the fiord, waiting to receive the treasure. One evening the earl sent a company of thralls to the house of the powerful peasant Brynjulf, commanding him to send him his wife, who was renowned for her beauty. Brynjulf refused, and the earl in great anger sent the thralls back with this message to the indignant husband, that he had the choice between death and the surrender of his wife. The peasant was obliged to yield, and with a heavy heart let his wife depart with the thralls. But no sooner was she gone than he recovered his manhood and swore vengeance. He summoned the inhabitants of the valley from far and near, and told them of the shame the earl had put upon him. All promised him their help, and resolved to hold themselves in readiness, awaiting the first opportunity for attacking the daring profligate. The earl, in the meanwhile, being quite ignorant of their designs, played into their hands. Very soon after his adventure with Brynjulf's wife, he sent a message of similar purport to Orm Lyrgja, whose wife Gudrun, on account of her beauty, was surnamed 'Lundarsol' (the Sun of Lunde). Orm, who was a man of great authority in his valley, sent word to all his neighbours, and after having feasted the earl's thralls, in order to detain them, refused to comply with their demand. Gudrun, who saw them depart, cried jeeringly after them: 'Give the earl my greeting, and tell him that I will not go to him unless he sends Thora of Rimul to fetch me.' Thora of Rimul was one of the earl's mistresses, whom his favour had made rich and powerful.

War-summons was now sent from farm to farm, and a great band of armed peasants came together, and marched toward Medalhus where Haakon was staying. He sent in haste a message to his son Erlend, to meet him at More, whither he intended to go, as soon as the army of the peasants had dispersed. Then his time for vengeance would be at hand. In the meanwhile he would be obliged to dismiss his men and hide, until the excitement should have subsided. With a single thrall named Kark, whom he had received as tooth-gift and who had been his playmate in his boyhood, he fled across the Gaul river, rode his horse into a hole, and left his cloak upon the ice, in order that his pursuers might believe that he had been drowned. Then he hastened to his mistress, Thora of Rimul, who hid him and the thrall in a deep ditch under her pigsty. Food, candles and bedclothes were given them, whereupon the ditch was covered with boards and earth, and the pigs were driven out over it. As it happened, Olaf Tryggvesson, whose young life Queen Gunhild had vainly endeavoured to destroy, had just then landed in Trondelag and had slain the earl's son Erlend. The peasants, hearing that he was of the race of Harold the Fairhaired, received him with delight and accompanied him to Rimul, where they thought it likely that the earl must be hidden.

After a vain search Olaf called them together, and mounting a big stone, close to the pigsty, declared in a loud voice that he would give a great reward to him who would find the earl and slay him.

In his damp and malodorous hiding place the earl sat, gazing anxiously at his thrall. Every word of Olaf's speech he could plainly hear, and by the light of the candle which stood on the earth between them, he saw that Kark, too, was eagerly listening.

'Why art thou now so pale?' asked the earl, 'and now again as black as earth. Is it not because thou wilt betray me?'

'No,' replied Kark.

'We were both born in the same night,' said the earl, after a pause; 'and our deaths will not be far apart.'

They sat for a long time in shuddering silence, each distrusting the other. From the stillness above they concluded that night was approaching; but neither dared to sleep. At last Kark's weariness overpowered him; but he tossed and mumbled excitedly in his sleep. The earl waked him and asked him what he had been dreaming.

'I dreamed,' answered Kark, "that we were both on board the same ship and that I stood at the helm."

'That must mean that thou rulest over thine own life as well as mine. Be therefore faithful to me, Kark, as behooves thee, and I will reward thee when better days come.'

Once more the thrall fell asleep and laboured heavily, as in a nightmare. The earl woke him again and asked him to relate his dream.

'I thought I was at Hlade,' said Kark, 'and Olaf Tryggvesson put a golden ring about my neck.'

'The meaning of that,' cried the earl, 'is that Olaf Tryggvesson will put a red ring about thy neck, if thou goest to seek him. Therefore, beware of him, Kark, and be faithful to me. Then thou wilt enjoy good things from me, as thou hast done before.'

The night dragged slowly along and each sat staring at the other, with rigid, sleepy eyes, which yet dared not close. Toward morning, however, the earl fell backward and sleep overwhelmed him. But the terrors of his vigil pursued him sleeping. His soul seemed to be tossed on a sea of anguish. He screamed in wild distress, rolled about, rose upon his knees and elbows, and his face was terrible to behold. Then Kark sprang up, seized his knife and thrust it into his master's throat. Soon after he presented himself before Olaf Tryggvesson with the earl's head, claiming the reward. But Olaf verified the murdered man's prophecy. He put not a ring of gold, but one of blood about the traitor's neck (995).

Earl Haakon was the last champion of paganism upon the throne of Norway. He was a man of great natural endowment, fearless yet prudent, formidable in battle, and in his earlier years justly popular for his kindliness and liberality. It appears, however, as if the dignity and power which he conquered by his own ability intoxicated him and disturbed the fine equilibrium of his mind. Morally, he was, barring the profligacy of his later days, a legitimate product of the old Germanic paganism and the conditions of life which must of necessity prevail in a militant community. The shrewdness and faithlessness which we are apt to censure in the heroic types of this age, were, in reality, enforced by the hostile attitude of man to man and the resultant necessity for distrust and simulation. Candour and veracity were virtues which, according to the old Norse code, were only to be practised between friends, while mendacity and deceit were legitimate weapons against enemies. Earl Haakon was, however, even according to his code, culpable in not discriminating between friend and foe. He rose by faithlessness, and by faithlessness he fell.

THE YOUTH OF OLAF TRYGGVESSON

The story of Olaf Tryggvesson's youth, as related in the sagas, is so marvellous that it can scarcely claim absolute credibility. The wonder-loving tradition seized upon him from his very birth as its favourite hero and adorned every incident of his career with a multitude of romantic details. To separate the framework of fact from the embellishments of fiction is, under such circumstances, no easy task.

That Olaf's career, even stripped of all fanciful additions, was as remarkable as any romance, there can be no question. We have seen how Queen Gunhild with untiring vigilance tracked him through forests and wildernesses while he was an infant, and how his mother Aastrid finally found a place of refuge with Haakon the Old in Sweden. Her sense of security could scarcely have been increased when Earl Haakon succeeded the sons of Gunhild; for the earl was not of royal blood, and must fear, no less than Gunhild, a scion of the race of Harold the Fairhaired. Aastrid therefore determined to go with her son to Gardarike, or Russia, where her brother, Sigurd Eriksson, held a position of authority under King Vladimir. She took passage for herself, her son and their attendants, upon a merchant ship bound for a Russian port, but the ship was captured by Vikings, who killed some of the passengers and sold others as slaves. The young Olaf, his foster father Thoralf Lousy-Beard, and the latter's son Thorgills, became the property of a Viking named Klerkon, who killed Thoralf because he was too old to command any price in the slave markets. The two boys he bartered away in Estonia for a big ram. The purchaser again disposed of them for a coat and a cape to a man named Reas, who treated Olaf kindly, while he put Thorgills to hard labour. With him Olaf remained for six years. His mother, Aastrid, in the meanwhile, had been found at a slave market by a rich Norse merchant named Lodin, who had recognized her in spite of her miserable appearance, and offered to ransom her on condition of her becoming his wife. She had gladly given her consent and had returned with him to Norway.

One day Olaf's uncle, Sigurd Eriksson, had occasion to visit the town in Estonia where his nephew was living. He was just riding across the marketplace, when his attention was attracted to a group of boys who were playing. There was especially one of them whose appearance struck him, and he called to him and asked him his name. The boy said that his name was Olaf. Sigurd now discovered by further questioning that it was his nephew he was addressing. He made haste to buy him and his foster brother Thorgills, and took them with him to his house. He enjoined upon Olaf to say nothing about his race and birth, and the boy promised to be silent. One day, however, when he was out walking, he caught sight of the Viking Klerkon who had slain his foster father. Without a moment's reflection, he went up and split his skull with an axe which he happened to have in his hand.

Now the penalty for breaking the public peace was death, and a crowd of people rushed together, demanding that the boy should be killed. His uncle, in order to save him, took him to the queen, Olga, or Allogia, told her who he was, and implored her protection. The queen became greatly interested in the beautiful boy, and had him educated, as behooved a king's son, in the use of arms and all athletic sports. At the age of 12 he received men and ships from Vladimir, and spent some years roaming about as a Viking. He is said to have done important service to his benefactor, reconquering a province which had rebelled; but the favour which he enjoyed raised him up enemies who slandered him, representing him as a dangerous rival of the king in the affections both of the queen and the people. Olaf then, at the advice of Olga, left Russia with his men and ships and went to Wendland, where he was received with distinction by King Burislav. He did not, however, reveal himself as an heir to the throne of Norway, but travelled under the name Ole the Russian. Burislav's eldest daughter, or, more probably, sister, Geira, fell in love with him, and he married her, performed many valiant deeds in the service of his father-in-law, and finally, at the death of his wife, sailed once more in search of adventures. He was then 21 years old.

A dream induced him to go to Greece and accept Christianity, and he is also said to have sent a bishop to Russia who converted Vladimir and Olga to the Christian faith. Thence Olaf went to Northumberland, Denmark, Scotland and France, and had adventures without number. At the age of 25 he found himself in England, and was summoned to appear before Princess Gyda, sister of the Irish king, Olaf Kvaran. She had been the wife of an earl, but was yet a young and beautiful woman. A great many wooers were importuning her, among whom a certain Alfvine, a great champion and manslayer. A day had been fixed on which Gyda had promised to choose a husband, and many high-born men had come together, hoping to be chosen. All were splendidly attired, and glittered in scarlet and gold. Olaf, with a few companions, came sauntering up to the marketplace, and stationed themselves somewhat apart from the rest as if merely to look on. He had pulled a fur hood and cape over his head and shoulders, and was otherwise plainly clad. Gyda, after having somewhat listlessly regarded the ranks of her wooers, caught sight of the tall stranger with the fur hood. She approached him, lifted up his hood, and looked long and earnestly into his eyes.

'If thou wilt have me,' she said, 'then I choose thee for my husband.'

Olaf replied that he was not unwilling to take her at her word; and their betrothal was forthwith published. Alfvine in great wrath now challenged the Norseman, fought, and was conquered. The wedding was then celebrated, and Olaf spent several years in England and Ireland. He became here more intimately acquainted with Christianity, was baptized, and became a zealous defender of the faith. In Greece, he had, according to the legend, only been *primsigned* – i.e., marked with the sign of the cross. This was regarded as a sort of compromise between the old faith and the new, and was supposed to secure a certain favour from Christ the White, without entirely forfeiting the goodwill of the old gods.

The Anglo-Saxon annals contain repeated references to Olaf Tryggvesson, and name him as the chieftain of a great Viking fleet, which, in the year 994, ravaged the coasts of Essex, Kent, Sussex and Hampshire. He even landed with a considerable army, and put up his winter quarters in Southampton, levying supplies from the neighbouring country. The unhappy proposition was then made to King Ethelred II to buy immunity from further depredations, and the sum of £10,000 was paid to Olaf and by him apportioned among his men. Sweyn Forkbeard, the son of Harold Bluetooth, then exiled from his native land, is also named as one of the chieftains concerned in this expedition, though in the treaty of peace between King Ethelred and the Vikings, which is yet preserved, his name does not occur. At the confirmation of Olaf, which took place with great pomp in the same year, King Ethelred was present, and it is said that Olaf solemnly vowed, on that occasion, that he would henceforth never more molest the inhabitants of England. This promise he appears to have kept. Sweyn, however, tempted by the great sums of money which he had extorted, returned again and again, expelled Ethelred for a time from his kingdom, and for many years was the virtual ruler of England.

The fame of Olaf Tryggvesson's deeds spread far and wide, and also reached Norway, where Earl Haakon anxiously listened to every rumour regarding him. That this daring young adventurer would, as soon as he felt himself strong enough, lay claim to his paternal kingdom, the earl could not doubt; and as his own popularity waned, he looked forward with increasing uneasiness to the conflict. He well knew the devotion of the people to the race of Harold the Fairhaired, and the thought took possession of him that his own safety demanded Olaf Tryggvesson's death. He confided his plan to his friend, Thore Klakka, and begged him to sail to Dublin, where Olaf was then staying, and either kill him, if the chance presented itself, or entice him over to Norway where he could easily destroy him. Thore Klakka accepted this mission, met Olaf in Dublin, and readily gained his confidence.

The young man was eager for information concerning his native land, and the earl's emissary lost no opportunity to urge him to sail thither, the sooner the better, and take possession of his inheritance. The earl, said Thore Klakka, was indeed powerful, but if the peasants heard that a descendant of Harold the Fairhaired was in the land, they would all forsake him and join the legitimate king. Olaf was easily persuaded to believe these flattering assurances, and in the spring of the year 995 sailed with five ships for Norway. In accordance with Thore Klakka's treacherous advice, he went straight to the north-western shires where Earl Haakon's power was the greatest, and landed on the island Moster in Hordaland. He raised his tent, planted the cross on the beach and had the mass celebrated. Being convinced of Thore's disinterestedness, he also accepted his advice not to reveal who he was, but sail northward to Trondelag in order to attack the earl unawares and slay him.

Great must have been Thore's surprise when, on landing at the mouth of the Drontheim fjord, he found that he had truthfully represented the condition of the country. The peasants were united in open rebellion against his master, and Olaf had only to make himself known in order to secure immediate allegiance. Of his speech at Rimul, and the ignominious death of the earl, we have already spoken. All the chieftains and peasants of Trondelag were now summoned to meet at the Oere-*thing*, at the mouth of the river Nid, and here Olaf Tryggvesson was formally proclaimed King of all Norway. The Tronders from this time forth reserved for themselves the right to proclaim the king in the name of the whole country, and even to this day the sovereigns of Norway are crowned in Drontheim. Nevertheless, the king was required to travel from district to district and receive the allegiance of the people. This Olaf now did, and was everywhere greeted with enthusiastic homage.

The above narrative exhibits several improbabilities, which, however, do not of necessity vitiate its essential truthfulness. Of Olaf's sojourn in Russia there can be no doubt, although, to be sure, the Vladimir who at that time reigned in Novgorod had no wife named Allogia or Olga, and if it was his grandmother Olga to whom reference is made, the king's jealousy seems altogether unreasonable. Likewise, Olaf's visit to Wendland and his marriage there are capable of proof from contemporary poems, while the deeds which are attributed to him in King Burislav's service have a suspiciously legendary character. The adventure with Gyda in England also conceals a framework of fact under its mythical embroidery.

OLAF TRYGGVESSON (995–1000)

King Olaf's first endeavour, after having ascended the throne, was to Christianize the country. He was by nature well adapted for this task, being zealous in the faith, resolute and uncompromising. Where gentle means did not avail he had no hesitation in employing sword and fire. Vehement as he was by temperament, brooking no argument, he wasted no time in weighing the probabilities of success or failure, but in the conviction of the sanctity of his cause stormed resistlessly onward and by his impetuosity and ardour, bore down all opposition.

His first appearance as the champion of the new religion was in Viken, where he called his relations and adherents together and told them that it was his intention to convert the whole kingdom of Norway to faith in Christ the White, even though he were to lose his life in the attempt. In Viken lived at that time his mother and his stepfather, Lodin, who had a large following of friends and relations. Some of these were, no doubt, already Christians, or had been *primsigned*, as Christianity had, 25 years before, been preached for a short time in this part of the country by two Germans. No particular opposition was therefore offered to the king's command, and within a brief period Olaf had the satisfaction of seeing all of Viken – the old kingdom of his father, Tryggve – nominally, at least, converted to Christianity. It is not to be inferred, however, that the converts, in accepting baptism, renounced their faith in the gods whom they had previously worshipped. On the contrary, they continued to believe in their existence, and perhaps even secretly to worship them. The Christian priests themselves professed belief in Odin and Thor, but represented them as evil powers who had been conquered by Christ and thrown into the outer darkness. As Christ had now all power in heaven and earth, it was futile to invoke the favour of the vanquished gods by sacrifice.

In this practical shape the new religion unquestionably appealed to many whom otherwise it could not have reached. The relation to the old gods had been in its essence a contract for protection and good crops, in return for certain tangible values sacrificed. As Christianity was then preached, it was in many respects the same thing under a different name. Prayers formerly addressed to Odin or Frey were now addressed to Christ and the Virgin Mary, and though offerings of horses and bullocks were discontinued, the fragrant incense was still supposed to rise to the nostrils of the new god and propitiate his favour. The salient and essential difference between the old and the new faith, and the only one which the Norsemen in the beginning vividly apprehended, was the great doctrine of peace upon earth and goodwill among men. While Odin and Thor took pleasure in bloodshed and rejoiced in war, Christ the White loved peace and accorded no merit to the manslayer.

That this doctrine, though it was slow to affect the lives of the new converts, nevertheless from generation to generation wrought a change in the moral consciousness of the Norsemen, can scarcely be questioned. The old Asa faith was inconsistent with any kind of civilization, because it meant, in the end, universal destruction. As long as killing was *per se* meritorious and secured the favour of the gods and honour among men, no trade but that of arms could flourish, and every peaceful industry became impossible. In Iceland, where the spirit of the old Germanic paganism survived, even long after the introduction of Christianity, internecine feuds of the most atrocious character prevailed for centuries, resulting in a gradual decadence, followed by stagnation and decay. The result in Norway, as the subsequent narrative will show, was scarcely better. A universal exhaustion followed the long carnival of bloodshed, and a heavy lethargy, lasting for 400 years, settled upon the people.

It would be vain to pretend that Olaf Tryggvesson, when he undertook the task of destroying the Asa faith, had any conception of the superior sociological value of the new faith over the old. Not even the conception of one God, instead of many, seems to have been emphasized in the preaching of those days. On the contrary, the Christian religion was adapted, as far as possible, to the pre-existing polytheistic notions, and a new hierarchy, consisting of the Trinity, the Virgin Mary and a host of saints, was exalted as objects of worship instead of the old gods. If the character of the religious teaching is to be inferred from the character of the teachers, it is safe to conclude that the early Germanic Christianity was ethically not far removed from the religion which it came to supplant. Thus we hear much in the Saga of Olaf Tryggvesson of a priest named Thangbrand, whose violence, pugnacity and readiness to kill must have made him an odd exponent of the gospel of peace.

Thangbrand was a Saxon, and had been sent north with many other missionaries to assist in converting the Danes. Bishop Siric, of Canterbury, presented him during a visit with a curiously wrought shield, upon which was the image of the crucified Christ. Shortly after this occurrence, Thangbrand made the acquaintance of Olaf Tryggvesson, who admired the shield greatly and desired to buy it. The priest received a munificent compensation, and finding himself suddenly rich, went and bought a beautiful Irish girl, whose charms had beguiled him. A German warrior who saw the girl claimed her, and when his demand was scornfully refused challenged the priest. A duel was fought and the German was killed. Some ill feeling was aroused against Thangbrand by this incident, and he fled to his friend, Olaf Tryggvesson, and became his court chaplain. As such he was under the authority of Bishop Sigurd, an Anglo-Saxon, probably of Norse descent, whom Olaf had brought with him from England. Bishop Sigurd was a man of grave and gentle spirit and a striking contrast to the ferocious court chaplain.

The Christianization of Viken was followed by that of Agder. Any decided opposition the king did not meet until he came to South Hordaland, where a number of mighty chieftains had gathered in the hope of intimidating him. His fearless and resolute behaviour, however, impressed them so much that, after some negotiations, they accepted the faith and were baptized. In return for this concession, they demanded of the king that he should give his sister Aastrid in marriage to the young and high-born chief, Erling Skjalgsson of Sole; and as the king thought this marriage in every way desirable, he gave his consent.

Encouraged by his success, Olaf hastened on to Trondelag, where was the old and magnificent temple of Hlade, the principal sanctuary of Norse paganism. Impelled by holy zeal, and heedless of the consequences, he broke down the altar of the gods, burned their images and carried off their treasures. The Tronders promptly responded to this challenge by sending the war-arrow from house to house, and preparing to fight with the king. Olaf, who had but a small force with him, did not venture to offer them battle; but sailed northward to Haalogaland, where another armed band, under the command of Thore Hjort and Haarek of Thjotta, stood ready to receive him. As discretion was here the better part of valour, the king was in no haste to land, but returned to Trondelag, where the peasants in the meanwhile had dispersed, and began to build a church in the place where the old temple had stood. He meant to show the Tronders that he was neither discouraged nor frightened, that neither threats nor arms could induce him to desist from his undertaking. With the desire to strengthen his power here, where it most needed strengthening, he began also the building of a royal residence, and laid the foundation of the future city of Nidaros or Drontheim (996).

At the beginning of the winter he again summoned the peasants to meet him at the *Frostathing*, and they again responded by an armed concourse, much greater than the preceding one. When the assembly was called to order, the king rose and eloquently expounded the new faith, repeating his demand that the Tronders should accept baptism and cease to sacrifice. But he had not spoken long when the peasants began to interrupt him by angry shouts, threatening to attack him and chase him out of the country, unless he was silent. One of them, a chieftain named Skegge Aasbjornsson or Ironbeard (Jernskjegge) was especially active in denouncing the king and exciting the people against him. Olaf came to the conclusion that nothing was to be accomplished here by persuasion, and he resolved reluctantly to postpone his propaganda until a more propitious time. He then began to talk in a more conciliatory spirit; promised the peasants to be present at their sacrificial feast at Yuletide, and discuss further with them the change of faith. This promise was received with great satisfaction, and the assembly peacefully dispersed.

Shortly before the time appointed for the sacrifice, Olaf invited the chieftains and the most powerful peasants from all the neighbouring shires to meet him at a feast at Hlade. He placed 30 well-manned ships out in the fjord, where he could summon them in case of need. The guests were royally entertained, and as the night advanced became very drunk. In the morning the king ordered his priests to celebrate the mass, and a crowd of armed men arrived from the ships to attend the religious service. The guests, who were scarcely in a condition to profit by the worship, observed with growing uneasiness the size of the congregation. When the service was at an end, the king rose and addressed them as follows:

'When we held *thing* the last time, at Frosten, I demanded of the peasants that they should accept baptism; and they, on the other hand, demanded of me that I should sacrifice with them, as Haakon, Ethelstan's foster son, had done. I made no objection to this, but promised to be present at the sacrificial feast at More. However, if I am to sacrifice with you, then I am minded to make a sacrifice of the biggest kind that has ever been made. I will not take thralls and criminals; but I will sacrifice the most high-born men and the mightiest peasants.'

He then named six of the most powerful chieftains present, who had been his most active opponents, and declared that he meant to offer them up to Odin and Frey for good crops. Before they had time to recover from their astonishment, they were seized, and presented with the alternative of being baptized, or sacrificed to their own gods. They did not meditate long before choosing the former. When the ceremony was finished, they begged to be allowed to depart, but the king declared that he would detain them, until they had sent him their sons or brothers as hostages.

At the Yuletide sacrifice at More, the king arrived with a large number of followers. The peasants, too, came in full force, armed to the teeth and defiant as ever. Conspicuous among them was the burly form of Ironbeard, who was everywhere active and seemed the head and front of the opposition. The king endeavoured to speak, but the noise was so great that nobody could hear him. After a while, however, the tumult subsided, and he repeated his former demand, that all present should accept baptism, and believe in Christ the White; to which Ironbeard haughtily responded, that the peasants were here to prevent the king from breaking the law, that sacrificing to the gods was in accordance with the law, and that Olaf, whether he would or not, would have to sacrifice, as his predecessors had done. The king listened patiently to this speech; and declared himself ready to keep his promise.

Accompanied by many men he entered the temple, leaving his arms without; for no one was allowed to enter the sanctuary, bearing arms. The king carried, however, in his hand a stout stick with a gold head. He inspected the images of the gods carefully; lingering especially before that of Thor, which was adorned with rings of gold and silver. Suddenly, while all were looking at him, he raised his stick and gave the god a blow, so that he fell from his pedestal and broke into many pieces. At the very same instant his men struck down the other idols; and Ironbeard who was outside was slain. It was all evidently pre-arranged; and the peasants, who stood aghast at the magnitude of the sacrilege, scarcely knew whither to turn or how to resent it. They looked to Ironbeard to give voice to their outraged feeling, but Ironbeard was dead; and there was no one among the rest who had any desire to speak. When the king, therefore, for the third time, repeated his demand that they be baptized, or fight with him on the spot, they chose the former alternative. After having given hostages for their perseverance in the faith, and their abandonment of heathen practices, they made haste to return to their homes. For the slaying of Ironbeard, Olaf offered to pay a large 'atonement' to his relatives, and to marry his daughter Gudrun. On the wedding night, however, Gudrun attempted to murder him, and was returned to her kinsmen. He can scarcely have regretted her much, as he immediately prepared for a new matrimonial venture.

This time his attention was directed to Sigrid the Haughty, the widow of King Erik the Victorious of Sweden. Sigrid was rich and wielded a large influence, being the mother of King Olaf the Swede, and the possessor of great landed estates in Gautland. She was, therefore, much afflicted with wooers, who came from many countries to share her heart and her possessions. One descendant of Harold the Fairhaired, Harold Gronske (the Greenlander), she had burned up, in order to punish his presumption in offering himself to her.

'I'll teach little kings the risks of proposing to me,' she said, as she ordered the hall where her wooers slept to be fired.

Olaf Tryggvesson's overtures, which were conducted by negotiations, she received favourably, and agreed to meet him at Konghelle, near the boundary line between Norway and Sweden. Olaf sent in advance, as a present, a large gold ring which he had taken from the door of the temple at Hlade. It was admired, but on being tested was found to be filled with copper. This incensed Sigrid, but she still concluded to keep her appointment with Olaf. They accordingly met and discussed the terms of the marriage. Olaf demanded, as an indispensable condition, that Sigrid should be baptized, to which Sigrid strenuously objected. Then the king sprang up in great wrath and struck her with his glove in the face, crying: 'What do I want with thee, thou old heathen jade?' She arose, speechless with anger, but when she had reached the door she turned back, saying: 'That shall be thy death.'

A short time after this meeting, Sigrid married Sweyn Forkbeard, of Denmark, possibly with a view to accomplishing her vengeance upon Olaf. Sweyn's sister Thyra, whom he had married against her will to the Wendic King Burislav, fled immediately after the wedding and arrived in Norway, imploring Olaf's protection. It is possible that he had met her before, and was well disposed toward her. At all events, he solved the problem by marrying her (998), although she was fully as old as Sigrid the Haughty, and had had two husbands before.

After this brief interval, devoted to personal affairs, Olaf returned once more to the task to which he had consecrated his life. The chieftains of Haalogaland, who had prevented him from landing when he came to convert them, still remained unsubdued; and the time was now convenient for teaching them a lesson in submission. There were especially three, viz.: Thore Hjort, Eyvind Kinriva and Haarek of Thjotta, the son of Eyvind Skald-Spoiler, who were the chieftains and leaders of the tribal aristocracy of those regions. It was natural enough that these men, who derived much of their dignity from their priesthoods and consequent identification with the old religion, should be most tenacious in their adherence to the faith which was the foundation of their power. Haarek, who descended from a daughter of Harold the Fairhaired, felt himself to be quite as great a man as King Olaf, and he was in no wise disposed to submit without a trial of strength. It so happened that two men from Haalogaland, named Sigurd and Hauk, had been captured by the king and escaped. These, pretending to be the king's enemies, sought refuge with Haarek, and were well received by him.

One day they proposed a sailing tour, to which their host willingly assented. They took provisions and beer with them in the boat, set sail and steered for Nidaros, where they delivered Haarek into the power of the king. He stubbornly refused to be baptized, but was, nevertheless, after a brief detention, given a ship and permitted to return unmolested to his home. From that day, however, Haarek, though making no pretence of friendship, acted as the ally of the king. He even helped to betray his friend, Eyvind Kinriva, into Olaf's hands. The king presented Eyvind with the usual alternative of baptism or death, but with the unusual result that the latter was preferred. Thore Hjort was now alone left; he allied himself with Raud the Strong, who had the reputation of being a wizard, and delivered a regular battle in which he was defeated by the king. Raud escaped on his fleet dragon-ship, while Thore was pursued by Olaf, who set a dog named Vige on his track, saying:

'Vige, catch thou the stag.'

The dog did actually overtake Thore, and the king cut him down with his own hands. Olaf strove in vain to get on the track of Raud, but the weather was so terrible that he did not venture to go to sea. He began to suspect, after a while, that it was Raud himself who, by his witchcraft, had aroused the elements; and after having waited for several days and nights for a change in the weather, he called Bishop Sigurd to him and asked his advice. The bishop, it is told, raised up a crucifix, surrounded by lighted tapers, in the prow of the king's ship, 'The Crane', and stood himself beside it, clad in sacerdotal vestments, praying and scattering holy water. Instantly the storm ceased about 'The Crane', though it still roared wildly under the heavens, and the smoke of the lashed waves stood like a wall on either side. The men now seized the oars and rowed in toward the island where Raud was living, 'The Crane' keeping the lead and the other ships following in the smooth water in her wake. Raud was surprised while asleep, and as he still refused to become a Christian, was tortured until he died. The king forced an adder down his throat, according to the legend; and it cut its way through his side, killing him by its poison.

There is much in this story which is obviously legendary. But there is one circumstance which stamps the adventure itself as essentially true, viz.: the detailed description of Raud's ship, 'The Serpent', which the king took, and which figures later in the battle of Svolder. One may be reluctant to believe that a man so chivalrous and noble as Olaf Tryggvesson on other occasions proved himself to be, can have been guilty of the cruelty which is here attributed to him. This instance is, however, not a solitary one. Eyvind Kinriva, when he refused to be baptized, had glowing coals put upon his stomach, at the king's command, and expired under horrible tortures. Olaf's fanaticism led him to believe that praise rather than censure was due to him for thus punishing the enemies of God. It is, indeed, probable that a man of gentler calibre, and more squeamish in the selection of his means, would never have accomplished even the nominal Christianization of Norway. In fact, so great was Olaf's zeal, and so single his purpose, that he subordinated all other concerns to this one great object, the thought of which filled him with a noble enthusiasm.

Even before he had secured the allegiance of the surviving chief of Haalogaland, Haarek of Thjotta, who, with all his household, accepted the Christian faith, he sent messengers to the Faeroe Isles, Iceland and Greenland, and commanded the chieftains there to renounce their old religion. Sigmund Bresteson, the Earl of the Faeroe Isles, whom he summoned to him, arrived in Norway (999) and was baptized. Thangbrand, who was sent to Iceland to preach the gospel, had at first a considerable success, baptizing such important chiefs as Hall of the Side, and Gissur the White, and the great lawyer Njaal of Bergthor's knoll. The pugnacious priest, however, soon got into difficulties by his readiness to draw his sword, killed several men, was outlawed and compelled to leave the island. In Norway, where Olaf had given him the church at Moster, he had, previous to his departure for Iceland, found it inconvenient to live on his income, and in order to increase his revenue, had been in the habit of making forays into the neighbouring shires, replenishing his stores at the expense of the heathen. This freebooting propensity incensed the king, and Thangbrand's missionary expedition to Iceland was undertaken as a penance for his misbehaviour. It had, however, far greater results than either Olaf or the priest could have anticipated. The public sentiment in Iceland, after Thangbrand's flight, changed with astonishing rapidity in favour of the new faith, which was legally accepted at the *Althing* June, 1000 CE.

Olaf's great achievement, as the first successful propagandist of Christianity on the throne of Norway, surrounded his name with a halo which dazzled his biographers and disposed them to exalt him beyond his deserts. For all that, it is a fact that his contemporaries, many of whom had small reason to love him, were no less dazzled by his brilliant personality than his biographers. In the first place, his manly beauty and his resemblance to Haakon the Good, which was frequently commented upon, predisposed the people in his favour. Secondly, his natural kindliness and winning manners attracted everyone who came in contact with him. Last, but not least, his extraordinary skill in athletic sports and the use of arms was greatly admired. He could, as Snorre relates, use his right and his left hand equally well in shooting; he could play with three spears at once, so that one was always in the air; he could run forward and backward on the oars of a ship while the men were rowing. In daily intercourse he was affable and generous, fond of a joke and easily moved to laughter and to wrath. In anger he could do things which he later regretted; and we have seen how, when fired with holy zeal, he committed acts which he ought to have regretted, though there is no evidence that he did. His love of splendour in attire and surroundings may be accounted a weakness, but it served, nevertheless, to endear him to his people.

Although surrounded by enemies on all sides, Norway suffered but little from foreign wars during the brief reign of Olaf Tryggvesson. Gudrod, the last surviving son of Erik Blood-Axe, made an attack upon Viken in the summer of 999, but was defeated and slain in the king's absence by his brothers-in-law, Thorgeir and Hyrning. Much more dangerous to King Olaf proved the hostility of Sigrid the Haughty, who was watching for an opportunity to take revenge upon him. Although he must have been well aware of the risks, he did not hesitate to furnish this opportunity. His queen, Thyra, had great estates in Wendland and Denmark, and was dissatisfied, because she was deprived of the revenues which they had formerly brought her. Whenever he spoke to her, she always contrived to bring in something about these estates, and by appeals to his vanity egg him on to war with her brother Sweyn Forkbeard, who withheld from her rightful property. When these tactics failed, she resorted to prayers and tears, until her husband's patience was well nigh exhausted.

If only for the sake of domestic peace, an expedition to Wendland began to be discussed as an approaching possibility. One Sunday in March – it was Palm Sunday – the king met a man in the street who sold spring vegetables. He bought a bunch and brought it to the queen, remarking that these vegetables were large, considering the earliness of the season. The queen, who was, as usual, weeping for her estates in Wendland, thrust the vegetables contemptuously away, and with the tears streaming down her face, cried: 'Greater gifts did my father, Harold Gormsson, give me when, as a child, I got my first teeth; he came hither to Norway and conquered it; while thou, for fear of my brother Sweyn, darest not journey through Denmark in order to get me what belongs to me, and of which I have been shamefully robbed.'

To this King Olaf wrathfully replied: 'Never shall I be afraid of thy brother Sweyn, and if we meet, he shall succumb.'

Summons was now sent through all the shires of the land, calling upon the chieftains to join the king with as many ships as were by law required of them. He had himself just finished a ship of extraordinary size and beauty, called 'The Long-Serpent', the fame of which spread through all the lands of the North. It was 56 Norwegian ells, or about 34 metres (112 feet) from prow to stern, had 52 oars on either side, and could accommodate 600 warriors. The crew was made up of picked men, none of whom must be over 60 or less than 20 years of age. Only one exception was permitted to this rule in the case of Einar Eindridsson surnamed Thambarskelver, who was but 18 years old, but the most skilful archer in all Norway. With his bow, called Thamb, from which he derived his surname, he could shoot a blunt arrow through a raw ox hide, depending from a pole.

In order to distinguish 'The Long-Serpent' from the dragon-ship he had taken from Raud the Strong, Olaf called the latter 'The Short-Serpent'. He had many other excellent ships besides, and his brothers-in-law, Erling Skjalgsson of Sole, Thorgeir and Hyrning, joined him, each with a large and finely equipped galley.

When he steered southward to Wendland, he had about 60 ships of war besides a similar number of smaller transports. King Burislav, in spite of his union with Thyra, received him well, possibly on account of the earlier relationship through Geira, or on account of their common hostility to Sweyn Forkbeard in Denmark. The question of the estates was amicably settled and Olaf, after having been splendidly entertained, prepared to start homeward. The rumour, in the meanwhile, had gone abroad that he was in Wendland, and his enemies, in order to gather a sufficiently large force to destroy him, employed Earl Sigvalde, the chief of the Jomsvikings, to detain him and lull him into a false security. In this the treacherous earl succeeded. He gained Olaf's confidence, scouted the thought that Sweyn Forkbeard should ever dare attack him; and finally offered to escort him on the way with his own fleet and pilot him through the dangerous waters along the Wendic coast. It was of no avail that Sigvalde's wife, Aastrid, the night before Olaf's departure, warned him against her husband as openly as she dared, and proposed to send a ship along in case of danger.

A strange infatuation bound him to his false friend. At Sigvalde's advice he even permitted part of his fleet to start in advance, as the straits between the islands were narrow. The traitor, in the meanwhile, was in constant communication with King Sweyn, at whose request he agreed to separate Olaf from his main force and lead him into the trap which his foes had prepared for him. Besides King Sweyn there were Earl Erik, who had the death of his father, Earl Haakon, to avenge, and King Olaf the Swede, the son of Sigrid the Haughty. All these were lying in wait with about 60 or 70 war galleys, behind the little island of Svolder, between the island Rugen and the present Prussian province, Pomerania. From their hiding place they looked for several days in vain for the Norse ships, and began to grow impatient. They had gone ashore with their crews in order to while away the time, and the three commanders were standing together, sweeping the horizon with their glances, when, to their delight, the Norse transport fleet hove in sight, spreading its sails before the favouring breeze.

The day was fair. The sun shone brightly, and the surface of the water barely curled into slight undulations. Gayly the proud ships stood out to the sea, one larger and finer than the other. When King Sweyn saw the beautiful ship of Erling Skjalgsson of Sole, he was sure that it must be 'The Long Serpent', though it had no dragon head in its prow. 'Afraid is Olaf Tryggvesson today,' he said, 'since he dares not carry a head on his dragon.' 'This ship I know well by its striped sails,' said Earl Erik; 'it does not belong to the king, but to Erling Skjalgsson. Let it pass; for if, as I suppose, he is himself on board, we shall be best served, if he and his band are not found among those with whom we are to fight today.'

By twos and threes the great ships of the Norse chieftains passed by, and every time the Swedish and the Danish king were sure that one of them must be 'The Long Serpent'. Presently Sigvalde's fleet of 11 ships became visible, and having received signals from the allied princes, turned its course suddenly around the island, to the great astonishment of Thorkill Dyrdill, who was steering the king's ship, 'The Crane', right in its wake. King Sweyn, at the sight of this splendid galley, could no more be restrained, but ordered his men aboard, in spite of Earl Erik's warning. He even insinuated that the latter was a coward who had no ambition to avenge his father; to which the earl replied, that before the setting of the sun it would be seen who was the more eager for battle, the Swedes and Danes, or he and his men.

Thorkill Dyrdill dropped the sails of 'The Crane', and, taking in the situation at a glance, determined to await the arrival of King Olaf. Then came 'The Short Serpent', casting golden gleams across the water from its shining dragon head; and King Sweyn cried exultingly: 'Loftily shall the Serpent bear me tonight, and I shall steer her.'

Earl Erik, in whom King Sweyn's recent taunt was rankling, replied: 'Even if Olaf Tryggvesson had no larger ship than this, Sweyn, with all his army of Danes, could not win it from him.'

When at last 'The Long Serpent' reared its flaming prow against the horizon, shooting long beams in the sun, the three princes marvelled at its beauty. Many a one trembled, too, with fear, when he saw the majestic ship approaching, and the dense rows of polished shields and swords flashing from afar.

'This glorious ship,' said Earl Erik, 'is fitting for such a king as Olaf Tryggvesson; for it may, in sooth, be said of him, that he is distinguished above all other kings as "The Long Serpent" above all other ships.'

All King Olaf's fleet, with the exception of 11 ships, were now out of sight, and many of his chieftains advised him not to fight against such heavy odds. He would not listen to their counsel, but ordered the ships to be bound together and everything to be prepared for battle.

'Down with the sails,' he cried with a loud voice, which could be clearly heard across the waters; 'never have I yet fled from any battle. God rules over my life. Never will I flee; for he is no king who shuns his foes because of fear.'

The whole hostile fleet now rowed forward from behind the island, and it seemed as if the sea was covered with ships as far as the eye could reach. King Sweyn, with his 60 galleys, became first visible.

'What chieftain is that right opposite to us?' asked King Olaf.

'That is King Sweyn with the Danish army,' answered one of his men.

'I have no fear of them,' said the king. 'Never yet have Danes beaten Norsemen, and they will not beat us today. But to what chieftain belong the standards there on the right?'

He was told that they belonged to Olaf, the king of the Swedes.

'The Swedes,' said he, 'would find it more agreeable to sit at home and lick their sacrificial bowls, than to meet our arms today on "The Long Serpent". Scarcely do I think that we need be afraid of those horse-eaters. But whose are those large ships on the left side of the Danes?'

'That,' answered his informant, 'is Earl Erik, Earl Haakon's son.'

'From them we may expect a hard battle; for, methinks, Earl Erik has considerable reason for attacking us; and he and his men are Norsemen like ourselves.'

While the king was speaking, Queen Thyra, who had accompanied him, came up on deck. Seeing the enormous hostile fleet before her, and the smallness of her husband's force, she burst into tears.

'Now thou must not weep,' said King Olaf; 'for now thou hast, indeed, gotten what was due to thee in Wendland; and today I mean to demand of thy brother Sweyn thy tooth-gift which thou hast so often asked me for.'

King Sweyn was the first to attack, but after a short and stubborn fight was compelled to retreat. One of his galleys was disabled after the other, and there was a great carnage. King Olaf himself stood on the poop royal of 'The Long Serpent', where all could see him, directing the defence, and himself fighting with spears and arrows. His helmet and his shield, which were gilt, shone in the sun. Over his armour he wore a short tunic of scarlet silk. While the Danes were in full retreat, the Swedes hastened to their rescue, and they now bore for a while the brunt of the battle. For every Swede or Dane that fell there were 10 ready to take his place; while the Norsemen, surrounded on all sides by hostile ships, had to endure an incessant shower of spears and arrows, and the shock of repeated onsets that had to be repelled by the sword in hand-to-hand conflicts.

However tired and thirsty they were, they could give themselves no respite. Every man that fell or was disabled by wounds left a gap that could not be filled. And yet, in spite of the great numerical superiority of their foes, they would have carried the day at Svolder, if Earl Erik had not commenced a destructive attack upon the right wing, while the Swedes and the Danes were engaging the centre. In fact, the latter were again retreating in disorder before the furious bravery of King Olaf's men, when Earl Erik rowed up alongside the outermost ship on the right, with his great galley, 'The Iron Ram', and made a vigorous onslaught. Here Norseman met Norseman, and the numbers had to decide.

The men on the king's ship fought desperately, but were overpowered, and leaped into the sea, or saved themselves on board the next ship. The first was then cut adrift, and Erik, in accordance with a well-matured plan, engaged the next and the next. At last all of King Olaf's ships except 'The Long Serpent' were cut adrift, and their defenders slain. Then a space was cleared in front of 'The Iron Ram', and she was rowed forward with tremendous force, striking 'The Long Serpent' amidships. The good ship creaked in all her beams; but as there was scarcely any wind no great damage was done. Einar Thambarskelver, who stood before the mast on 'The Long Serpent', saw Earl Erik standing near the prow of 'The Iron Ram', covered by many shields. He bent his bow and sent an arrow whizzing over his head, and in the next instant another, which flew between the earl's arm and his body. The earl, turning to the archer, Finn Eyvindsson, said: 'Shoot that tall man on the forward deck.'

Finn aimed an arrow at Einar just as he was bending his bow for a third shot at the earl; the arrow hit the bow in the middle, and it broke with a loud crash.

'What was it that broke?' asked Olaf.

'Norway from thy hands, my king,' cried Einar.

'So great was not the breach, I hope,' the king made answer; 'take my bow and shoot with that.'

He flung his own bow to the archer, who seized it, bent it double, and flung it back. 'Too weak is the king's bow,' he said.

Earl Erik was now preparing for the final attack, and he could not doubt its result.

King Olaf's men were in a desperate strait, from which no escape was possible. The king flung forth his spears, two at a time, from his station on the poop, and many men were transfixed by his keen shafts. He watched at the same time the combat on the forward deck, whither the earl was just directing his attack, and it seemed to him that his men made no headway.

'Do you wield your swords with so little strength,' he cried, 'since they bite so poorly?'

'No,' answered a warrior; 'but our swords are dull and broken.'

The king then hastened to the forward deck, where there was a large chest of arms. He opened it and took out armfuls of bright, sharp swords, which he flung to his men. As he stooped down, the blood trickled down over his hands from under his armour. His men then knew that he was wounded, but it was no time then for nursing anyone's wounds. The earl's men were storming forward, and the tired Norsemen fell in heaps, and could no longer keep them back. The arrows rained thick and fast about the king, and it was obvious he could not hold out much longer. He was visible to all; for he made no attempt to hide or shelter himself.

One of his trusted men, Kolbjorn Stallare, who saw his danger, sprang upon the poop and placed himself at his side. His resemblance to the king had often been remarked upon; moreover, he was of the same height, and was similarly dressed. The storm of missiles was now directed against both, and, as they raised their shields, they were thickly fringed with arrows. The clash of arms, the groans of the dying and the whizzing of flying missiles, filled the air. The king let his shield drop and looked out over the ship. There were but eight men alive, besides himself and Kolbjorn. He raised the shield above his head and leaped overboard. Kolbjorn followed his example, but was picked up by the earl's men, who mistook him for the king. That the latter was drowned, there can be no reasonable doubt, although there is a legend, which was fondly cherished, that he swam to the galley which Aastrid, Earl Sigvalde's wife, had sent out for his rescue. According to this story, he made a pilgrimage to Rome, and lived long as a hermit in the Holy Land.

King Olaf Tryggvesson was 36 years old when he died (1000). Queen Thyra, who, with good reason, held herself responsible for his death, was inconsolable. When she came up on deck after the battle and saw the destruction she had wrought she broke into lamentation. Earl Erik was moved by her sorrow and spoke kindly to her, assuring her that if she would return to Norway she would be accorded the honour which was due to her as the widow of so great a king. She thanked him for his offer, but said that she had no heart to survive her lord. On the ninth day after the battle she died.

THE NEW MILLENNIUM

The Viking Age, which lasted from the late eighth to the early eleventh century, came to an end for several reasons. Some of the most important factors were changes to the political structures in European powers, the increasing importance of Christianity in medieval European life, changes in the economy, several key – and absolutely crushing – military defeats and even climate change. The daily struggles of life centuries ago in Scandinavia do not look so different from those of today, it seems. As *Hávamál* says, 'He who has few workers should rise early to see to his work himself. He who sleeps in the morning loses much, half of wealth is gotten by initiative.'

Over time these mighty kingdoms of Europe consolidated and became more centralized, reducing the need for Viking expeditions and raids. The Nordic peoples gradually converted to Christianity, a movement spurred by the kings themselves, especially St. Olaf (he didn't get his name because he looked pretty in a halo, you know). The new religious doctrine served to change their attitudes toward violence, the penalties for violence under the law and trade. The rise of more powerful trading centers in Europe and the growth of cities put pressure on the traditional Viking economy, based on raiding and bribes, not to attack population hubs such as York in England

and Paris in France. The Vikings then suffered military defeats at the hands of stronger European kingdoms, for example those of England and France. Finally, climate changes such as a cooling atmosphere made growing seasons shorter and crop yields poorer; it thus set the stage for famine and disease due to malnourishment.

Vikings who could not – or would not – adapt were forced to abandon settlements in remote, inhospitable places such as Greenland. At the same time, they came under the authority of new lords, both religious and political, and ended their summertime habits of raiding farmland and monasteries on foreign shores. Instead, they looked around at what their exploits had won them and took these new riches, from golden rings and coin hoards bursting with treasure to a storehouse of legendary tales repeated over a fire in the endless winter months, with them into an uncertain future.

THE DISCOVERY OF AMERICA

During the reign of Earl Haakon a man from Jederen, called Erik the Red, being obliged to leave Norway because he had killed a man, proceeded to the western part of Iceland. Here he committed a similar offence and was condemned at Thorsnes Thing to banishment. He had heard that a man called Gunbiorn, son of Ulf Krage, had some time ago been driven by the storm far westward and had seen a great country. Erik the Red fitted out a vessel and told his friends that he intended to find the country Gunbiorn had seen. He took with him a man by the name of Heriulf Bardson.

They found the country (984), and on a visit later to Iceland Erik the Red gave such a fine description of the new country that it was called Greenland. A number of colonists returned with him to the new country, and the foundation of several settlements were laid. In the summer of 999 Leif Erikson, a son of Erik the Red, made a visit to Norway, and as he met King Olaf Tryggvasson he adopted Christianity, and passed the winter with the king. In the following spring King Olaf sent Leif Erikson, together with a priest and other teachers, to Greenland to proclaim Christianity there. Flourishing colonies, with churches, monasteries and bishoprics, are known to have been maintained in Greenland until the end of the fourteenth century.

Biarne Heriulfson, a son of the above-named Heriulf Bardson, while sailing westward from Iceland in search of his father, met with stormy weather, northerly winds and fogs, and was driven out of his course. As he came to different shores, which, from the description he had received, could not be those of Greenland, he turned around, and, sailing in a north-easterly direction, finally arrived at his father's home in Greenland. When telling of his discovery he was much ridiculed for not having landed and examined the new countries. Leif Erikson bought Biarne's ship, and with a crew of 35 men set out, in the year 1000 CE, to look for these lands.

He came first to a land on his right as he sailed southward. It had great icy mountains in the interior and a shore of flat stones. He therefore named the country Helluland (from the Norse *helle*, a flat stone). He continued his course southward, and came to another country, which was level and covered with woods and had a low coast. He called this country

Markland (outfield or woodland). The antiquaries consider Helluland to have been Newfoundland, and Markland some part of Nova Scotia. Leif and his party put to sea again with a northeast wind, and after two days' sailing made land, and came to an island lying on the north side of the mainland. They entered the channel between the island and a point projecting northeast from the mainland, and at last landed at a place where a river which came from a lake fell into the sea. They found the country very agreeable, and, resolving to winter there, erected some houses. Leif divided his people into two parties, to be employed in turns in exploring the country and working about the houses. One evening it happened that one of the exploring party, a German by birth, named Tyrker, was missing. They went out to search for him, and when they met him he told them he had been up the country, and had discovered vines and grapes, a fruit with which he was acquainted from his native country. They now occupied themselves in gathering grapes and cutting vines and felling timber with which they loaded the vessel. Leif called the country Vinland. Toward spring they made ready and sailed away, and returned to Greenland.

In the year 1002 Leif Erikson's brother, Thorvald, fitted out a ship and sailed southward with 30 men, after consulting with Leif. They came to Vinland, to the houses put up by Leif, where they remained quietly all winter, and lived by fishing. In the spring Thorvald sent a party in the longboat to explore the country to the south. They found the country beautiful and well wooded, but with little space between the woods and the sea, and the strand full of white sand. There were also many islands, and shallow water. They came back in the autumn to

Leif's houses. The following spring Thorvald sailed with his vessel eastward, then northward along the land. Outside of a cape they met bad weather and were driven ashore and broke their keel. They remained there a long time to repair their vessel. Thorvald said to his men: 'We will stick up the keel here upon the ness and call the place Keelness.' Then they sailed eastward along the country and landed on a headland, which Thorvald liked so well that he said he would like to make his home there. On going on board they saw three little hills on the sandy shore. They went up to them and found they were three canoes, made of skin, with three natives – or Skraelings, as the Northmen called them – under each canoe. They killed eight of them, while one made his escape in his canoe. Afterward a great number of the natives attacked Thorvald's party. They were repulsed, but Thorvald was wounded by an arrow and died. He was buried on the headland which he had said he liked so well. His men remained there during the winter, and in the spring returned to Greenland.

In the summer of 1006, an Icelander by the name of Thorfin Karlsefne came to Greenland, and, in the winter, married Gudrid, the widow of Thorstein, third brother of Leif Erikson. By her advice he resolved to undertake an expedition to Vinland and establish a colony there. In the spring (1007) they set out with three ships, 160 men and all kinds of livestock, and sailed to Vinland. Sometime after their arrival there Gudrid bore a son, who was named Snorre. The colonists occasionally traded with the Skraelings, giving them pieces of cloth and dairy products for their skins; but when they refused to sell them weapons, the Skraelings became hostile to the settlers and attacked them repeatedly. These constant hostilities so disheartened the settlers that they resolved to leave the country, and, after three years' sojourn in Vinland, Thorfin Karlsefne and his party returned to Greenland.

Another expedition to Vinland was undertaken, shortly after their return, by Freydis, the illegitimate daughter of Erik the Red, her husband Thorvald and two Norwegians named Helge and Finboge. This party quarrelled among themselves, and Freydis, who is described as a very bad woman, caused a great number of them to be murdered. The survivors returned to Greenland in the spring of 1013. The next summer, Thorfin Karlsefne went to Norway with his Vinland cargo and sold it to great advantage. He returned to Iceland and bought land there, and, according to the saga, many men of distinction are descended from him and his son Snorre, who was born in Vinland.

THE EARLS ERIK AND SVEIN, SONS OF HAAKON (1000-15)

After the battle of Svolder, the three allied princes divided the kingdom of Norway between them. King Olaf the Swede got four districts in the Throndhjem country, and the districts of North More and South More and Raumsdal, and in the eastern part of the country he got Ranrike from the Gaut River to Svinesund. Earl Erik got four districts in the Throndhjem country, and Halogaland, Naumudal, the Fjord districts, Sogn, Hordaland, Rogaland and North Agder, all the way to the Naze (Lindesnes, the southernmost point in Norway). The Danish king, Svein Tjuguskeg, retained Viken, which he had held before, and Raumarike and Hedemarken.

After the division, the Swedish king gave his Norwegian possessions into the hands of his brother-in-law Svein, the brother of Earl Erik, on the same conditions as the sub-kings or earls held such possessions formerly from the chief king. At the same time the Danish king gave most of his possessions in Norway in fief to Earl Erik. Thus the two brothers together ruled over a larger territory than their father, Earl Haakon, had held; but they were not able to wield the same power. During his whole time, Earl Erik received no taxes from Rogaland, which Erling Skialgson ruled over with unlimited authority. The earls Erik and Svein were baptized, and adopted the Christian faith; but as long as they ruled in Norway they allowed everyone to do as he pleased as to the manner of observing his Christianity. On the other hand, they upheld the old laws, and all the old rights and customs of the country. They were popular men and good rulers. Of the two brothers Earl Erik had most to say in all public matters.

The earls tried to gain the friendship of Olaf Tryggvasson's old friends, and in many cases they succeeded. The brave young Einar Thambaskelfer was won over by their giving him great fiefs in Orkadal, so that he became one of the most powerful and esteemed men in all the Throndhjem country. They also gave him their proud sister Bergliot in marriage. One mighty man, however, they tried in vain to conciliate. That was Erling Skialgson, the brother-in-law of Olaf Tryggvasson. He could not forgive Earl Erik for having joined the Swedes and Danes in an unexpected attack on Olaf Tryggvasson and causing his death. He managed to maintain a firm hold on the dominions his brother-in-law had given him. If the earls visited a neighbourhood where they knew that Erling was staying, they always took with them a large armed force, and they never thought of visiting Erling on his estate, Sole. He had with him never less than ninety free men. If it was reported that the earls were in the neighbourhood, he had 200 men or more. He never went by water from one place to another except in a fully manned ship of 20 benches of rowers. In the summer he used to make Viking cruises in order to procure means with which to support his many men.

Erling was a good master. At home, on his estate, he always had 30 slaves besides the many servants engaged in work outside. He gave each of them a certain day's work; when one of them was through with that, he had the balance of the day at his own disposal. Each one received a piece of land to cultivate, and what grain he produced he could sell and use the proceeds toward buying himself free. The amount needed for this purpose was fixed by the earl, and it was so low that many bought their freedom at the end of a year, while all who were at all industrious could make themselves free within three years. He also assisted his men after they had become free. Some of them were given land to clear and cultivate, while others were shown how to conduct the herring fisheries.

After the death, in England, of the Danish king, Svein Tjuguskeg, his son, Canute (Knut) the Mighty, sent word to Earl Erik in Norway (his brother-in-law) to come over and help him to conquer England. The earl immediately called together the mightiest peasants, and in their presence divided the country between his brother Svein and his son Haakon. As the latter was only 17 years old, the earl appointed his brother-in-law, Einar Thambaskelfer, guardian for him. Thereupon Earl Erik set sail for England. He met King Canute there, and was with him when he captured London. He was given Northumberland to govern, and remained there until his death.

From the short joint reign of Earl Svein and Earl Haakon in Norway only one event of importance is known. As soon as Earl Erik had left the country, they effected a reconciliation with the mighty Erling Skialgson at Sole, who had never been able to forgive Earl Erik for the assault on Olaf Tryggvasson, but readily made peace with Svein and Haakon; and the new friendship was further cemented by Aslak, Erling's son, marrying Earl Svein's daughter Gunhild (or Sigrid, as the name is given in another place). One good reason why the earls sought to strengthen their power by an alliance with the powerful chieftain, Erling Skialgson, was no doubt the unexpected appearance of a most threatening enemy, the young pretender to the throne, Olaf, son of Harald Grenske.

THE YOUTH OF OLAF HARALDSSON

Olaf Haraldsson, after his death called Olaf the Saint, was the son of Harald Grenske and Aasta. Harald Grenske, who, as we have seen, at one time governed Viken under the suzerainty of the Danish king, was the grandson of Bjorn the Merchant – who was killed by Erik Blood-Axe – and a great-grandson of Harald the Fairhaired. Olaf was born shortly after the death of his father. His mother Aasta was then staying at the home of her father, Gudbrand Kula, a mighty man in the Uplands. Soon afterward, Aasta was married again to Sigurd Syr, who was king in Ringerike and a descendant of Harald the Fairhaired, and in his house Olaf was brought up. When King

Olaf Tryggvasson came to Ringerike to spread Christianity, he induced Sigurd Syr and his whole family to be baptized, and he acted as godfather at the baptism of little Olaf.

One day, when Olaf was 10 years old, King Sigurd wanted to ride out, and, as there was nobody else about the house, he told his stepson Olaf to go and saddle his horse. Olaf did not refuse, but he went to the goats' pen, and put the king's saddle on the largest he-goat, led him up to the door, and went in and told King Sigurd that his horse was saddled. When King Sigurd came out and saw what Olaf had done, he said: 'Easy it is to see that thou wilt little regard my orders; and thy mother will think it right that I do not order thee to do anything against thy own inclination. I see well enough that thou art far more proud than I am.' Olaf answered little, but went his way laughing.

When Olaf grew up he became of medium height, but very stout and strong. He had light brown hair, and a broad face which was white and red. He had particularly fine eyes, which were beautiful, but piercing, so that one was afraid to look him in the face when he was angry. Olaf was very expert in all bodily exercises, understood well how to handle his bow, and was especially an expert in throwing his spear. He was well liked by his friends and acquaintances, was ambitious in his sports and always strove to be the first.

Olaf was 12 years old when, for the first time, he went on board a ship of war (1007). His mother, Aasta, got Rane, who was called foster father of kings, to command the ship and take Olaf under his charge. The men on board, however, gave Olaf the title of king. With two ships, Olaf first steered to Denmark and then to Sweden, where he harried the coasts and fought with Vikings. Afterward he made cruises to Finland,

Russia and Gotland. Later he turned westward to Friesland and England, where he took part in the fights between the Danes and the Anglo-Saxons. From the poems of the Skalds it appears that he took part in the battle of Hringmara (1010), and in the storming of Canterbury (1012). In company with Thorkel the Tall (a brother of Earl Sigvald) he entered the English king Ethelred's service, took part in his battles against the Danish Vikings, and accompanied Ethelred on his flight to Normandy. From here he thought of making a pilgrimage to the Holy Land; but on the way he had, according to tradition, a remarkable dream. He thought he saw a tall and handsome man, who told him to return to Norway and take his Udal, adding 'for thou shalt be king over thy country forever'. (The land owned by a peasant was called his *udal*. By udal-right the land was kept in the family, and it could not be alienated or forfeited from the kindred who were 'udal-born' to it.)

OLAF THE SAINT (1015–28)

Leaving his longships (battleships) behind him at Northumberland, Olaf sailed, in the autumn of 1015, with two merchant ships and 120 well-armed men, across the North Sea to Norway. After a stormy voyage he landed on the west coast of Norway, near a small island called Saela. King Olaf thought this was a good omen, because that word means luck. He sailed southward to Ulfasund, where he heard that Earl Haakon was south in Sogn, and was expected north with a single ship as soon as the wind was favourable. King Olaf then sailed further south, and when he came to Saudungssund he laid one of his vessels on each side of the sound, with a thick cable between them. Soon after Earl Haakon came rowing into the sound with a manned ship; they saw Olaf's ships, but thought they were only two merchant vessels, and rowed in between them. When the ship was over the cable, Olaf's men on each side wound it up with the windlass, so that Haakon's ship upset, and all his men plunged into the water. Most of them, however, were picked up and taken on board Olaf's ship; only a few were drowned.

Among those saved was Earl Haakon. He was a very handsome boy of 18 years, with fair, silken hair, bound about his head with a gold ornament. When Olaf saw him, he said: 'True it is what has been said of your family: you are handsome people; but now your luck has deserted you.' Haakon replied: 'It is always so, that sometimes one is victorious, and sometimes another. I am little beyond childhood in years; besides, we did not expect any attack. It may turn out better with me another time.' 'But dost thou not fear that thou art now in such a condition that, hereafter, there will be neither victory nor defeat for thee?' asked the king. 'That all depends upon thee,' said the earl. Olaf then asked what he would give if he were allowed to go unhurt. The earl asked what he demanded. 'Nothing,' said the king, 'except that thou shalt leave the country and take an oath that thou shalt never go into battle against me.' Earl Haakon agreed to this, took the oath and rowed away with his men. As soon as possible he sailed over to England, to his mother's brother, King Canute, who received him well. His father, Earl Erik, whom he afterward joined, considered his son's oath binding upon him also, and he therefore made no attempt to win back the lost kingdom, but remained in Northumberland until his death (1024).

King Olaf now went southward along the coast, holding Things with the peasants in many places. Many went willingly with him, while others, who were Earl Svein's relations or friends, refused him allegiance. He therefore decided first to apply to his relations, the kings in the Uplands, and see what support he could gain from them for his cause. He sailed east to Viken, set his ships on land and proceeded with 120 men up the country to Ringerike, to meet his stepfather, Sigurd Syr. The story of his reception at his mother's home, as detailed in Snorre Sturlason's *Heimskringla*, is very interesting, and gives a vivid picture of the life and customs at the home of a rich and mighty Norwegian in those days. The main portion of the description is here given.

As Olaf was approaching Sigurd Syr's home some of the servants ran ahead to the house. Olaf's mother, Aasta, was sitting in the room, and around her some of her girls. When the servants told her that King Olaf was coming, and that he might soon be expected, Aasta immediately got up, and ordered men and girls to put everything in the best order. She ordered four girls to bring out all that belonged to the decoration of the room, and put it in order with hangings and benches. Two men brought straw for the floor, two brought forward four-cornered tables and the drinking jugs, two bore out victuals and placed the meat on the table, two she sent away from the house to procure in the greatest haste all that was needed, and two carried in the ale; and all the other serving men and girls went outside of the house. Messengers went to seek King Sigurd wherever he might be, and brought to him his dress-clothes, and his horse with gilt saddle, and his bridle which was gilt and set with precious stones. Four men she sent off in different directions to invite all the great people to a feast, which she was preparing as a rejoicing for her son's return. She made all who were in the house dress themselves with the best they had, and lent clothes to those who had none suitable.

King Sigurd Syr was in the field superintending the harvest work when the messengers came to him with the news, and told him all that Aasta was doing at the house. He had many people with him working in the field. He probably did not like the interruption of the work caused by his wife's message, but he dressed himself in the fine clothes sent him, mounted his horse and rode home together with 30 well-dressed men whom he had sent for. As they rode up to the house, Olaf, under his banner, was seen coming up from the other side with 120 men all well-equipped. People were also gathered all around. King Sigurd saluted his stepson, and invited him and his men to come and drink with him. But Aasta went up and kissed her son, and invited him to stay with them, saying that all the land and people she could furnish would be at his service. King Olaf thanked her kindly for her invitation. Then she took him by the hand, and led him into the room to the high-seat, while King Sigurd got men to take care of their clothes, and see that the horses were cared for. Then Sigurd went in, and a great feast was had.

King Olaf had not been at the place many days before he called his stepfather, King Sigurd, his mother Aasta, and his foster father Rane to a conference and consultation. He informed them that it was his intention to win back from the Danes and the Swedes the land of his forefathers or die in the attempt. He asked Sigurd to help him, and give him the best possible advice in the matter. King Sigurd thought the plan was very risky, but knew from experience that it would be useless to try to dissuade Olaf from it. He would, therefore, help him with goods and money; but he would not bind himself to anything more, before he knew the views and intentions of the other Upland kings.

In the Uplands there lived at that time many descendants from Harald the Fairhaired. They all bore the title of king, although their possessions were small. After the death of Olaf Tryggvasson they had acknowledged the suzerainty of the Danish king. One of them ruled over Raumarike, Hadeland and Thoten, another over Valders. In Gudbrandsdal there was a king named Gudrod, and in Hedemarken two brothers, Rorek and Ring, were the rulers. With these district kings Sigurd Syr had a meeting in Hadeland which King Olaf also attended. Here Sigurd announced his stepson Olaf's purpose, and asked their aid to accomplish the plan. He also told of the many brave deeds which Olaf had performed on his war expeditions.

King Rorek then made a speech against the proposed change. The people, he said, had had many experiences. When King Haakon, Athelstan's foster son, was king, all were content; but when Gunhild's sons ruled over the country, they became so hated for their tyranny that the people would rather have foreign kings, who usually left the people to themselves if only the taxes were paid. When Earl Haakon had succeeded in establishing himself firmly as a ruler with the help of the people, he became so hard and overbearing toward them that they could no longer tolerate him. They killed him, and raised to the kingly power Olaf Tryggvasson, who was udal-born to the kingdom, and in every way well qualified to be a chief.

The whole country's wish was to make him supreme king, and raise again the kingdom which Harald the Fairhaired had established. But when King Olaf had become secure in his power, no man could manage his own affairs for him. With the small kings he was very hard, and collected even greater tribute than Harald the Fairhaired had done. A man was not even allowed to believe in what god he pleased. After Olaf Tryggvasson had been taken away, they had kept friendly with the Danish king, and had received great help from him in everything; they had been allowed to rule themselves, and had experienced no oppression. Rorek was, therefore, inclined to let well enough alone, and declined to take any part in the proposed plan.

His brother Ring was of a different opinion. He said that even if he only could keep the same power and property that he held now, he would prefer to see one of his own race as supreme king rather than a foreign chief. And if Olaf succeeded in making himself supreme king, those of them would fare best who had best deserved his friendship. He believed Olaf to be an honourable man, and if they gave him aid now he would certainly show his gratitude afterward. He was in favour of giving Olaf all possible friendship and support. The others, one after the other, expressed the same opinion, and the result was that the most of them entered into a league with King Olaf. This league was confirmed by oath.

Thereafter the kings summoned a Thing, and here Olaf explained in a long speech what claims he had to the throne of Harald the Fairhaired. He requested the peasants to elect him king, and he promised them to uphold the old laws, and to defend the country. His speech was very well received.

Then the different kings spoke in support of his request, and the result was that King Olaf was proclaimed king over the whole country according to the laws of the Uplands. The king thereupon proceeded through the Uplands accompanied by 360 men, and from all directions the people flocked to him and hailed him as their king.

From the Uplands King Olaf hastened over the Dovre Mountain to the Throndhjem country. It was of importance to come there before the reports of his proceedings reached Earl Svein, who was about to celebrate Christmas at Steinker. At Medaldal, in Orkedal, he summoned the peasants to a Thing, where he requested them to accept him as king. They were without a leader and did not have sufficient strength to offer opposition to the king; so the result was that they took the oath of allegiance. At Griotar he met an army of about 800 men, which had been collected by Einar Thambaskelfer, but had been left without a leader while Einar went to Gauldal to get more men. Olaf offered the men peace and law, 'the same as King Olaf Tryggvasson offered before me', and then presented them with two conditions – either to enter his service or fight him. The result was that they hailed him as their king. When Earl Svein heard of this, he fled from Steinker with a longship and proceeded to Frosta. After having reached Steinker, Olaf again summoned a Thing, and compelled the people to recognize him as their king. He thereupon sailed to Nidaros, where he made preparations to celebrate Christmas. Earl Svein and Einar Thambaskelfer meanwhile gathered an army of 2,400 men, with which they suddenly descended upon Nidaros. Olaf and his men barely escaped, and fled southward to the Uplands by the same way they had come. Earl Svein took the Christmas provisions which Olaf's party had been obliged to leave and then burned the town of Nidaros.

Olaf spent the winter in the Uplands, and in the spring gathered an army with which he intended to meet Earl Svein. The kings in Hedemarken furnished him with many armed men, and his stepfather, Sigurd Syr, joined him with a great force. During the winter he had built a ship, which was named 'Karlshoved' (Carl's Head, possibly intended to represent the head of Charlemagne, whose name was held in great veneration). On the bow of the ship was a crowned head, which the king himself had carved. With a fine and well-equipped fleet Olaf set out from Viken, going first to Tunsberg.

Earl Svein in the meanwhile collected a great force in the north. Many of the chiefs were his relatives and friends, and were able to give him great assistance. His brother-in-law, Einar Thambaskelfer, was on his side, and with him many other lendermen (a sort of local governors); and among them were many who had taken oath of allegiance to King Olaf the winter before. Earl Svein sailed south along the coast, drawing men from every district. When they came to Rogaland, Erling Skialgson of Sole joined them with a considerable force. Svein's fleet is said to have consisted of 45 ships, with probably upward of 2,500 men; Olaf hardly had half the number of ships, but his ships were considerably larger, so that the number of men was probably about the same. Toward the end of Easter he entered Viken with his fleet and put in at Nesiar (Nesje), a headland on the east side of the bay (near Fredriksvaern).

On Palm Sunday, March 25, 1016, the two fleets met in battle. Before opening the battle Olaf had his ships tied together, his own ship, 'Karlshoved', occupying a place in the centre. On this ship were 120 men armed in coats of mail, French helmets and white shields, on which was a gilt or painted cross. Olaf had a white banner on which the figure of a serpent was sewed. The king instructed his men to defend themselves with the shields in the beginning, and take care of their lances and arrows, so that they were not thrown away to no purpose. This advice was followed with good results. When the conflict had become exceedingly sharp, and the missiles began to be scarce on the earl's side, Olaf's men were well supplied, and their attack was very severe.

Men fell in great numbers on both sides, but mostly on the earl's ships. King Olaf with the 'Karlshoved' engaged Earl Svein's ship, and his men were soon preparing to enter it. The earl, seeing his defeat, ordered his ship cut loose from the others, and at the last moment his brother-in-law, Einar Thambaskelfer, succeeded in pulling the ship out of the line of battle from behind, using his own vessel as a towboat. When the earl's ship was gone, the flight became general. Some of the earl's men fled up the country, others surrendered on the king's mercy, but Earl Svein and his followers escaped out through the bay. Svein proceeded to Sweden to seek the aid of the Swedish king, while Erling Skialgson and some other chiefs sailed westward and returned to their homes. Earl Svein was well received by King Olaf the Swede, and it was agreed that next winter they should proceed with an armed force overland through Helsingland and Jemteland and down to the Throndhjem country, for the earl depended upon the faithful help of the people there. The summer was to be spent in Viking expeditions in the Baltic. Svein made a cruise to

Russia and plundered the coasts; in the autumn he was taken sick there and died (1016).

King Olaf went north after the battle of Nesje, and settled down in Nidaros, where he rebuilt the royal residence and the church, and helped the merchants to rebuild the town. After the death of Earl Svein he was readily recognized by all the people in that part of the country as the rightful king. The Swedish king became very angry when he heard that he had lost the possessions in Norway which he had won by the battle of Svolder, and he threatened to take great revenge upon Olaf the Big, a nickname which he had given his Norwegian opponent on account of his stoutness. He sent tax collectors into Norway, and when these were harshly treated, some of them even being killed, Olaf the Swede was highly enraged, and war between the two kings was threatened. King Olaf made preparations for an emergency, although he much preferred peace, and even wished to marry the Swedish king's daughter. He built fortifications on a headland in the river Glommen, near the falls of Sarpen, and around these fortifications he laid the foundation of the town of Borg or Sarpsborg.

The people on both sides of the boundary were very much displeased with the feud between the kings, and on both sides the kings were urged to make peace. The Norwegian king was willing enough, and sent conciliatory messages to Olaf the Swede, but the latter rejected all overtures. Finally the matter was brought to a crisis at a general Thing assembled at the Swedish city of Upsala. Here the king at first also refused to hear the propositions for peace, when Thorgny Lagman (lawman, a kind of judge at the Thing) rose, and made the following speech: 'The disposition of Swedish kings is different now from what I hear it was formerly. My grandfather, Thorgny, could well remember the Upsala king Erik Eymundson, and used to tell of him that when he was in his best years he went out every summer on expeditions, and conquered Finland and Karelen, Estonia and Courland and many parts of the eastern country. Even at the present day the earth-bulwarks and other great works which he made are to be seen. And yet, he was not so proud that he would not listen to those who had something to say to him. Thorgny, my father, was a long time with King Bjorn, and well knew his ways and manners. At that time the kingdom was in great power and suffered no losses. He, too, was sociable with his men. I also remember Erik the Victorious, and was with him on many a war expedition. He enlarged the Swedish dominion and bravely defended it, and with him also it was easy to talk about public affairs. But the king we now have allows no one to talk with him of anything but what he himself desires to hear. He wants to have Norway laid under him, which no Swedish king before him ever desired, and thereby causes many men to be alarmed. But now it is the will expressed by us peasants that thou, King Olaf, make peace with the king of Norway, and give him thy daughter Ingegerd in marriage. If thou wilt reconquer the countries on the Baltic which thy relations and ancestors had there, we will all go with thee. But if thou wilt not now consent to what we demand, we will no longer suffer law and peace to be disturbed, but will attack thee and kill thee. So our forefathers did when, at the Mora Thing, they drowned five kings in a morass because they were filled with the same insupportable pride thou hast shown toward us. Now tell us, in all haste, which of these two conditions thou wilt choose.' The whole public approved, with clash of arms and shouts, the speech of Thorgny Lagman. Then the king rose and said he would do as the people desired. 'All Swedish kings,' he said, 'have done so, and have allowed the peasants to rule in all according to their will.' The murmur among the people then came to an end, and it was decided that the terms of peace offered by the Norwegian king were to be accepted, and that Ingegerd, the king's daughter, was to be married to King Olaf of Norway.

In the meanwhile King Olaf travelled through the country, and carefully investigated the manner in which Christianity was observed. Where he found the people lacking in Christian knowledge, he taught them and furnished them with Christian teachers. If he met with obstinate opposition, he acted with severity and cruelty. 'If any there were,' says the saga, 'who would not renounce heathen ways, he took the matter so zealously that he drove some out of the country, mutilated others on hands or feet, or stung their eyes out; hanged some, slew some with the sword; but let none go unpunished who would not serve God.' In this way he proceeded through the country, accompanied by 360 armed men.

King Olaf soon found that Christianity was thriving less the further he proceeded into the interior. In the Uplands five small kings came together at Ringsaker, and under the leadership of King Rorek conspired to kill King Olaf. 'But it happened here,' says the saga, 'as it usually does, that everyone has some friend even among his enemies.' Ketil Kalf of Ringenes, who was present at the meeting of the conspirators, went down after supper to the lake (Miosen), and boarded a little vessel which King Olaf had made him a present of after the battle at Nesje. He had 40 well-armed men with him, and rowed in all haste down the lake. He arrived early in the morning at Eid (Eidsvold), where he found the king and told him of the intention of the small kings of Upland. King Olaf immediately gathered his men, sailed north to Ringsaker, surprised the conspirators and captured them.

King Olaf now availed himself of the opportunity that chance had given him, to rid himself of royal rivals who, as descendants of Harald the Fairhaired, claimed under the law to have as much right to their possessions as any supreme king, and who had always been in the way of a national unity. King Olaf now, by one decisive act, secured the unity and independence of the country, and prepared the way for the victorious entrance of Christianity.

King Ring and two other kings were banished from Norway, under oath never to return. Rorek was a treacherous man and could not be depended upon, so the king ordered both his eyes put out, and afterward took him with him in that condition wherever he went. He ordered Gudrod Valley-king's tongue to be cut out, and of the lendermen and peasants who were implicated in the conspiracy some he banished from the country, some he mutilated and with others he made peace. King Olaf took possession of the land that these kings had possessed. His stepfather, Sigurd Syr, who had had nothing to do with the conspiracy of the other small kings, died during the winter (1018), and now Olaf alone bore the title of King in Norway.

Shortly after his stepfather Sigurd Syr's death, Olaf went to visit his mother, Aasta, and on this occasion it is told that she took her boys (half-brothers of Olaf) to show them to the king. King Olaf took Guthorm on one knee and his brother Halfdan on the other. He made a wry face at the boys, and pretended to be angry, and they became frightened and ran away. Then Aasta brought in her youngest son, Harald, who was then three years old. The king made a wry face at him also, but the boy only stared back at him. The king then took hold of the boy's hair as if to pull it, but the boy in return pulled the king's whiskers. 'Thou wilt probably be revengeful someday, my friend,' said the king.

The following day Olaf and Aasta were watching the boys at play down by the lake (at the Tyrifjord). Guthorm and Halfdan had built houses and barns and had little figures representing cattle and sheep. Little Harald was down by the water, where he had little chips of wood floating. The king asked him what they were, and Harald answered that they were warships. The king laughed, and said: 'The time may come, kinsman, when thou wilt command ships.' Then the king called Guthorm and Halfdan up to him, and asked them what they would like to have above all. 'Fields,' answered Guthorm. 'And how large?' asked the king. 'I would have that headland yonder sown with corn every summer,' answered the boy. The headland included 10 farms. 'There would be a great deal of corn there,' said the king. Turning to Halfdan, he asked what he would like best to have. 'Cows,' said Halfdan. 'And how many?' asked the king. 'So many that when they came to the lake to drink they would stand close together around the whole lake,' was the answer. 'You both take after your father in wanting a great husbandry,' said the king. 'But what wouldst thou have?' he asked Harald. 'Men,' replied the boy. 'And how many?' 'So many that in a single meal they would eat all of Halfdan's cows,' was the answer. The king laughed, and said to Aasta: 'Here, mother, thou art bringing up a king.' 'And more is not related of them on this occasion,' says the saga; but the prophecy was fulfilled, for Harald, Sigurd's son, in time became king of Norway.

The Swedish king broke the promises he had given at the Upsala Thing, and did not send his daughter Ingegerd to the appointed meeting place on the boundary, when King Olaf of Norway came to fetch his bride. Shortly afterward the Swedes revolted, and the Swedish king again had to make concessions, and promise to make peace with the king of Norway. The latter had, in the meanwhile, against the wishes of her father, married Astrid, a younger half-sister of Ingegerd. At the peace summit of Konungahella, where the kings finally met, this marriage was approved by the Swedish king, the boundary lines between the two countries were finally agreed upon, and friendly relations were established.

KING OLAF ESTABLISHES CHRISTIANITY IN NORWAY

After the peace of Konghelle, King Olaf ruled for many years without being molested by foreign enemies. It was his ambition to make Norway a strong Christian monarchy like other Christian states of Europe, and he laboured assiduously to carry through a great program of organization and reform by which the foundations were laid for the future national development of Norway. The problems confronting him were many and difficult. Norway would have to regain its integrity and independence, Christianity had to be re-established, the laws were in need of revision and the aristocracy had to be reduced to submission and to full obedience to the laws.

In the years prior to 1019, while he was yet engaged in the struggle with the king of Sweden, he introduced Christianity in Oplandene. He visited every district and petty kingdom, placed missionaries there to instruct the people, and punished severely all those who refused to accept the Christian faith. The kings of these districts were much displeased, and assembled to form an alliance against him; but a friend informed him of their plot. He surprised them and took them prisoners while they were still deliberating upon the uprising, and punished them severely. Some he banished, others he maimed or blinded, says the saga; the rule of petty kings in Norway was ended. Oplandene, which hitherto had been nearly independent, was now placed immediately under the crown.

After the treaty of peace with Sweden in 1019, Olaf could devote himself to the missionary work with greater energy, and he was ably assisted by the bishops which he had brought from England and Normandy. Of those mentioned – Rudolf, Bernhard, Grimkel and Sigurd – Grimkel was the most important. He was a man of learning, tact and ability. The name indicates that he was of Norse descent, but he must have been born in England. He was King Olaf's chief adviser and assistant both in the missionary work and in lawgiving. Among the king's most powerful and devoted friends were also: Bjørn Stallare, Sighvat Thordsson the great skald, Thord Foleson, Aslak Fitjaskalle, Thormod Kolbrunarskald, and Hjalte Skjeggesson.

In 1019 Olaf went to Nidaros, where he remained that winter. The following summer he introduced Christianity in Haalogaland, the most northern district of Norway, and Haarek of Tjotta and Thore Hund of Bjarkey, the most powerful chieftains in those parts, pledged their submission to the king. In Uttrøndelagen, Christianity had been maintained since the days of Olaf Tryggvasson, but in Indtrøndelagen the people had returned to paganism, and the powerful Ølve of Egge continued to officiate as priest in the heathen temple in spite of King Olaf's warning. Olaf, therefore, marched against the Indtrønders while they were assembled for the spring sacrifices, captured Ølve, and caused him to be executed. He gave his widow and his estates to Kalv Arnesson, whom he made a *lendermand*.

The people of Gudbrandsdal were converted to Christianity in 1021, after some resistance. When the army which they sent against the king was defeated at Breidevangen, south of Sell, a *thing* was assembled at Hundtorp, where the *herse* Dale-Gudbrand was baptized, and the people accepted Christianity. Dale-Gudbrand built a church at Hundtorp, and Olaf left missionaries to instruct the people. The story told in the sagas that the people carried out an idol representing the god Thor, thinking that it would frighten King Olaf, and that Kolbein the Strong, one of Olaf's men, demolished it with a club, is a piece of fiction introduced by Snorre for dramatic effect. It symbolizes the combat of Christianity against heathenism, and King Olaf's war against the idols. It marks the beginning of a whole literature of folktales connected with the name of Saint Olaf.

In 1023 Olaf also introduced Christianity in the Gulathingslag and in Valdres. In many places, as in Viken, in Uttrøndelagen, and in localities on the west coast where churches had been built by Olaf Tryggvasson, Christianity had not altogether disappeared, but it had been obscured and corrupted through heathen ideas and customs. It, therefore, became King Olaf's second great task to give the Church of Norway a permanent organization, and to establish for it a code of church laws according to which it might be governed. With the assistance of Bishop Grimkel and other ecclesiastics, he produced such a code of laws written in the Norwegian language. The *Heimskringla* says: 'The church laws he made according to the advice of Bishop Grimkel and other teachers, and devoted all his energy to eradicate heathenism and old customs which he considered contrary to the Christian spirit.'

He called a general *thing* in the island of Moster, where people from Viken, Gulathingslag and Frostathingslag were present. Here King Olaf and Bishop Grimkel explained the new laws to the people, and they were finally adopted. For the Eidsivathingslag Olaf made a new code in which the church laws were incorporated. The districts of Viken were also organized into a *thinglag*, called 'Borgarthingslag', because the *thing* met at Borg, or Sarpsborg. It received a code of laws to which the church laws were also added. It is not certain, however, that the Borgarthingslag was originally organized by King Olaf. In the Gulathingslag and Frostathingslag there was one principal church in each *fylke*; in the Borgarthingslag two, and in the Eidsivathingslag three. The principal churches had resident priests who received the income from church lands set aside for their maintenance.

The final step taken by King Olaf in the organization of the Church of Norway was to place it under the higher ecclesiastical authority of an archbishop. This might have led to a closer affiliation with the Church of England, since Christianity had been brought to Norway from that country, but the political situation proved unfavourable. Knut the Great, who was now king of England, had not relinquished his claim on Norway, and any closer relations between the two countries, even in religious matters, might have contributed to strengthen his hold. King Olaf, therefore, sent Bishop Grimkel to negotiate with Archbishop Unvan of Bremen, with the result that the Church of Norway was placed under the supervision of the Archbishop of Bremen.

Christianity began henceforth to gain general favour. The old pagan conceptions were not eradicated, however, through the hasty conversion. They gradually assumed Christian forms and continued to live in the religious life as well as in the songs and stories of the people. Christ was substituted for Odin as the divine ruler. The poet Eiliv Gudrunsson sang about Christ the mighty king of Rome, who sits in the South at the Well of Urd, and rules over the lands of the mountain kings. King Olaf takes the place of Thor as the red-bearded champion of light, who is ever victorious in his war against trolls and evil spirits. Freyja reappears as the Virgin Mary, who rules over the animals of the forest. She is also the midwife, and assists at the birth of children. This naive but poetic blending of Christian forms and pagan ideas marks the advent of the intellectual life of the Christian Middle Ages, from which the folk songs and fairy tales have sprung.

It became necessary for Olaf also to revise the civil laws, to bring them into closer conformity with Christian principles. The *Heimskringla* states that 'he made the laws according to the counsel of the wisest men; he took away, or added, as he considered it just.' We have already seen that he gave the Eidsivathingslag a new code, and it is probable, though not certain, that he established the Borgarthingslag. The laws of the Gulathingslag and of the Frostathingslag were so thoroughly revised that these old codes were henceforth known as the 'Laws of Saint Olaf'. The revision of the laws by the king and his learned assistants, who were familiar, not only with Christian principles, but also with the laws of the Christian kingdoms of western Europe, was a legal work of the greatest importance. The 'Laws of St. Olaf' were destined to become the foundation of future Norwegian jurisprudence.

King Olaf's lawgiving represents in itself a centralization of power, and a growth of royal authority which carries with it the greatest change in the political institutions of Norway. King Haakon the Good had, indeed, been a lawgiver, but not to the extent which this function was now exercised by King Olaf. The old laws were regarded as having been given by the gods themselves; they were inherited, time-honoured custom, the expression of the sense of legal justice of the whole people, who originally had exercised the power of law-making. But after the union of Norway, and the introduction of Christianity, when the laws had to be revised and brought into harmony with the new conditions, the king gradually assumed this power; and after Olaf Haraldsson's time the people had little direct influence on legislation.

The old *lagthings*, which had been well-suited to the old tribal organization, were conspicuously defective as law-making assemblies for the united kingdom of Norway. They were four in number, not a single assembly for the whole country, and they were provincial, not national in character.

They had no power of taxation, and the laws were introduced by the king, or in his name. The powers of administration, taxation and legislation were, therefore, quite naturally united in the hands of the sovereign. The king, not the *lagthings*, became the exponent of the national will.

But he was not an absolute monarch; the people still exercised indirectly no small influence on legislation. If they desired a new law, or the revision of an old one, they negotiated privately with the king, and when an understanding was reached, the measure was proposed at the *lagthing* in the king's name. If he wished to propose a new law, he negotiated with men of influence to gain the necessary support. In these preliminary negotiations the people could exercise considerable influence through their spokesmen. To become a law, the new measure had to be proposed at the *lagthing* and accepted by the people. In matters of taxation the king was also dependent on the will of the people. If new taxes had to be levied, even for special emergencies, a proposal was brought before the various local or *fylkesthings*, where the assent of the people had to be secured.

The establishment of the kingdom of Norway based on the theory of a strong national monarchy with centralized legislative and administrative powers necessitated many important changes in the whole system of government. Many new departures of far-reaching importance had been made, especially by Harald Haarfagre, and Olaf Haraldsson continued his great predecessor's work of reorganization. The *herser*, or tribal chieftains, who had ruled over larger local districts, were now replaced by *lendermaend*, or officials appointed by the king. The *herser* had been the leaders of the people – an old aristocracy; the *lendermend* became the representatives and adherents of the king. The *aarmaend*, who in Harald Haarfagre's time were men of humble station, appointed as overseers of the royal estates, were now replaced by *sysselmaend*, or royal officials. They collected the taxes in their districts, and arrested and punished criminals in the name of the king.

The *hird* was also reorganized. Three classes are mentioned: *hirðmaend*, *gestir*, and *huskarlar*. The *hirðmaend*, usually sons of *lendermaend* and other leading men in the country, constituted the king's court. The *gestir* were sent on difficult and dangerous missions, and executed the police duties exercised by the king throughout the kingdom. The *huskarlar* had charge of the work about the royal residence, and furnished the necessaries for the king's household. This class does not seem to have belonged to the *hird* proper. The 'King's Mirror' says: 'All men who serve the king are called "huskarlar", but honour and power are divided among them according to their ability to serve him, and according as he wishes to grant preferments to each. There are some *huskarlar* in the king's *hird* who receive no salary, neither are they permitted to eat or drink with the rest of the *hird*. They must do all things about the royal residence which the overseer demands.' They seem to have been young men of good family, who sought this kind of service as a possible road to promotion and royal favour.

At the head of the *hird* stood the great officials of the king's court, who acted in the capacity of ministers of state. They were called *hirðstjorar* (leaders of the *hird*). The chief officials were: the *stallari*, who had charge of the royal equipages, and acted as the king's representative at the thing; the *merkismaðr*, or royal standard-bearer, the *fehirðir*, or treasurer, and the *hirdbishop*, who was the king's adviser in ecclesiastical affairs. All public offices, from the lowest to the highest, had thus been organized into an articulate system of national administration.

During the reign of Eirik Jarl and Svein, the powerful chieftains in the colonies had cast off all allegiance to Norway, and ruled as independent princes. The task of reuniting these island possessions with the kingdom required, therefore, the most vigilant attention. Through energetic and tactful measures King Olaf soon succeeded in bringing the Orkney and Shetland Islands back to their old allegiance. The Faroe Islands accepted the king's code of church laws, but so long as the crafty Trond i Gata lived, no taxes were paid to the king of Norway.

King Olaf investigated diligently how Christianity was maintained in Iceland. He persuaded the Icelanders to abolish many heathen customs which were still practiced, but his church laws do not seem to have been established there. He sought to gain the friendship of the Icelandic chieftains, and many of them visited him in Norway. He negotiated with them in regard to the relation between Norway and Iceland, and an agreement was made about 1022, called 'The Institutions and Laws Which King Olaf Gave the Icelanders'. According to this agreement the Icelanders should virtually enjoy the rights and privileges of citizens of Norway. 'They had the same right of *odel* as other freeholders, and could inherit property in Norway on the same terms as native citizens. They paid no taxes except the landøre, which was paid for the privilege of trade and intercourse with Norway. In return, the king's men should have the same rights in Iceland as native citizens, and the suits at law should be brought directly to the highest court. In time of war the Icelanders who happened to be in Norway owed the king military service, and could not leave the country. Two out of every three would then have to join the royal standards. This arrangement lasted till 1262, when Iceland was finally united with Norway. King Olaf rebuilt the city of Nidaros, which Olaf Tryggvasson had founded, and restored the royal hall and the St. Clemens church, which had been erected in Olaf Tryggvasson's time.

More difficult than any other task in King Olaf's great work of reorganization was that of reducing the recalcitrant aristocracy to proper submission. Many of the great chieftains who reluctantly had pledged the king a nominal allegiance, soon manifested a hostile opposition to his plans, but King Olaf, none the less, proceeded with characteristic energy to restrict their power to what he considered reasonable limits. The powerful Haarek of Tjotta had to divide his *syssel* with King Olaf's friend Osmund Grankelsson, and Aslak Fitjaskalle was made *sysselmand* in Hordaland, in southwestern Norway, where Erling Skjalgsson of Sole ruled with almost royal power. The king enforced the laws with strict impartiality, and punished with uncompromising severity even the most powerful offenders. The *Heimskringla* says: 'He meted out the same punishment to the powerful and to the small, but the great men of the country regarded this as arrogance, and they were greatly offended when they lost their kinsmen through the king's just decision, even if the case was true. This was the cause of the uprising of the great men against King Olaf, that they could not tolerate his justice. But he would rather surrender his kingdom than his uprightness.'

Erling Skjalgsson and others sent their sons to King Knut the Great in England, who received them well, gave them rich presents, and did what he could to encourage the defection of the Norwegian chieftains. King Knut was a powerful monarch who ruled over England, Scotland, Wales and Denmark. He, also, called himself king of Norway, and claimed even the throne of Sweden. He was tall and stately, with light hair and bright eyes, generous and sociable, a king whom the young nobles loved to serve. So long as Knut was fully occupied with affairs in England, the aristocracy did not venture to rebel openly against King Olaf, but the growing power and influence of King Knut was a steadily growing menace to Norwegian independence. The new king of Sweden, Anund Jacob, was a brother of Olaf's queen, Astrid. The two kings made a joint attack on Denmark in an endeavour to seize the country, but King Knut met them with a large fleet, and an undecisive battle was fought by Helgea, near Skåne, after which all thought of conquering Denmark had to be abandoned.

Erling Skjalgsson and Haarek of Tjotta had thrown off all allegiance to King Olaf, so that he could find no support in northern and western Norway. King Knut, who had made active preparations to invade the country, left England with a fleet of 50 ships, in 1028, and a Danish fleet lay ready to join him. When this news reached Norway, the chieftains of Trøndelagen assembled the Ørething and proclaimed Knut king, and Erling Skjalgsson hastened to his assistance at the earliest opportunity. But Olaf would still strike a blow for his throne and his country. He left Viken with 13 ships, and met Erling Skjalgsson's squadron near Utstein in southwestern

Norway. A battle was fought which resulted in the defeat and death of Erling. It was now late in the autumn, and a great fleet was advancing against him from Trøndelagen. All further resistance was useless. He steered his ships into a fjord in Søndmør, took leave of his friends, and through the winter's snow he made his way across the mountains to Sweden. He spent some time in the island of Gothland, where he introduced Christianity. From there he proceeded to Novgorod, and finally to Kief, where he found refuge at the court of his brother-in-law, Duke Jaroslaf of Gardarike.

NORWAY UNDER DANISH OVERLORDSHIP – KING OLAF THE SAINT

King Knut the Great, who was now over-king of Norway, placed Haakon, the son of Eirik Jarl, in charge of the kingdom as his deputy or vassal. Haakon went to England, where he married Gunbild, a daughter of King Knut's sister, but on his return voyage he was drowned in the Pentlandsfjord, and the great Ladejarl family became extinct in the male line. Both Kalv Arnesson and Einar Tambarskjaelver aspired to become his successor, but Knut let them understand that he intended to make his own son king of Norway. This was a great disappointment to the ambitious nobles. It became apparent that the benefit which they were to derive from their rebellion against King Olaf would be considerably smaller than they had been led to anticipate. Einar Tambarskjaelver became quite disgusted, and remained absent from Norway till after the battle of Stiklestad.

Olaf Haraldsson languished in exile at Grand Duke Jaroslaf's court. He was moody and unhappy, and could never wholly relinquish the idea of rescuing Norway from foreign rule. The *Heimskringla* states that Olaf Tryggvasson appeared before him in his dreams, and told him to return to Norway and claim the kingdom which God had given him. 'It makes a king renowned to gain victory over his enemies, but it is a glorious death to fall on the battlefield with one's men.' Many of Olaf's men had joined him in Gardarike, and they encouraged him to attempt to wrest Norway from the foreign conquerors. When the news spread that Haakon was dead, he determined to return to Norway. He left his son Magnus at the court of Jaroslaf, and proceeded to Sweden, where King Anund Jacob gave him great aid, though he did not dare to form an alliance with him against King Knut. He gave him a number of soldiers, and allowed him to recruit many more. His adherents in the eastern districts of Norway also aided him. His half-brother Harald Sigurdsson, son of King Sigurd Syr and Aasta, the later chieftain of the Varangians in Myklegard (Constantinople), joined him with a force of 720 men. People of all sorts drifted to his standards, and he was able to enter Norway with a considerable army. He had some good troops, but the greater portion of these hasty levies were of inferior quality.

In Trøndelagen the chieftains, on hearing of King Olaf's return, had gathered a large army of the best forces in the country under such able generals as Kalv Arnesson, Tore llund, and Haarek of Tjotta. Kalv Arnesson had the chief command. The *Heimskringla* states that their army numbered 12,000 men, while Olaf had only 3,600 men; but these figures are, no doubt, too large. Henrik Mathiesen estimates the forces of the chieftains to have numbered about 5,000 men. Sighvat Skald says that they gained the victory because they had twice as many men as King Olaf, who, accordingly, must have had a force of about 2,500 men. Olaf marched across the mountains to Vserdalen in Trøndelagen, and selected a very advantageous position at Stiklestad. According to the 'Olafssaga ins helga' he remained here a few days before the arrival of the chieftains and their forces, waiting for Dag Ringsson, who was bringing reinforcements; but Dag reached Stiklestad too late to be of any assistance.

On the morning before the battle, legend tells, while the army was still resting. King Olaf fell asleep, leaning his head upon the knee of Finn Arnesson, Kalv Arnesson's brother, who had remained faithful to him. He dreamed that a ladder reached from the earth to heaven, and that he had reached the highest round. Here Christ stood and beckoned to him, and promised him reward for his faithful work. At noon, on July 29, 1030, the two armies faced each other on the field of Stiklestad in full battle array. King Olaf stood in the midst of his army in brynie and gilt helmet. He carried the sword 'Hneiter' and a white shield on which a golden cross was painted. His white standard with a dragon in the centre was carried by his standard-bearer, Thord Foleson. About one o'clock, the war trumpets sounded the signal for advance. The serried columns of warriors rushed down the sloping ground to the combat; the most notable battle in Norwegian history had begun.

Olaf's plan was to throw his opponents into disorder by a vigorous assault, and in this he was partly successful. The lines in his front yielded before the furious onset, and great confusion resulted. But the experienced generals and well-disciplined forces of the enemy soon regained their foothold. Olaf's small army was outflanked and surrounded, attacked in front and rear, and overwhelmed by superior numbers. The king was soon wounded in the melee. He had dropped his sword and stood leaning against a stone when Kalv Arnesson and Tore Hund, who pressed forward toward the royal standard, found him and cut him down. Thord Foleson the standard-bearer, Bjørn Stallare, and many other leading men of the royal army were now dead, and many were wounded. Among the latter were Thormod Kolbrunarskald, who on the morning of the battle had awakened King Olaf's army with a song. He withdrew from the conflict with an arrow in his bosom and died before evening. Dag Ringsson now arrived and made a spirited attack, but he could not prevent the complete rout of the royal forces. Those who could sought safety in flight; among others Harald Sigurdsson, who was severely wounded. After his recovery, Harald went to Russia to Grand Duke Jaroslaf, and later he proceeded to Constantinople, where he became captain of the Varangians in the service of the Greek Emperor.

Christianity was no longer the issue in the battle of Stiklestad. The Christian faith had been so firmly established that the chieftains did not attempt, and, probably, did not even desire, to subvert it. The memorable battle was a struggle between the old system of aristocratic rule, and the new royalty leagued with the ideas of national union, independence and progress toward higher cultural ideals. For this cause King Olaf had laboured, and in devotion to it he gave his life. But the aristocracy had triumphed. The king lay dead on the field of battle, and the national cause seemed hopelessly lost when the rumour got abroad that Olaf was a saint. The glory of his martyrdom emanating from the battlefield of Stiklestad kindled the first sparks of patriotism, and gave the lost national cause a new and sacred consecration. Those who had opposed Olaf the king now willingly bent the knee before Olaf the saint. His name became the rallying cry of patriots; his great work and still greater sacrifice for his high ideals had united all hearts; his defeat at Stiklestad had turned into a national victory.

An English lady Elfgifu bore King Knut a son, Svein, who was now about 14 years of age. Svein was made viceroy of Norway, and his mother accompanied him, acting as his adviser, though it is generally acknowledged that she was the real ruler during Svein's short reign. The old form of aristocratic government was not re-established as might have been expected. King Knut was not satisfied with maintaining merely a nominal overlordship, as Harald Gormson had done in earlier days, but demanded for his son powers and privileges far exceeding those which King Olaf had claimed. Svein and Alfiva established Danish laws, and began to rule as if they were exercising unlimited dominion over a conquered people, though it was the Norwegian nobles, and not the Danes, who had defeated King Olaf.

No one was permitted to leave the country without permission from the king. The property of persons convicted of murder was confiscated by the king, and the inheritance of persons outlawed for crime was swept into the royal coffers. The fishermen had to give a part of their catch to the king; a tax called 'Christmas gifts' was levied; all ships leaving Norwegian harbours had to pay a tax called 'landøre', and the people had to erect all buildings needed on the royal estates. Each seventh man had to do military service, and the testimony of a Dane (a member of the king's *hird*) was to be worth that of 10 Norsemen. King Knut's failure to keep his promise to the Norwegian nobles had caused great disappointment, but the government which he established added insult to injury, and awakened the bitterest resentment even among the chieftains who had given him the kingdom.

King Olaf, who had fought so bravely for national independence, was contrasted with the foreign oppressors. His justice and heroism were extolled, and the deep mutterings of popular discontent soon grew into angry avowals that disloyalty to him was treason, and that slavery under foreign rulers had been substituted for national independence. The rumour that King Olaf was a saint added new strength to the growing storm of discontent. The eclipse which occurred on August 31st, a month after the battle of Stiklestad, was thought to be in some way connected with King Olaf's defeat and death, and the association of ideas soon established the conviction that the eclipse took place at the time of the battle. Miracles were said to have happened while the king's body was lying on the battlefield. Thorgils Halmason and his son Grim, who were living near Stiklestad, saw on the night after the battle a light issue from the place where the king's body was lying. They carried the corpse away, and hid it carefully from his enemies, but the same light was seen every night. King Olaf's cheeks did not fade, but retained their ruddy colour. His hair, beard and fingernails continued to grow, and sick persons who prayed to the dead king were healed. King Svein and his mother made every effort to hush down and explain away these stories about Olaf, but this only nursed the wrath of the people against the enemies of their patriotic and sainted king.

The disappointed nobles supported the growing opposition to the Danes. 'It was Einar Tambarskjtelver's boast that he had not taken part in the uprising against King Olaf. He remembered that King Knut had promised him a jarldom in Norway, and that he had not kept his word. Einar was the first of the chieftains to maintain that King Olaf was a saint.' Olaf's body was brought to Nidaros and interred in the St. Clemens church, which he had built. Bishop Grimkel proclaimed him a saint, and the 29th of July, the day of his death, was dedicated as a church holiday, the Olafmas, in his honour.

A pretender by the name of Tryggve now appeared, who claimed to be a son of Olaf Tryggvasson. He came to Norway with a small force, but was defeated and slain by Svein. But the powerful *lendermemd* gave the king no support. They summoned a *thing* at Nidaros, where the people presented their complaints, but Svein and his mother were unable to give any answer. Einar Tambarskjselver arose and said, 'Go home, ye people! A bad errand you have now, as you have had before when you appealed to Alfiva and King Svein. You might as well await injustice at home as to seek it all at once in this one place. Now you listen to the words of a woman, but you refused to listen to King Olaf, who was in truth a saint. A vile treason was committed against him, and our punishment has been severe, while such great humiliation has fallen on our people since this rule was established over them. God grant that it may not last long! It has already lasted too long.'

King Svein and his mother tried in vain to assemble a new *thing*. No one came in answer to their summons. They began to fear a general uprising, and in the winter (1033–34) they left Nidaros, and Danish dominion in Norway was ended. The people of Trøndelagen determined to place St. Olaf's son, Magnus, on the throne. Einar Tambarskjelver and Kalv Amesson were sent to Gardarike as special envoys to offer him the crown. He accompanied them to Norway, and was proclaimed king in 1034, or 1035.

Olaf's canonization was an event of the greatest importance, not only because of the immediate results which it produced, but also through the influence which St. Olaf was destined to exercise on the religious and national development in the future. The hero-king and great lawgiver had become the patron saint and supreme representative of the nation, the *perpetuus rex Norwegiae* under whose egis both royalty and hierarchy could henceforth exercise permanent and unquestioned authority. The old church still standing at Stiklestad was built, it is thought, on the very spot where King Olaf fell, and the rock near which he suffered death is said to have been enclosed in the altar of the church. But Nidaros, where the king was buried, became the chief St. Olaf sanctuary in Norway, and pilgrims from many lands visited the saint's grave every year. They came from Sweden, Denmark and Russia; from the Baltic Sea countries, and from the British Isles.

In course of time their rich offerings to the Saint enabled the archbishop of Norway to erect a cathedral in Trondhjem, the most magnificent in the Scandinavian North. Crosses and chapels were erected in various places made sacred by Olaf; but the commemoration of the saint spread also to other countries, and many churches were dedicated to him in foreign lands. In the island of Gothland; in Angermanland, Helsingland, Upsala and other districts in Sweden he was especially honoured. There were St. Olaf churches in Norrkoping and Lodose, and the monasteries in Abo, Strengnes, Skara and Enkoping were dedicated to him. In Denmark the commemoration of St. Olaf was very widespread, which can be seen from the number of churches dedicated to him in all parts of the Danish kingdom. In England a number of churches were named in his honour. In London alone there were four St. Olaf churches: one in Southwark, one in Silver street, and two in the eastern part of the city. There was also a Tooley street ['Tooley' being a corruption of the Southwark church's name: St Olave's to 'Synt Toulus' and so on], and Exeter had a St. Olaf church. Chester has still an Olaf's church and an Olaf street. York has an Olaf's church, and Norfolk a St. Olafe's bridge. Churches were also dedicated to St. Olaf in Reval in Estonia, in Novgorod and Constantinople, and there is evidence that he was commemorated, also in Ireland, Scotland and Normandy.

MAGNUS THE GOOD – THE UNION OF NORWAY AND DENMARK

Magnus Olafsson met with no resistance on his arrival in Norway. King Knut the Great died in England in 1035, and Svein and Alfiva (Elfgifu) fled to Denmark, where Svein died the year following. What plans King Knut had with regard to the succession is not known, but it is probable that he desired his realm to remain united under his one legitimate son Hardeknut, son of Emma, who had already been crowned king of Denmark. But Harald Harefoot, the son of Knut and his English mistress Alfiva, the mother of Svein, was staying in England, and when Knut died he became an active candidate for the throne. Hardeknut was, therefore, compelled to come to an understanding with King Alagnus. In order to terminate the hostilities between Norway and Denmark, which had already been in progress for some time, the two kings met at Brennøerne, near the mouth of the Gota River, in 1038, and concluded a treaty of peace. Hardeknut recognized the independence of Norway, and a compact was entered into by the kings that if one of them died without an heir, the other should inherit his kingdom, and 12 leading men of each country took an oath to maintain the compact.

The treaty of Brennøerne is a counterpart of the treaty of Konghelle concluded with Sweden in 1019. The integrity and independence of Norway had now been duly recognized, and the kings of the Yngling dynasty were regarded as possessing the same full legitimacy as the royal families of Denmark and Sweden. King Olaf's great fame both as king and saint had made a deep impression on the whole Scandinavian North, and contributed greatly to win for Norway an unqualified recognition as a sovereign and independent state. When Magnus returned to Trondhjem, says the saga, he placed King Olaf's body in a beautiful casket ornamented with gold, silver and precious stones. He also began the erection of a St. Olaf's church, in which the remains of the saint were to be deposited; but this structure was not completed till the next reign.

Before Magnus became king, he had to promise full amnesty to those who had taken part in the armed opposition to his father. It seems that he also agreed to abrogate the noxious laws introduced by King Svein, and to re-establish the laws of King Olaf. But youthful impetuosity soon led him to deal harshly with his father's old enemies. When Haarek of Tjotta was killed by a personal enemy, the offender was not punished. Tore Hund died on a pilgrimage to the Holy Land, and Kalv Arnesson had to flee to the Orkneys to Thorfinn Jarl, who was married to Ingebjørg, the daughter of his brother Finn Arnesson. There had been much secret rivalry between Kalv and Einar Tambarskjaelver, both of whom had aspired to become jarl. Einar, who had taken no part in the uprising against King Olaf, gained the friendship of Magnus, but the young king was unable to forgive Kalv, who had been the leader of the opposition to his father. Einar was styled the king's foster father, or chief councillor, and exercised great influence. Many who had taken part in the battle of Stiklestad against Olaf were made to feel the king's wrath, and the laws of Svein were not repealed as quickly as had been expected.

The people grew dissatisfied and chose as their spokesman the skald Sighvat Thordsson, who had been King Olaf's closest friend, and who now occupied a similar position of honour and confidence at the court of King Magnus. In a song called 'Bersøglisvisur' the skald reminded the young king of his promises to the people, showed him how ill it befits a king to break his word, and pointed to the growing dissatisfaction and the danger of such a situation. So deeply was Magnus impressed with the song that he immediately changed his ways. He became so just and kind that the people henceforth called him Magnus the Good. He granted amnesty to all, and promised to improve the laws by gradually revoking the more oppressive measures of King Svein's reign.

The ties which united the island colonies with the mother country were weakened by the repeated overthrow of the government, as well as by the establishing of foreign dominion in Norway. As the Danish kings paid little attention to the Norwegian colonies, the jarls and chieftains who ruled over the island groups found opportunity to make themselves independent. In the Orkneys Thorfinn Jarl had regained his old independence after the fall of St. Olaf, and the crafty and powerful Trond i Gata had ruled the Faroe Islands according to his own pleasure since the death of Sigmund Brestesson. But when Trond died in 1035, Leiv Assursson, another Faroe chieftain, went to Norway and tendered his submission to King Magnus, who placed him in charge of the colony. Thereby Norwegian sovereignty was again established in the Faroe Islands.

The king's measures with regard to the Orkneys proved less successful. It has been noted elsewhere that, on the death of Sigurd Lodvesson, the Orkneys were divided among his sons Sumarlide, Bruse and Einar; but none of them lived long, and their half-brother, Thorfinn Sigurdsson, became jarl, and seized all their possessions. Bruse's son, Ragnvald, who was staying at the court of the Grand Duke Jaroslaf, in Gardarike, had accompanied Magnus to Norway. Magnus gave him the title of jarl, and granted him his father's possessions in these islands. Ragnvald was well received by Thorfinn, who at this time was engaged in wars in Scotland. He granted him two-thirds of the islands, and they became friends and allies. But while Kalv Arnesson, the uncle of Thorfinn's wife Ingebjørg, was stajdng in the Orkneys, Thorfinn and Ragnvald became enemies, and hostilities resulted in which Ragnvald lost his life. The colony did not return to its allegiance to Norway till 1066, in the reign of Harald Haardraade.

King Knut the Great is thought to have been about 40 years old at the time of his death. He came to England as a conqueror, but proved to be one of the ablest and wisest of English kings. During the last five years of his reign he ruled over a great empire including England and Scotland, Denmark, Norway, the Orkney Islands and the Viking colonies in the Hebrides and the Isle of Man. The extensive possessions under his own immediate rule he governed with a wisdom and moderation which entitles him to be numbered with the greatest monarchs. He did not confiscate the people's lands for the benefit of his own followers, or in other ways treat England as a conquered country. His soldiers received a money payment, and the people were allowed to keep their lands. He established the old English laws, known as the 'Laws of Edward the Confessor', and ruled as a native English sovereign. He was one of the wisest and most prolific of early English lawgivers; he became an earnest Christian, and remained throughout his reign deeply attached to the intellectual life and higher culture of western Europe.

But Knut's worthless sons did not walk in their father's footsteps. In 1036 Harald Harefoot (son of Elfgifu or Alfiva) succeeded him on the throne of England, but his reign was short and inglorious. He was ambitious and violent, and seemed more devoted to hunting than to the affairs of the state, wherefore the people, fitly enough, nicknamed him Harefoot. He died at Oxford in 1040 at the moment when his half-brother Hardeknut (son of Emma) finally arrived in England. Hardeknut was, if possible, even less qualified to occupy a throne than his worthless brother. He promised amnesty to all who had hitherto sided with Harald Harefoot, but as soon as he was crowned king he began to levy heavy taxes to pay his large army. He was harsh and narrow-minded, and lacked every kingly quality. When this unworthy son of the great King Knut suddenly died in his 25th year, in the second year of his reign, the people felt it as a riddance. He was succeeded by his half-brother, Edward the Confessor, the last surviving son of King Ethelred and Emma.

According to the treaty of Brennøerne, King Magnus of Norway succeeded Hardeknut as king of Denmark. King Knut's family was now extinct in the male line, and Svein Ulvsson, or Svein Estridsson, a son of Ulv Jarl and Knut's sister Estrid, who was the nearest heir to the throne, was unable to rally the people to his support. King Magnus Olafsson was now 18 years old, a well-built young man with light auburn hair and noble features. He was brave, well skilled in the use of arms, and had already gained a reputation for justice. The Danes welcomed him with unfeigned enthusiasm, mixed with a veneration accorded him as the son of the greatest saint in the North. With characteristic generosity King Magnus made Svein Estridsson a jarl, with the understanding that he should defend the borders of Jutland against the Wends. He married his sister Ulvhild to Ordulf, son of the Duke of Saxony, and secured thereby the friendship and support of that powerful family.

Magnus, who enjoyed great power and renown, claimed also the throne of England as the heir of King Hardeknut according to the treaty of Brennøerne. The 'Saga of Magnus the Good' states that he sent the following message to King Edward the Confessor; 'You may have heard of the agreement which was made between King Hardeknut and myself, that the one who lived longest should inherit the lands and subjects of the other, if he died without a male heir. Now it has come to pass, as I know you have learned, that I have fallen heir to all the Danish possessions of King Hardeknut. But at the time of his death he held England no less than Denmark, and I, therefore, claim England according to the agreement made. I desire that you give up the kingdom to me, otherwise I will attack it with an army both from Denmark and Norway, and he will then govern it who wins the victory.'

The *Anglo-Saxon Chronicle* shows that in 1046 an invasion from Norway was expected, and that the English fleet was stationed at Sandwich ready to defend the coast. But 'Svein's fight with him (i.e. with Magnus) hindered him from coming hither,' says the chronicle. Subsequent events in Denmark prove the correctness of these statements. Einar Tambarskjeelver is said to have shaken his head when he heard that Magnus had made Svein Estridsson a jarl. 'Too powerful a jarl', was his comment. Svein was soon tempted to begin an uprising against King Magnus. He made an alliance with the Wends, against whom he was to protect the borders, and Magnus had to call out half the military forces of Norway to put down the rebellion. Svein was compelled to flee, but at any favourable moment he might renew the attack, and with so dangerous an enemy at his back Magnus did not venture to undertake an invasion of England.

The fortified city of Jomsborg was also an inconvenient neighbour. So long as this independent Viking stronghold did not submit to King Magnus it was a constant source of danger to his kingdom, and he resolutely marched against it and captured it after a spirited resistance. In the meanwhile the Wends, who had not been held in check by Svein Estridsson, poured over the borders, and committed fearful depredations in southern Jutland. Magnus gathered a large army at Hedeby, and his brother-in-law, Ordulf of Saxony, came to his assistance with a considerable force. On Michaelmas, Sept. 29, 1043, he faced the Wendish host on Lyrskog Heath, and defeated them in a most sanguinary battle. Under these circumstances the intended invasion of England had to be abandoned, but Magnus had won great renown through his many victories. He had overcome all opposition, and the peace and security of the Danish kingdom was safely established.

Everything now augured well for a prosperous and peaceful reign, but Magnus was still to learn that 'uneasy lies the head that wears a crown'. A most formidable rival suddenly appeared to place new difficulties in his path. This was Harald Sigurdsson, a half-brother of St. Olaf, son of Aasta and King Sigurd Syr. During the 15 years which had passed since the battle of Stiklestad, he had gained great renown as chief of the Varangians in the service of the Greek Emperor at Byzantium. He had married Elizabeth (Ellisiv), daughter of Grand Duke Jaroslaf of Gardarike, and brought great treasures with him to Norway. Elizabeth seems to have died soon after their marriage, as Harald married Thora of the Arnmødling family shortly after his arrival in Norway. Harald was a talented leader of the old martial type, who never hesitated to make the sword the arbiter of every controversy. The sagas describe him as very tall and strong, resolute and energetic. He possessed in an eminent degree the spirit of enterprise and reckless daring which characterized the great Viking chieftains, and his military achievements in the Levant were soon extolled in a whole literature of fictitious tales, in which he is represented as the central figure in every historic event with which he was in any way connected.

The saga narratives, based partly on these tales, and partly on skaldic songs which were often misunderstood, because they told of unknown and distant lands, are wholly unreliable in details. Only the more general features which are corroborated by other sources can be accepted as history. P. A. Munch has shown that the skaldic songs agree in all main features with the Byzantine writers, and that a reliable account of Harald's early career can be extracted from these sources. The correctness of Munch's position was later proven through the discovery of a document which threw new light on the subject. In 1881 Professor Wassilievsky of Moscow published a treatise on a newly discovered Greek manuscript from the eleventh century, written by a contemporary of Harald Sigurdsson. The author tells us that Araltes (Harald) was a son of the king of Varangia, and that his brother Julavos (Olaf) had made him next to himself in rank. But Araltes, who was young and had learned to admire the power of the Romans, wished to do homage to Emperor Michael Paflagon (also called Michael Katalaktus), and came to Constantinople with 500 brave warriors. This agrees with the *Heimskringla*, which states that Harald had many men. The author further states that the emperor sent him to Sicily, where the Roman army was carrying on war. He must have served under the imperial general Georgios Maniakes, whom he aided in the conquest of Sicily, 1038–40. He performed great feats of arms, says the author, and on his return the emperor gave him the title of 'manglabites'.

Then it happened that Delianos in Bulgaria rose in rebellion. Harald accompanied the emperor into that province, and performed such deeds as befitted his rank and valour. On his return to Constantinople the emperor conferred on him the title of 'spatharo-kandidatos'. Harald's campaign in Bulgaria is not mentioned in the sagas, but it is referred to in a song by the skald Thjodolv Arnorsson. Harald was staying in Constantinople when the emperor died in December 1041, and also during the short reign of Michael Kalifates, who was dethroned April 21, 1042. He did military service for a while also under the next emperor, Konstantin Monomachos, but he sought permission to leave, 'because he wished to return to his own country'. This request was refused, but Harald made good his escape, 1043 or 1044. The author is also able to state that Harald became king in his own country after his brother Olaf, and that as king he maintained his old friendship with the Romans. From the skaldic songs, which corroborate the statements of the author, and on many points supplement the account, we learn that Harald also took part in campaigns in Syria and Mesopotamia, and that he went to Jerusalem with a body of Varangians, probably to guard the architects and laborers sent by the emperor to erect a new church in that city.

After Harald left Constantinople, he went to Grand Duke Jaroslaf in Gardarike. He married Ellisiv, the grand duke's daughter, as already stated, and after having spent some time at his court, he crossed the Baltic with a single ship, and came to Sigtuna in Sweden. Here he met Svein Estridsson, who sought to persuade him to join in an attack on King Magnus; but Harald decided to try negotiations. He proceeded to Denmark, and found Magnus stationed with his fleet in Øresund (the Sound), on the coast of Skåne. Harald had a stately vessel, beautifully painted, with gilt dragon head and dragon's tail, and with a sail of costly material. The sudden appearance of such a ship caused no small surprise on the royal fleet, and King Magnus sent a vessel forward to hail the stranger. In answer to the inquiry of the king's messengers a tall and stately man came forward and told them that he was sent by Harald Sigurdsson, King Magnus' uncle, to learn how he would receive him. The tall stranger was Harald Sigurdsson himself. When this news was brought the king, he immediately sent word that he would receive his uncle with open arms. Harald then landed and was received by King Magnus and all his leading men.

In a few days negotiations were begun. Harald asked if Magnus would recognize his right of succession to the throne, and grant him one-half of his kingdom; to which Magnus replied that in such matters he would follow the advice of his chief counsellors. Einar Tambarskjaelver then arose and said that if Harald received half the kingdom, it was but fair that he should divide his treasures with King Magnus; but this Harald refused to do. Einar, who was ruffled by the refusal of so generous an offer, said to him; 'Far away you were, Harald, while we won the kingdom back from the Knytlings (King Knut and his sons), and we have no desire to be divided between chieftains. Hitherto we have served only one at a time, and so it shall be as long as King Magnus lives. I will do all in my power to prevent you from getting any part of the kingdom.'

Harald now returned to Sweden, where he formed an alliance with Svein Estridsson. Denmark was attacked, and Harald harried the Danish islands in true Viking fashion, as it appears, against the will of Svein, who could only gain the people's ill-will through such depredations. When Magnus came with a fleet, Harald made his way to Norway, where he hoped to be proclaimed king in Magnus' absence. He first tried to win his own home districts in Oplandene, but the people remained indifferent. In Gudbrandsdal he was more successful. His powerful relative, the youthful Thore of Steig, aided him. Harald called a *thing*, where Thore gave him the royal title, which, together with the band of followers which he had gathered, gave him new prestige. When Magnus learned of Harald's whereabouts, he quickly returned to Norway, but a clash of arms was averted by the chieftains, who did not want to see two near relatives wage war against each other.

A meeting was arranged, and negotiations were renewed. It seems that the chieftains were determined not to divide the kingdom, and not to tolerate two kings except as joint sovereigns. An agreement was finally reached on the basis of Einar Tambarskjaelver's earlier proposition. Harald should share the throne of Norway with Magnus, and in return he should divide his treasures with him. The joint sovereignty appears to have been limited to Norway, which was now for the first time to be ruled by two kings exercising equal authority. The kings had each their own *hird*, but rivalry and jealousy between their followers and adherents soon bred serious trouble. Harald, who was harsh and uncompromising, was nicknamed Haardraade (Hard-ruler), and was often contrasted in a disparaging way with the kind and generous Magnus the Good. The people, especially the chieftains, sided with Magnus, and Harald grew very embittered against Einar Tambarskjaelver, who became the leader of an opposition to the new king, whom he regarded as an usurper.

In 1047 Magnus and Harald made an expedition to Denmark, and drove out Svein Estridsson, but Magnus died suddenly in Iceland. According to Saxo Grammaticus, Svein Aagesson, and Adam v. Bremen, he was thrown from his horse while pursuing Svein, and received so severe an injury that he died shortly after on board his ship, 1047. Before he died he willed the kingdom of Denmark to Svein Estridsson, whom he had learned to respect as a courageous and able prince. Magnus was highly beloved by the Norwegian people, and his death caused general mourning. He left no son to succeed him on the throne; a fortunate circumstance, perhaps, as civil strife between rival candidates was thereby averted. Harald immediately assembled all the warriors of the fleet, and announced to them that he did not want to abide by the decision of King Magnus, as he regarded Denmark as well as Norway his rightful inheritance. But the warriors refused to follow him on a campaign in Denmark until he had properly buried King Magnus. Einar Tambarskjaelver told him that he would rather follow Magnus dead than any other king living. With a large part of the fleet he left King Harald, and set sail for Trondhjem, where Magnus was interred in the St. Clemens church by the side of his father, St. Olaf. Harald could do nothing against Denmark for the present. He went to Viken in southern Norway, and assembled the Borgarthing, where he was proclaimed king of all Norway. He was also proclaimed King Magnus' successor at the Ørething, in Trøndelagen, according to old custom, and the following year he married Thora, the daughter of Thorberg Arnesson of Giske, as already mentioned.

THE REIGN OF HARALD HAARDRAADE

Olaf Tryggvasson and Olaf Haraldsson had to win the throne as a prize in armed conflict with the aristocracy, but Harald Sigurdsson Haardraade became king of Norway without opposition, though he was very unpopular. Since St. Olaf's time a complete change had taken place in the people's attitude towards the centralized power of monarchical government. Kingship was now looked upon as a fully legitimated national institution, and Harald succeeded to the throne by right of inheritance, or *odel*, which no one ventured to challenge. There was no longer any organized opposition to the king. The aristocracy had accepted the new form of government, and submitted loyally to the king's authority when it was exercised with proper moderation.

They had given King Magnus their undivided support in all his undertakings, and he was very popular and highly beloved by all. But his rule had been benign, and the nobles had exercised a great influence in public affairs. During his minority Kalv Amesson had acted as regent, and later Einar Tambarskjaelver became his chief counsellor. Magnus was not a tool in the hands of the nobles, but he listened to their advice, and showed them no unnecessary effrontery. King Harald Haardraade was of a different type. He was harsh and greedy, not always conscientious as to the means which he employed, disposed to be arbitrary and to have slight regard for others. His character was of the kind that breeds discord, and quarrels with recalcitrant nobles were numerous in his reign. But he was able and ambitious, and came to the throne with the fixed purpose of making the royal power supreme in church and state, and of extending full authority over all the lands which belonged or which had belonged to the Norwegian crown. He was a most able and energetic ruler, who brooked no interference from nobles at home or from powers abroad. He loved independence as passionately as he coveted renown, and wielded the sword of state with a grim recklessness, like a soldier's broadsword, to gain for himself and his kingdom the greatest possible prestige and power.

From the outset he met with considerable opposition and ill-will, caused by his own greed and harshness. He was greatly chagrined by what he considered the arrogant behaviour of some of the chieftains. One of the principal offenders was Einar Tambarskjaelver in Trøndelagen, who acted as the spokesman of the people, and on more than one occasion forced the king to recede from his harsh, and sometimes unjust, demands. King Harald had a suspicion that many of the chieftains were carrying on secret negotiations with King Svein of Denmark. In order to test their loyalty he engaged spies who claimed to be secret agents sent by King Svein to offer the Norwegian nobles riches and great honours if they would aid him against King Harald. When these spies came to Einar Tambarskjaelver, he told them that although he was not Harald's friend, he would do everything in his power to aid him in defending the kingdom against King Svein. The king praised Einar for his loyalty, and Invited him to a festive gathering in Nidaros. It now looked as if old differences would be forgotten, that peace and friendship would, finally, be established between them.

But King Harald gave the great noble new offense, as if from pure love of mischief. The old enmity was still further aggravated, and Einar and his son Eindride were treacherously murdered at the instigation of the king. This wanton deed caused the greatest resentment in Trøndelagen, and the people threatened to rise in open rebellion. Einar's widow, Bergliot, sent word to her powerful relative, Haakon Ivarsson in Oplandene, and asked him to avenge Einar's death. Harald sent Finn Arnesson to Haakon, who promised to remain loyal if the king would give him Ragnhild, the daughter of Magnus, in marriage, together with a dowry suitable to her rank. This was promised him, and the threatened uprising was averted.

Finn Arnesson, who had been St. Olaf's special friend, and who had adhered no less faithfully to his successor, was not much better rewarded than Einar Tambarskjaelver. His brother Kalv, who at Finn's request had been permitted to return from his exile, accompanied Harald on an expedition against Denmark, but the king sent him against the enemy with a handful of men, and he was overpowered and slain. Finn felt so aggrieved that he abandoned both his king and his country, and went to King Svein in Denmark, who made him jarl over the Danish province of Halland, on the southwest coast of Sweden. After some time Haakon Ivarsson asked King Harald to fulfil his promise of giving him Ragnhild, King

Magnus' daughter, in marriage. Harald said that he had no objection, but Haakon would have to obtain the maiden's own consent. Haakon agreed to do this, but he was unsuccessful in his courtship. Ragnhild told him that although he was a handsome and noble-looking man, she, being a princess, could not many him so long as he was only a *lendermand*. He then asked Harald to give him the rank of jarl, so that he could marry Ragnhild, but this he would not do. It had been a rule, he said, ever since the time of St. Olaf, not to have more than one jarl in the kingdom at one time. Orm Eilivsson was now jarl, and he could not deprive him of his title and dignity.

This strange answer convinced Haakon that Harald did not intend to keep his promise, and he went to King Svein in Denmark, where he was well received. He was later reconciled to King Harald, and married Ragnhild, who had learned to love him, and now accepted him without interposing any conditions. Harald promised to raise him to the rank of jarl on the death of Orm Eilivsson, but when Orm died, he again failed to keep his promise, and Haakon and Ragnhild returned to Denmark to King Svein, who invited them to stay at his court, and welcomed St. Olaf's granddaughter with special fondness. Haakon was made jarl of Halland to succeed Finn Arnesson, who had died.

It is quite clear from these and other similar episodes that Harald Haardraade was bent on destroying the power of the aristocracy, and he could ill conceal his feeling of satisfaction when the powerful nobles one after another disappeared. He is even said to have stated in skaldic verse that he had caused the death of 13 men, but who they were is not mentioned. It cannot be doubted that by pursuing such a policy of removing the old chieftains who possessed sufficient prestige to be able to offer resistance, the king gradually strengthened his own power. He possibly even gave the throne increased stability, but this practice weakened Harald in his foreign wars. It deprived him of the aid of many of the ablest men. Some left the country to use their influence in stirring up opposition to him both at home and abroad, and many who remained at home gave him but a half-hearted support.

The enmity between Harald and King Svein developed into a feature of European politics, and shaped Harald's attitude in the administration of church affairs. In order to strengthen his position, Svein allied himself more closely with Archbishop Adalbert of Bremen, and with the German emperor, while Harald continued in the old friendship with the Saxon dukes. He severed all connections with Archbishop Adalbert, received bishops from the Greek Church, and maintained friendly relations with Byzantium. The Norwegian bishops were no longer consecrated by the Archbishop of Bremen, but in Rome, England, France or in the Orient.

Archbishop Adalbert protested to Pope Alexander II against Harald's flagrant disregard of the authority of the archbishop over the Church of Norway, and the Pope wrote a letter reprimanding the king. Adalbert also sent messengers to Harald to protest against his course of action, and threatened him with ban and other punishments, but Harald replied: 'I know of no archbishop in Norway except myself. King Harald.' He maintained the independence of the Church of Norway throughout his whole reign with such unbending pertinacity that he was accused of all sorts of vile practices by his angry opponents. Adam v. Bremen, who stayed at the court of Archbishop Adalbert, indulges in the bitterest invectives against Harald, whom he pictures as the most cruel and unprincipled tyrant. This is not history, but the expression of acrimonious partisan spirit. Konrad Maurer quotes the following from Kemble: 'Every wise and powerful government has treated with deserved disregard the complaint that the "Spouse of Christ" was in bondage. Boniface, himself an Englishman, papal beyond all his contemporaries, laments that no church is in greater bondage than the English – a noble testimony to the nationality of the institution, the common sense of the people, and the vigour of the state!'

The hostility existing between Harald Haardraade and King Svein seems to have led Harald to establish the city of Oslo (now incorporated in the city of Christiania) on the Foldenfjord in Viken. Here he would be within more easy reach of Denmark, and in better position to defend the country than if stationed in the far-away Nidaros. A new national sanctuary was established in the city to give it greater prestige, as Harald seems to have entertained the hope that Oslo might become to southern Norway what Nidaros and the shrine of St. Olaf was to Trøndelagen. The saint interred in the new city was Halvard, a native of the district, and a cousin of the king.' He is said to have been the son of a landed proprietor, Vebjørn, and his wife Torny, a sister of Aasta, the mother of St. Olaf and King Harald Haardraade. Already in his youth he was noted for great piety and purity of life. His father was a merchant, and Halvard assisted him in his work, but he was so conscientious that he made two weights, a lighter one for weighing the part which he himself was to receive, and a heavier for weighing his brother's part.

One day, as he left home to go across the Drammensfjord, a woman came running to him, beseeching him to rescue her. She was pursued by three men who claimed that she had committed theft in their brother's house. She protested her innocence, and Halvard took her into his boat and started across the lake, but the pursuers soon caught up with them. In vain he pleaded for the woman. When he refused to give her up, they killed both him and her, fastened two millstones to his body and lowered it into the lake. Sometime afterward, his body, with the millstones still fastened to it, was found floating on the lake, and twigs, which had been used in searching for the corpse, budded several times in succession. The Icelandic annals state that St. Halvard was slain in 1043, and Adam v. Bremen says that many miraculous cures occurred at his grave. He must, therefore, have been generally regarded as a saint at the time when Adam v. Bremen wrote (about 1070), but when and in what way he was proclaimed a saint is not known. His body was probably interred in the St. Mary's church erected by King Harald.

In the twelfth century a new cathedral church, dedicated to St. Halvard, was erected at Oslo. King Harald also built a St. Mary's church in Nidaros, in which the shrine of St. Olaf was deposited. As the city had grown, and private houses were erected around the St. Clemens church and the royal hall, the king selected for the new church a location farther from the centre of the city. Here he also erected a new royal residence. He completed the St. Olaf's church which King Magnus had begun, and the unfinished royal hall from King Magnus' time was remodelled into a church dedicated to St. Gregorius.

King Harald maintained the supremacy over the colonies with energy and firmness. Thorfinn, the powerful jarl of the Orkney and Shetland Islands, who had remained independent since the death of St. Olaf, hastened to Norway as soon as he heard of the death of Magnus the Good, and was well received at the court. It must be inferred that he submitted to Harald, and that these island colonies returned to their old allegiance as dependencies under the king's overlordship. Thorfinn seems to have been the more willing to offer his submission, because King Macbeth of Scotland, with whom he was closely associated, was threatened by Malcolm Canmore, the son of Thorfinn's cousin King Duncan. Thorfinn was sure to be involved in the struggle in Scotland, and he would not risk the possibility of coming into collision with King Harald.

Hostilities between Macbeth and Malcolm began in 1054. Aided by his foster father, the powerful Earl Siward of Northumbria, Malcolm defeated Macbeth at Dunsinane the same year, and in 1057 Macbeth was slain in the battle of Lumphanan. What part Thorfinn played in the struggle cannot be stated, but it is quite certain that he aided his old friend Macbeth. Thorfinn had also added the Hebrides (Sudreys) to his dominions, and when he submitted to the king, they became a Norwegian dependency. Kalv Arnesson acted as governor in the islands till his return to Norway in Harald Haardraade's reign. The Faroe Islands remained in firm allegiance to Norway. Since Leiv Assursson was made governor by King Magnus after the death of Trond i Gata, no attempt was again made by the colony to assert its independence. Harald also made earnest efforts to attach Iceland more closely to the crown. He sought by rich gifts to gain the goodwill of the leading men, and when a famine occurred in Iceland, he sent several shiploads of provisions. Many Icelandic skalds became his *hirdmaend* and were shown great honours. As a result of these favours the Icelanders held Harald in high esteem, but they did not formally acknowledge themselves subject to the king of Norway. The intercourse with the colonies in Greenland was well maintained, and voyages were made every year across the Atlantic directly from Norway to Greenland.

Harald refused to abide by the arrangement made by King Magnus that Svein Estridsson should receive the kingdom of Denmark, and continued to claim the Danish throne. He repeatedly harried the coasts of Denmark, but as these attacks, which seem to have been mere raids, proved unavailing, Harald finally challenged Svein to a pitched battle. The challenge was accepted, and a naval engagement was fought off Nisaa near the mouth of the Gota River on the 9th of August, 1062. Throughout the whole bright summer night the combat raged. Harald gained the victory, but he returned to Norway immediately afterwards, and this battle was as barren of results as former expeditions.

King Anund Jacob of Sweden had died, and his successor, Stenkil Ragnvaldsson, had granted Vermland to Haakon Ivarsson, who had been made jarl of Halland by King Svein. At the head of an army Haakon entered Ringerike in south-eastern Norway, and collected taxes as if he were a jarl. Haakon was popular in these districts, while Harald was disliked, because he levied excessive taxes and deprived the people of many old rights and privileges. A serious uprising seemed imminent, and Harald finally decided to make peace with Denmark, 1064. King Svein was henceforth left in undisturbed possession of the Danish throne. Harald attacked and defeated Jarl Haakon, and the uprising in Oplandene was speedily put down.

THE SECOND CONQUEST OF ENGLAND

The weak King Edward the Confessor, who succeeded Hardeknut on the throne of England, was better fitted to be a monk than a king, and throughout his reign he was a tool in the hands of the powerful earls, Godwin of Wessex, Leofric of Mercia and Siward of Northumbria. Godwin, who was his father-in-law and the most powerful man in England, exercised for a long time almost royal powers, and his sons Sweyn, Harold and Tostig were granted large possessions. Harold was a man of eminent ability, and his generosity and uprightness of character made him very popular.

When his father died in 1051, he was about 31 years of age, and during the declining years of Edward the Confessor he administrated the affairs of the realm with great wisdom and ability. His brothers Sweyn and Tostig were men of a different type – greedy and lawless ruffians, who were a constant source of strife and mischief. Sweyn abducted the beautiful abbess Eadgifu from a nunnery, and committed other vile deeds, for which he was finally banished. Tostig, who was King Edward's favourite, was made Earl of Northumbria on the death of Earl Siward, but he seldom visited his possessions except to extort unjust taxes. The long-suffering people finally rebelled and drove him away, and Morkere, a grandson of Leofric, was chosen to succeed him. King Edward died on the 5th of January, 1066.

As he left no son, the kingdom of England became a prize to be contended for by a number of rival candidates, all men of fame and ability, whose claims to the throne were equally clouded and uncertain. The four candidates who claimed to be the lawful heirs of the deceased king were: Duke William of Normandy, Earl Harold, son of Godwin, King Svein Estridsson of Denmark, and King Harald Haardraade of Norway. Earl Harold claimed that King Edward had bequeathed him the kingdom. This would give him no valid title to the throne, since the king could not elect his successor. But Harold was the only native English candidate who could be considered at this critical moment, and he was chosen king by the Witenagemot, which alone possessed the right of choice. This made Harold rightful king of England, but it did not extinguish the title which the other candidates claimed to have. Duke William urged that King Edward the Confessor had promised him the throne of England. He also maintained that Harold had sworn fealty to him, and had solemnly promised to support his claim. Harold had been shipwrecked on the coast of Ponthieu in France some years before. The count of that district took him prisoner, and turned him over to Duke William of Normandy, and he was forced to give William the stated pledges to obtain his liberty. Neither of these reasons gave Duke William any right to the throne of England, as neither King Edward nor Earl Harold could give away the kingdom, but what he needed was a fair pretext; for the rest he trusted to his valiant sword.

Svein Estridsson of Denmark claimed the English throne as the heir of his cousin King Hardeknut, and of his uncle King Knut the Great. Harald Haardraade of Norway based his claim on the treaty of Brennøerne by which Hardeknut made Magnus the Good his heir. This was, in a way, the same claim which Magnus himself had urged against Edward the Confessor, but it had been reduced to an empty pretence, since Magnus on his deathbed had surrendered Denmark to Svein Estridsson. The plotting Earl Tostig had negotiated with all the three foreign pretenders, and stood ready to sell his support to the highest bidder.

As soon as rumour got abroad that Harold had been crowned at London, January 6, 1066, Duke William of Normandy sent messengers to remind him of his promise, and began active preparations for an invasion of England. He mustered all his barons, and induced a great number of knights from Anjou, Brittany, Poitou, Flanders and other places to join in the enterprise by offering them lands and treasures. He had prevailed on Pope Alexander II to issue a bull approving of the expedition, and ships were built to carry the army across the English Channel. According to William of Aquitaine, he also sent an embassy to Svein Estridsson to solicit his aid. This must have been Tostig, who, according to the sagas, went to King Svein as soon as his brother Harold was crowned king, to induce him to invade England. Svein did not venture upon such an undertaking, and Tostig then turned to King Harald Haardraade of Norway without any authority from Duke William. Harald is said to have promised to send an expedition to England in the summer, and Tostig promised to aid him with all the forces which he could gather. When the conquest was completed, he was to be made jarl over one-half of England as King Harald Haardraade's vassal. But Tostig, who was as impatient as he was unreliable, hastened to Flanders, and before either Duke William or King Harald were ready to set sail, he gathered a fleet of 60 vessels, manned partly by his own adherents, partly by adventurers and freebooters of all sorts, and made an attack on the southern coast of England. King Harald came against him with a large fleet and army, and he fled northward, and entered the Humber, where his fleet was destroyed by Earl Edwin of Mercia. With 12 ships he reached Scotland, where he was harboured by King Malcolm III.

In the summer of 1066 Harald Haardraade was busy making preparations for his expedition to England. He had chosen the Solund Islands, on the coast of Sogn, in southwestern Norway, as the rendezvous for his fleet, and by the beginning of September he had gathered a large armament of 250 war vessels and about 20,000 men. Before his departure he made his eldest son, Magnus, regent, and caused him to be crowned king. His younger son, Olaf, accompanied him on the expedition. He sailed first to the Shetland Islands, and thence to the Orkneys. The Orkney jarls, Paul and Erlend, had to join the expedition with a large number of ships and troops. When he reached the Tyne in Scotland, about the 10th of September, he was also joined by Tostig, who acknowledged him as his lord. They landed at various places along the coast, captured Scarborough after some resistance, and took possession of the coast districts as far as the Humber.

The fleet ascended the Humber and the Ouse, but came to anchor at Riccal, 13 kilometres (8 miles) south of York. Here Harald landed his army, and marched along the river towards the city. The earls Morkere of Northumbria and Edwin of Mercia, who had gathered a large army in York, came out to meet Harald at Fulford, about 3 kilometres (2 miles) from the city. A bloody battle was fought, in which the earls suffered a crushing defeat. The remnants of their army fled back to York, while Harald took possession of the neighbouring district, and entrenched himself at Stamford Bridge on the Derwent River. The city of York offered to capitulate, and on September 24 Harald advanced with his army to meet the citizens outside the city, where the terms of peace were arranged. They acknowledged him their lord, promised to supply him with provisions, and agreed to give 500 hostages. In the evening Harald returned to his fleet, but planned to advance on the following morning to Stamford Bridge, where the hostages were to be delivered.

In the meantime, Harold Godwinson had arrived at York with his army, and had been watching Harald's movements. In the night he was secretly admitted into the city. The next morning Harald advanced with a part of his army; the other part was left in charge of his son Olaf and the Orkney jarls Paul and Erlend to guard the fleet. The day was warm, and, as no hostilities were anticipated, the men marched without their brynies. When they arrived at Stamford Bridge, Harold suddenly fell upon them with his whole force. The saga says that Harald did not follow Tostig's advice to retreat to the ships, but sent messengers to bring the rest of the army to his support. This was a fatal mistake. Before help arrived, Harald's forces were overwhelmed and defeated, and he was mortally wounded in the fight.

The *Heimskringla* gives a vivid description of the battle of Stamford Bridge. It tells how Harald, when he found himself face to face with the whole English army, planted his banner, formed a shield-ring and made ready for the combat. But before the battle began, a horseman rode up, spoke to Earl Tostig, and offered him the earldom of Northumbria if he would join the English. Tostig asked how much he would give Harald Sigurdsson, the Norwegian king. The horseman said that he would gladly give him six feet of ground, and as much more as he was taller than other men; but Tostig rejected the offer, says the saga. When the horseman rode away, they discovered that it was King Harold Godwinson himself. The fight commenced, and the Norsemen in their shield-ring resisted stoutly the attack of the English cavalry. But when they thought that the attack had failed, and that the English began to retreat, they rushed eagerly forward in pursuit. The shield-ring was broken, and they were attacked from all sides. A fearful carnage resulted. King Harald rushed into the midst of the fray, but an arrow pierced his throat, and he fell mortally wounded. Tostig now assumed command. Supported by the reinforcements which arrived from the fleet, he rallied the broken columns to renewed efforts, but the men had become exhausted on the forced march from the fleet. Towards evening the Norse army broke and fled in wild disorder, and darkness alone saved the broken remnants from destruction.

This dramatic description of the battle is manifestly erroneous. The English are represented as fighting on horseback, though we know that their army was very deficient in cavalry. The English were foot soldiers, as we see from the battle of Hastings, which occurred less than three weeks later. The saga writer seems to have confused the battle of Stamford Bridge with that of Hastings, where the Norman mounted knights made repeated attacks on the English foot soldiers, who stood firm behind their shield-wall, until by a feint they were led to pursue the enemy, and suffered a crushing defeat. The cavalry fight in the battle of Stamford Bridge is not mentioned in the older Norse sources, nor in the *Anglo-Saxon Chronicle*. We are left completely in the dark, therefore, as to the details of the battle. We only know that at Stamford Bridge King Harald Haardraade suffered an overwhelming defeat. 'There King Harald of Norway and Earl Tostig were slain,' says the *Anglo-Saxon Chronicle*, 'and a great number of men with them, both Norsemen and English.' The chronicle states that Harold Godwinson suffered Harald's son Olaf and the Orkney jarls to depart with 24 ships and the remnant of the army.

We may well doubt the accuracy of the statement that only 24 ships left. Olaf and the jarls, who were in charge of the fleet, had both time and opportunity to hold the ships in readiness, as they knew that a battle was in progress. That the whole large army of 30,000 men should be so utterly destroyed that only 24 ships could be manned seems quite incredible. The statement in the *Heimskringla* that Harold let Olaf depart with the fleet and the remnant of the army seems more worthy of belief. Harold had no time to waste. On September 28th, three days after the battle of Stamford Bridge, Duke William landed at Pevensey, in southern England, with 60,000 men, and on the 6th or 7th of October Harold was again in London making preparations for the still greater battle fought at Hastings, October 14, 1066. In this hard-fought battle Harold Godwinson fell, and William the Conqueror became king of England.

The defeat and death of the warlike Harald Haardraade changed the political situation in the North. Svein Estridsson of Denmark felt that all danger of an attack from Norway was now removed, and as he considered his claim to the throne of England as valid as ever, he resolved to invade England and expel King William. Many Danes who had been banished from England, or had suffered other wrongs, were also urging him to assert his claim. But the preparations proceeded very slowly, and three years passed before the expedition was finally ready to start.

In the month of August, 1069, 240 ships set sail for England, led by Svein's brother Asbjørn, his sons Harald and Knut, and Jarl Thorkil. After attacking Dover, Sandwich and Norwich without success, the fleet entered the Humber, and advanced toward York. Northern England, where the Viking element still was strong, had not submitted to King William. The boy Eadgar the Etheling, grandson of Edmund Ironside, was chosen king when Harold fell at Hastings, but he had fled to Scotland after the battle. He was now in Northumbria, where the earls Morkere and Edwin were aiding him in organizing a great revolt against William. The arrival of the Danish fleet in the Humber became the signal for a general uprising. York was taken by the combined forces of Danes and Northumbrians, but the Norman garrison burned the city before surrendering, and the victors levelled the fortifications with the ground.

When King William arrived, the Danes retreated to their ships, and the Northumbrians returned to their homes, but as soon as he departed the attack was renewed. William was unable to assail the Danish fleet for want of ships, but he succeeded in bribing the Danish commander, Asbjørn, to remain inactive, and finally to depart from England. On northern England he wreaked a fearful vengeance, wasting it with fire and sword. No such devastation had ever passed over an English community as that wrought by William the Conqueror in Northumbria. The prosperity of this flourishing district was wiped out, and its spirit and power of resistance was broken. Asbjørn returned to Denmark with his ships laden with booty, but the enterprise had failed, and his own conduct had been reprehensible. In 1075 another Danish fleet of 200 vessels, led by Svein's son Knut, and Jarl Hagen, again visited England, and entered the Humber, but not a hand was raised to aid or welcome them, and they returned home after collecting some booty in the neighbourhood of York. This was the last Viking expedition to England.

OLAF KYRRE – A PERIOD OF PEACE

Olaf, Harald's son, spent the winter 1066–67 in the Orkneys, and returned to Norway in the spring. His brother Magnus had been crowned king before the expedition left for England, but Olaf was also made king on his return. The *Heimskringla* says that they were made joint kings, but Magnus was to rule the northern and Olaf the southern half of the country. The loss of the great army sent to England was a severe blow; nothing less than a national calamity. The country's resources were badly drained, and the available stores and military forces were gone. Under these circumstances King Svein of Denmark found the time opportune to put forward a claim to overlordship over Norway. Magnus and Olaf refused to listen to these demands, and he gathered a fleet and prepared to invade the country. This he could now do without violating any agreement, since the treaty of peace concluded between him and King Harald in 1064 should remain in force only so long as the kings lived.

Hostilities commenced, but the peace-loving Olaf began negotiations with King Svein, which resulted in a new treaty of peace between Norway and Denmark in 1068. This treaty should be binding for all times, and neither kingdom should claim supremacy over the other. King Magnus, who had been sickly for some time, died in 1069, and Olaf became king of all Norway. The *Heimskringla* describes him as follows: 'Olaf was a large man, and well built. It is a common opinion that no one has seen a man better looking, or of nobler appearance. His yellow, silky hair fell in rich locks; he had fair skin, beautiful eyes and well-proportioned limbs. He was, generally, reticent, and spoke little at the thing, but he was glad and talkative at the drinking feast. He drank much, and was cheerful and peace-loving to the end of his days.' Because of his quiet disposition and peaceful reign he was called Olaf Kyrre (the quiet). His efforts to maintain peace at home and abroad had a most beneficent effect at this time, not only because the kingdom needed to recover from the heavy losses incurred in the fruitless military exploits of his martial father, but also because the people's mind needed to be turned away from the strut and vainglory which usually attends war and adventure, to seek employment and honour in peaceful pursuits.

Conditions in the neighbouring kingdoms were also favourable to the maintenance of peace, as both Denmark and Sweden were so occupied with internal strife or foreign conquests that they could not pursue any aggressive policy in their relations with Norway. Christianity bad not been firmly established in Sweden, and many people were displeased because of King Stenkil's efforts to promote the missionary work. The violent reaction against the church which occurred when he died in 1067, was caused, perhaps, in part by the overzealous Bishop Egino of Skåne, who had threatened to destroy the great heathen temple at Upsala. Many people returned to their old faith, and sacrificed to the heathen gods. Several rival candidates were also contending for the throne, and the country was torn by civil strife for many years, until Inge Stenkilsson finally overpowered his rivals, and succeeded his father on the throne.

In Denmark King Svein was engaged in preparing his great expeditions to England, which brought him only loss and disappointment. When he died in 1076, his son Harald became his successor, but he soon died, and a younger brother, Knut, became king of Denmark. He was an ambitious and warlike young man, who could not forget that his ancestors had occupied the throne of England. Not discouraged by his father's fruitless attempts at conquest, he determined to send a new expedition to England. He was a great friend of Olaf Kyrre, and solicited his aid for the undertaking. Olaf refused to join the expedition, but as a good friend he placed 60 warships fully manned at his disposal. In 1084 Knut began to collect a large fleet, but time passed, and when the preparations finally were near completion, most of the Danish chieftains grew impatient and returned to their homes. Norway was thereby saved from renewed hostilities with England. King Knut, who thus suddenly found himself deserted, was very wroth. He began to rule harshly, and collected unjust and excessive taxes. This produced a general rebellion, and he was killed by an angry mob in St. Alban's church in Odense where he had

sought refuge. In the reign of his successor, Olaf Hunger, he
was declared holy, and he soon became the national saint of
Denmark, though his only merit seems to have been that he
was slain in a church.

Olaf Kyrre, who was pious as well as peaceful, was deeply
interested in the labours of the clergy, and worked zealously
throughout his long reign to give the Church of Norway a
more stable and efficient organization. The defiant attitude
which his father Harald Haardraade had assumed over against
the Archbishop of Bremen he seems to have regarded as
improper, if not unfortunate. His own disposition, as well as
his friendly relations with Denmark, which was a part of the
archdiocese of Bremen, inclined him to favour the archbishop,
and to uphold his authority over the Norwegian clergy. He
was also encouraged in his loyalty to the Roman See and its
representative the archbishop by the Pope himself, who in his
letters to the king expressed deep solicitude for the church in
the North.

The powerful Gregory VII, who occupied the papal throne
at this time (1073–85), was the real founder of the papal power,
and the organizer of the Roman hierarchy. The constant strife
between ruling princes, the violence and turmoil everywhere
rampant convinced him that the church alone possessed
the wisdom and authority to maintain peace, and to act as
arbiter in every controversy. He wished to reform the world
by organizing a universal religious monarchy with the Pope as
supreme ruler. 'Human pride,' he wrote, 'has created the power
of kings. God's mercy has created the power of bishops. The
Pope is the master of the emperors. He is rendered holy by the
merits of his predecessor, St. Peter. The Roman Church has

never erred, and Holy Scripture proves that it can never err. To resist it is to resist God.' The growing power of the hierarchy, and the increased devotion to the Roman Church, which was the result of Pope Gregory's activity, was fast ripening into the great religious movement which culminated in the crusades, the impulse of which was felt in every land in western Europe. Cathedrals were built, and crusading missionary work was carried on with zeal, while all nations were drawn closer to Rome, which was the centre of religious and intellectual life.

That Olaf Kyrre was imbued with the spirit of the age is rendered evident by his labours to organize the Church of Norway according to the general plan of the Catholic Church in other countries, as well as by his efforts to introduce in Norway the culture and refinement of the aristocratic circles in England and continental Europe. His reign marks a final victory of medieval ideas, which found their best expression in crusades and knight-errantry, but the Roman incubus, which was so potent in controlling the governments, and in shaping the intellectual life of the age, was far less marked in Norway than elsewhere in Europe. Celibacy of priests, which the Pope now enforced as a part of the Roman church discipline, was not introduced in Norway. The clergy remained subject to the king, who exercised firm control in ecclesiastical affairs. The skaldic poetry flourished, the national saga literature and history writing were yet to blossom forth, and there were but scant traces of a religious literature fostered under the influence of the church. The separation of the North from the archdiocese of Bremen gave the Norwegian people a new opportunity to preserve their independence in church affairs, and to develop a strong national spirit.

The attempt of Pope Gregory VII to assert his supremacy over the German emperor precipitated the famous struggle between the Pope and Emperor Henry IV, which divided the whole Empire into the warring factions of Welfs and Ghibellines, friends of the Pope and supporters of the emperor. Archbishop Adalbert of Bremen was one of the emperor's staunchest supporters. His successor, Liemar, also adhered to the Ghibelline party, even after the emperor had been excommunicated, and Pope Gregory VII punished the disobedient prelate by depriving him of his office. King Svein Estridsson of Denmark and his successors were adherents of the Pope, and this finally led to the separation of the Scandinavian countries from the Bremen archdiocese, and the creation of a new archbishopric in the Danish city of Lund, in Skåne, in 1104.

During this period of strife, which paralyzed the power of the Archbishop of Bremen, the highest ecclesiastical authority in Norway was exercised by the king. The state-church principle, which had been practiced by St. Olaf, and which had been so imperiously maintained by Harald Haardraade, was now further strengthened by circumstances which made the king the natural leader of the Church of Norway. King Olaf Kyrre divided Norway into three bishoprics: Nidaros, Selja and Oslo, each with its diocesan bishop, who received the rank of jarl. New incumbents were chosen by the chapters of the diocese, but they had to present themselves before the king, who in reality selected the candidates. Each diocese had its own saint: Nidaros, St. Olaf; Oslo, St. Halvard; and Selja, St. Sunniva. In Trondhjem Olaf erected a cathedral church on the spot where St. Olaf was thought to have been buried the first time. It was dedicated to the Trinity, but was generally called the Christ church. The altar was placed on the spot where St. Olaf's body was supposed to have rested, and the shrine of the saint was moved to the new church. On the foundations of this church the Trondhjem cathedral was later erected. King Harald Haardraade's body, which had been brought back to Norway, was interred in the St. Mary's church, which he had built.

On the west coast of Norway, Olaf Kyrre founded the city of Bergen, which, because of its favourable location, soon became one of the chief commercial towns in the North. The bishop of the diocese was to reside here, and the king began the erection of a large cathedral of stone, the Christ church. This was finished in 1170, and the St. Sunniva relics were then transferred from Selja to Bergen. In the Orkneys Jarl Thorfinn founded a bishopric and built a cathedral church at Birgsaa 1050–64. In Iceland Gissur Isleivsson, who became bishop in 1081, erected a cathedral on his estate Skalholt, which he donated to the church as a permanent bishop's residence.

The long period of peace during the reign of Olaf Kyrre produced a marked improvement in economic conditions. The cities grew, and commerce increased; no extra taxes were imposed for military purposes, and good harvests seem to have added to the general prosperity. It is evident from the saga accounts that this reign was long remembered as a sort of golden age of peace and plenty. 'In the reign of Olaf Kyrre there were good harvests and such abundant good fortune that Norway had never been more prosperous under any king since the days of Harald Haarfagre,' says the saga. Under these circumstances a taste for luxury and comfort was naturally developed, and the king laboured earnestly to bring the civilization and culture of his people into full harmony with the Christian spirit, and to introduce in Norway the elegance and courtly manners which were being developed everywhere in Europe during this age of chivalry. The *hird* was doubled in number, so that it consisted of 120 *hirdmaend*, 60 *gestir* and 60 *huskarlar*. The *hirdmaend* were divided into groups, at the head of which stood *skutilsveinar*, or officers of the king's guard. After the creation of this new office the *lendermaend* do not seem to have sought the king's *hird* as before, but they held now the highest rank in the country, as King Olaf did not appoint any jarls after the death of Haakon Ivarsson. The *kertisveinar*, corresponding to the French pages, waited at the king's table. Behind each guest at the table stood a *kertisveinn*, with a burning candle.

The people of the higher classes began to wear costumes of foreign pattern borrowed especially from England and Normandy. 'The people began to dress with great splendour according to foreign fashions,' says the saga. 'They wore fine hose ruffled about the knee. Some put gold rings about the legs; many wore long mantles with slit sides tied with ribbons, and with sleeves five ells long, and so narrow that they had to be pulled on with a cord, and arranged in folds up to the shoulders. They wore high shoes, embroidered with silk and even ornamented with gold.' From the upper classes, who were in sympathy with the spirit and higher culture of the age, the new tastes and ideas were soon communicated to the common people, who through a natural instinct for imitation gradually adopted as much of the new customs as environment and circumstances would permit. King Olaf also introduced many improvements in the construction of dwelling houses. Hitherto the fireplace, *arinn*, was placed in the centre of the house, and the smoke escaped through an opening in the roof, the *ljori*. Olaf built houses with stone floors and introduced the oven, which was erected in a corner of the room with a flue for carrying away the smoke. The *ljori* disappeared, and the houses received a loft, the beginning of a second story. Windows became more common, though glass windows seem yet to have been limited to the king's own dwellings.

From the earliest times the Norsemen took great delight in social and religious festivities; their great hospitality and the liberal entertainment of friends and travellers have already been mentioned as a conspicuous national trait. The period of prosperity and peace in the time of Olaf Kyrre gave new stimulus to the development of social life. Permanent clubs or guilds, organized under the protection of the church, were instituted by King Olaf to afford better opportunity for social intercourse. These guilds had their own guild halls, women were also members, the rules were strict, and much attention was paid to fine manners and good conversation. Christian spirit was also fostered in the guilds, as they were placed under the supervision of the church. The members were mutually pledged to assist one another in times of need, a very fortunate arrangement at a time when municipal government was yet in its infancy. Thereby the guilds became the forerunners of political clubs, insurance companies, pension funds and like organizations which have sprung from the feeling of social interdependence.

The members were jointly responsible for each other's houses and stables. If a member suffered loss of house or stable by fire, the guild would rebuild it. If a man's granary burned, he received a certain amount of grain; if he lost three head of cattle or more, each member should give him a measure of grain; if the member was a merchant, and lost his goods by shipwreck, he also received a compensation. If a member was imprisoned in a foreign land, he was ransomed by the guild; if he was slain by one who did not belong to the guild, the other members would assist in prosecuting the slayer; but if a member committed murder, he was expelled from the guild, and was not again allowed to appear in the guild hall. When a member died, all the other members were present at the funeral.

The guilds were generally named after patron saints, under whose special protection they were supposed to stand. In Bergen they were especially numerous, and the names of many are still familiar in that city. The most important was the St. Jatmund's (St. Edmund's) Guild, to which, according to an old writer, even 'kings, dukes, counts, barons, knights and other noblemen belonged'. In Trondhjem the oldest was the Mykle Guild (the Great Guild), organized by Olaf Kyrre, and dedicated to St. Olaf. Tunsberg had the St. Olaf's Guild and the St. Anna's Guild; Oslo, the Guild of the Holy Body, St. Anna's Guild and the Shoemakers' Guild. The country districts, too, had their guilds. They are mentioned as having existed in Salten, Aalen, Opdal, Medalen, in Herø in Søndmør, and in many other places. That many guilds existed of which no records have been preserved can be seen from placenames like Gildeskaale, Gildehus, Gildevang, Gildevold, Gildesaker, etc. In course of time when the cities became industrial centres, the guilds very naturally developed into craft guilds, in which men of the same profession or handicraft were associated together. But in Norway the guilds were controlled by the king and the church, and at no time did they become independent political organizations hostile to the ruler, something which happened not infrequently in some countries of Europe.

Among the more prominent men in Norway in Olaf Kyrre's time may be mentioned especially Skule Kongsfostre, the king's chief adviser, a man of high rank, who had followed him from England. He seems to have been the king's foster father, not the son of Earl Tostig, as some sources have it. Skule was placed at the head of the *hird*, and he was also sent to England to bring back the body of King Harald Haardraade. The king gave him the old royal hall in Oslo, when a new royal dwelling was erected, and he granted him also a number of estates at Oslo, Konghelle and Trondhjem; and also Rein in Nordmør, from which his descendants derived their name. From Skule Kongsfostre descended Duke Skule (Skule Jarl), famous in the reign of King Haakon Haakonsson. Dag Eilivsson, the father of Gregorius Dagssøn, in Viken, Sigurd Ulstreng in Trøndelagen, the son of Rut af Viggen who fell at Stiklestad, Thore af Steig, in Oplandene, who was the king's secret opponent, and Sveinke Steinarsson, who ruled the border districts on the Gota River, were among the most powerful men in the kingdom at this time. King Olaf Kyrre died in 1093, in the 27th year of his reign.

A REVIVAL OF THE VIKING SPIRIT – MAGNUS BAREFOOT

When Olaf Kyrre died, his son Magnus was proclaimed king in Viken, while the people of Oplandene were led, as it appears, by Thore of Steig, to choose his nephew Haakon.

The arrangement of joint kingship, first introduced in the time of Magnus the Good and Harald Haardraade, was now repeated. The kingdom does not seem to have been divided, though some sources seem to indicate it. According to the *Morkinskinna*, the two kings ruled together for two years, but the older sources, Theodricus Monachus and *Agrip*, state that the joint kingship lasted only one winter. Haakon was then killed by a fall from his horse. Thore of Steig, the old opponent of Olaf Kyrre, did not even now acknowledge King Magnus, though, after the death of Haakon, the young king was the only legitimate heir to the throne. Thore formed an opposition party in support of the pretender Svein, and started a revolt; but this was easily put down, and the two leaders, Thore of Steig and Egil Askelsson, were captured and executed.

The king found another opponent in Sveinke Steinarsson, who was a *lendermand*, a sort of *markgraf* [marquis] in the border districts on the Gota River. In these far-off districts his will was law, and he protected the people against the robbers and outlaws who infested the region along the border. He had not taken part in the revolt, but he did not submit to the king, and managed all affairs according to his own mind. He was summoned to the Borgarthing, where the *stallare*, Sigurd Ulstreng, represented the king. After the *thing* was assembled, they saw a body of warriors approaching, dressed in steel so bright that they looked like a moving block of ice. This was Sveinke, who came to the *thing* with 500 armed followers. He ridiculed the *stallare*, and after some altercations, Sigurd had to flee. The king marched against the arrogant *lendermand*, but hostilities were averted through the intercession of friends.

Sveinke was banished for a short period, but he was soon recalled, and became one of the king's best friends.

Magnus Barefoot was a warrior like his grandfather Harald Haardraade. In his reign the air was again filled with the sounds of war trumpets and the din of arms. The Viking spirit flared up anew from the smouldering embers, fanned into life by the martial spirit of the young king, who is reported to have said that a king ought to court honour rather than a long life. King Magnus was brave to foolhardiness, and energetic to rashness, a sort of demigod, who was loved by his followers even for his faults. But it would be manifestly unjust to regard him as a mere Viking chieftain, or as a romantic dreamer, who spent the 10 years of his reign in the pursuit of the phantom of military glory. It is evident that he followed a clearly conceived plan, and that he was never led by vain ambition to waste his means in rash and impossible adventures. He did not aspire to the throne of England, like his grandfather had done, nor did he attempt to conquer Ireland, as some old writers would have us believe. The chief, if not the only, purpose of his expedition to the British Isles seems to have been to reduce the Norse island possessions to full submission to the home government. But the ever-recurring war expeditions increased the burdens of taxation, removed great numbers of the ablest men from productive employments, and retarded the peaceful development inaugurated by Olaf Kyrre. The history of Magnus Barefoot's reign is a record of his military campaigns; of the internal affairs of the country in his time little is known; of real progress history has nothing to record.

As soon as Magnus was securely seated on the throne, he provoked a war with Sweden by claiming the Swedish province of Dal, or Dalsland, lying between Ranrike and Lake Venern. He crossed the Gota River with an army, and harried the districts until they had to offer their submission. On Kaland Island, in Lake Venem, be built a fort, and left a garrison of 360 men, but when he returned home for the winter, the Swedish king, Inge Stenkilsson, captured the fort and drove away the garrison. The following spring Magnus renewed his campaign, and a battle was fought at Fuxema, on the Gota River. According to *Agrip*, Magnus was victorious, but according to Theodricus Monachus he lost the battle. The last version is probably correct, since a peace conference was called at Kongbelle in 1101, where the three kings, Magnus Barefoot of Norway, Inge Stenkilsson of Sweden and Eirik Eiegod of Denmark were all present. According to the terms of the treaty here concluded, the kings should retain the territories which their predecessors had held, but Magnus should receive the hand of Margaret, King Inge's daughter, in marriage, and her dowry should be the districts in dispute. She was nicknamed Fredkulla (the peace maiden). Snorre gives the following description of the three kings as they appeared together at Konghelle: 'Inge was the largest and strongest, and looked most dignified, Magnus seemed the most valiant and energetic, but Eirik was the handsomest.'

The most noteworthy features of King Magnus' reign were his expeditions to the British Isles. Two earlier expeditions, which Magnus was thought to have made in 1092 and 1093–94, have been described by the old scholar Torfaeus. Buchanan, a Scotch historian of the sixteenth century, who bases his account on Fordun's *Scotichronicon*, also tells how King Magnus in 1094 aided Prince Donaldbane to gain the throne of Scotland. The account of the last-named expedition has been considered to be historic also by the great Norwegian historian P. A. Munch, but Gustav Storm has shown that Magnus made neither of these expeditions. The passage in the *Scotichronicon* is shown to be an interpolation by a late writer, and the foundation for the statement referring to Magnus' operations in Scotland in 1094 disappears wholly when it is made clear that at this time he was still in Norway, busily engaged in securing his succession to the throne. Norse sagas mention only the two expeditions in 1098–99 and 1102–03, about which Welsh chronicles, Irish annals and verses of contemporary skalds give the most reliable information.

After the peace at Konghelle, Magnus sailed to the British Isles with a fleet of 150 ships. He landed in the Orkneys, where he deposed the jarls Paul and Erlend, and sent than to Norway, possibly, because they had been neglectful of their duties as vassals. Soon afterward he took King Gudrød Crowan of the Hebrides prisona, and forced him to submit. He then proceeded to the Isle of Man, which was regarded by the Norsemen as belonging to the Hebrides group (Sudreyjar). Civil strife between rival chieftains had here been in progress, and he found on the battlefield of Sandvad the corpses still lying unburied, says the chronicle. He took possession of the island and erected a number of houses and castles. According to Ordericus Vitalis, he brought over a large number of colonists from Norway, because the inhabitants had been greatly reduced in numbers by the incessant feuds. The real reason for the new colonization may have been that he could put little trust in the loyalty of the Manx, who were partly of Gaelic descent, and who had lived isolated in their island homes too long to feel any attachment for Norway.

During the reign of William Rufus (1087–1100) the Normans in England were engaged in subduing Wales. The king was unsuccessful in his campaigns against the Welsh mountaineers, but Norman barons and adventurers had gradually pushed their way into the country, where they seized one district after the other, and erected castles. When the king of South Wales fell in the battle of Brecknock, in 1093, three Norman lordships came into being in South Wales. In Northern Wales the Normans had been less successful, but the conquest was pressed with energy. The Earl of Chester had pushed across the Menai Strait to Anglesea, where he built a castle at Aberlleiniog. But the Welsh rallied in 1095–96, and destroyed all the Norman castles on Welsh soil except that of Pembroke. King William marched against them, and vowed that he would exterminate the entire male population, but he had to return home without having won a single victory. The Norman earls were more successful. In 1098 the earls of Shrewsbury and Chester marched through northern Wales, crossed over to Anglesea, and rebuilt the castle of Aberlleiniog. The Welsh turned to Magnus Barefoot for aid. He accepted the invitation, and quickly crossed over from the Isle of Man with his fleet. In attempting to prevent the Norsemen from landing, the Earl of Shrewsbury was mortally wounded, and the Normans, who had become thoroughly alarmed, evacuated Anglesea. Magnus returned to the Orkneys for the winter. King Lagman of Man, whom he had taken captive, was made vassal king of Man and the Hebrides, and he seems to have ruled till 1101.

When the king and his men returned to Norway, they wore Scotch national costumes. As these had never before been seen in Norway, they attracted much attention, and the people, who were ever fond of descriptive nicknames, called the king Magnus Barefoot.

King Lagman of Man and the Hebrides disappears in 1101. Whether he died in that year, or departed on a pilgrimage to the Holy Land as stated in the *Chronica Regum Manniae* cannot be definitely determined. The chronicle also states that Magnus sent another king, Ingemund, to Man; but he was slain, and Magnus went to the Islands to restore order and submission. This gives a credible explanation of Magnus' second expedition, which he seems to have undertaken for the purpose of organizing the western possessions for his son Sigurd, who was made 'king of the Islands' in 1102. His plan seems to have been to make Sigurd ruler of this new island kingdom, while his older son Eystein was to inherit the throne of Norway. The Welsh chronicle states that Magnus visited Anglesea, cut a great deal of timber, and brought it to Man, where he built three castles, which he garrisoned with his own men. From Man he sailed to Dublin in 1102. The *Heimskringla* states that he captured Dublin and Dublinshire, and spent the winter with King Myriartak (Muirchertach) in Kunnakter (possibly Connaught), but this is wholly erroneous.

The *Ulster Annals* have the following entry for the year 1102: 'In this year King Magnus came to Man, and he made peace with the Irish for one year.' The Four Masters give a more detailed account: 'An Irish army was assembled at Dublin to resist Magnus and the Norsemen, who came to ravage the country, but they made peace for one year, and

Muirchertach gave King Magnus' son Sigurd his daughter in marriage, and many costly presents with her.' This shows that Magnus' second expedition could not have been undertaken with a view to conquer Ireland, but that it has been his aim to attach the island possessions more closely to the Norwegian crown. In these efforts he had been very successful. He re-established order in the islands, built and garrisoned forts for the maintenance of peace, brought in new colonists to settle and develop the districts which had been laid waste during the period of anarchy and misrule, and united the islands under a king, who was to govern them, subject to the authority of the king of Norway. These wisely conceived and ably directed efforts to establish an efficient government in these distant islands which had hitherto been the spoils of reckless adventurers, and the haunts of freebooters, might have had abiding results; a new era of peace and development might have dawned for them, had not death suddenly cut short King Magnus' career.

It appears that in the summer of 1103 he left the Isle of Man, bound on a homeward voyage. He landed on the northeast coast of Ireland, where he made a raid into the country with but a small force. After he had penetrated quite a distance inland he was suddenly attacked by an Irish army. Trusting in his bravery he refused to retreat, but his men were overpowered by superior numbers in the marshes where the battle was fought, and Magnus himself fell. lie was at this time 30 years of age. The accounts of this raid into Ireland as given by the different sources are much at variance. The sagas describe it as a foraging expedition, and state that Magnus was waiting for cattle to be brought him 'ofan af Kunnoktum', when the Irish suddenly fell upon him. Ordericus Vitalis relates that Magnus landed on the coast of Ireland. The Irish were much afraid, and did not dare to meet him in battle, but, speaking fair words, they prevailed on him to debark, and when he had marched two miles into the country he was ambushed and slain. The *Chronica Regum Manniae* states that Magnus hastened ahead of his fleet with 16 ships; that he imprudently landed in Ireland, where he was surrounded by the Irish, who slew the king and nearly all his men. He was buried at the St. Patrick's church at Down (Downpatrick), the chronicle adds. The essence of the whole matter seems to be contained in the statement of the *Ulster Annals* that Magnus was attacked and killed by the Ulstonians on a plundering expedition.

When Sigurd heard of his father's death, he became disheartened and returned to Norway. King Muirchertach had formed an alliance with King Henry I of England, as both seem to have regarded Magnus as a dangerous neighbour, and Olaf Bitling, a son of the former King Gudrød Crowan, was placed on the throne of Man.

Though Magnus' plans thus suddenly came to naught, his work had, none the less, produced permanent results. The jarls of the Orkneys and the kings of Man and the Hebrides became more closely attached to Norway than hitherto, and the system and organization introduced by King Magnus continued to exist in the Islands for well-nigh 150 years.

ANCIENT
KINGS & LEADERS

Ancient cultures often traded with and influenced
each other, while others grew independently.
This section provides the key leaders from a
number of regions, to offer comparative insights
into developments across the ancient world.

NORSE MONARCHS

This list is not exhaustive and dates are approximate. The legitimacy of some kings is also open to interpretation. Where dates of rule overlap, kings either ruled jointly or ruled in opposition to one another. There may also be differences in name spellings between different sources.

BEGINNINGS

The Norse people or Vikings migrated from Norway, Denmark and Sweden during the Middle Ages to many places including Britain, Ireland, Scotland, Normandy, Iceland, Greenland and even as far as North America. They brought their religious beliefs and mythology with them. The first two humans were created by three Norse gods, including Odin. Ask, a man created from an ash tree, and Embla, a woman created from an elm tree, went on to create the whole human race who dwelled at Midgard.

HOUSE OF YNGLING

Descendants of the family, whose name means children of the god Frey, became the first semi-mythological rulers of Sweden, then Norway. There are several versions of this dynasty showing different names or orders descending from Fiolner, son of Frey, son of Njord, who was part of the Vanir tribe. The family is also known as the Sclyfings.

Fiolner (son of the god Frey)
Sveigoir (son of Fiolner, mythological king of Sweden)
Vanlandi (son of Sveigoir)
Visbur (son of Vanlandi)
Domaldi (son of Visbur)
Domar (son of Domaldi)
Dyggvi (son of Domar)
Dag 'the Wise' spaki (son of Dyggvi)
Agni (son of Dag)
Alrekr and Eirikr (sons of Agni)
Yngvi and Alfr (sons of Alrekr)
Jorundr (son of Yngvi)
Aunn (son of Jorundr)
Egill/Ongentheow (father of Ohthere and Onela)
Ottarr/Ohthere and Onela (son of Egill)
Aoils/Eadgils and Eanmund (son of Ohthere)
Eysteinn (son of Eadgils)
Yngvarr (son of Eysteinn)
Onundr (son of Yngvarr)
Ingjaldr (?)

From the Yngling family came these semi-mythological kings.

Olaf the Tree-feller	approx. 700s CE
Halfdan Whiteleg	approx. 800s CE

Gudrod the Hunter   approx. 850s CE
Halfdan the Swarthy (Halfdan the Black)   821–860 CE

The following list runs from 872 which is when King Harald Fairhair was victorious in the Battle of Hafrsfjord, after which he merged the petty kingdoms of Norway into a unified kingdom.

FAIRHAIR DYNASTY (872–970 CE)

Dates for the Fairhair dynasty are estimated.

Harald I Halfdansson (Harald Fairhair)   872–928/932 CE
Eirik I Haraldsson (Eric Bloodaxe)   928/932–934 CE
Haakon I Haraldsson (Haakon the Good)   934–960 CE
Harald II Ericsson (Harald Greycloak)   961–970 CE

HOUSE OF GORM/EARL OF LADE (961–995 CE)

Harald Gormsson (Harald Bluetooth; ruled with
   Harald Greycloak)   961–980 CE
Earl Hakkon Sigurdsson (Hakkon Jarl, Eric
   the Victorious)   965/970–995 CE

FAIRHAIR DYNASTY (RESTORED) (995–1000 CE)

Olav I Tryggvason   995–1000 CE

HOUSE OF GORM/EARL OF LADE (RESTORED) (1000-1015 CE)

Sweyn Forkbeard; joint ruler	1000–1013 CE
Earl Eirik Haakonsson; joint ruler	1000–1015 CE
Earl Sweyn Haakonsson; joint ruler	1000–1015 CE

ST. OLAV DYNASTY (1015-1028 CE)

Olav II Haraldsson (Saint Olav)	1015–1028 CE

HOUSE OF GORM/EARL OF LADE (SECOND RESTORATION) (1028-1035 CE)

Cnut the Great (Canute)	1028–1035 CE
Earl Haakon Ericsson; joint ruler	1028–1029 CE
Sweyn Knutsson; joint ruler	1030–1035 CE

ST. OLAV DYNASTY (RESTORED) (1035-1047 CE)

Magnus I Olafsson (Magnus the Good)	1015–1028 CE

HARDRADA DYNASTY (1046-1135 CE)

Harald III Sigurdsson (Harald Hardrada)	1046–1066 CE
Magnus II Haralldsson	1066–1069 CE
Olaf III Haralldsson (Olaf the Peaceful)	1067–1093 CE

Hakkon (II) Magnusson (Haakon Toresfostre)   1093–1095 CE
Magnus III Olafsson (Magnus Barefoot)   1093–1103 CE
Olaf (IV) Magnusson; joint ruler   1103–1115 CE
Eystein I Magnusson; joint ruler   1103–1123 CE
Sigurd I Magnusson (Sigurd the Crusader)   1103–1130 CE
Magnus IV Sigurdsson (Magnus the Blind)   1130–1135 CE

GILLE DYNASTY (1130–1162 CE)

Harald IV Magnusson (Harald Gille)   1130–1136 CE
Sigurd II Haraldsson; joint ruler (Sigurd Munn)   1136–1155 CE
Inge I Haraldsson; joint ruler (Inge the Hunchback)   1136–1161 CE
Eystein II Haraldsson; joint ruler   1142–1157 CE
Magnus (V) Haraldsson; joint ruler   1142–1145 CE
Haakon II Sigurdsson (Hakkon the
  Broadshouldered)   1157–1162 CE

HARDRADA DYNASTY (RESTORED, COGNATIC BRANCH) (1161–1184 CE)

Magnus V Erlingsson   1161–1184 CE

SVERRE DYNASTY (1184–1204 CE)

Sverre Sigurdsson   1184–1202 CE
Haakon III Sverresson   1202–1204 CE
Guttorm Sigurdsson   January to August 1204 CE

GILLE DYNASTY (COGNATIC BRANCH) (1204–1217 CE)

Inge II Bardsson   1204–1217 CE

SVERRE DYNASTY (RESTORED) (1217–1319 CE)

Haakon IV Hakkonsson (Hakkon the Old)   1217–1263 CE
Haakon (V) Haakonsson (Hakkon the Young)   1240–1257 CE
Magnus VI Haakonsson (Magnus the
    Law-mender)   1257–1280 CE
Eric II Magnusson   1273–1299 CE
Hakkon V Magnusson   1299–1319 CE

HOUSE OF BJELBO (1319–1387)

Magnus VII Eriksson   1319–1343 CE
Hakkon VI Magnusson   1343–1380 CE
Olaf IV Hakkonsson   1380–1387 CE

HOUSE OF ESTRIDEN (1380–1412)

Margaret I   1380–1412 CE

HOUSE OF GRIFFIN (1389–1387)

Eric III   1389–1442 CE

HOUSE OF PALANTINATE-NEUMARKT (1442-1448)

Christopher   1442–1448 CE

HOUSE OF BONDE (1449-1450)

Charles I   1449–1450 CE

HOUSE OF OLDENBURG (1450-1814)

Christian I   1450–1481 CE

Interregnum (1481–1483) in which Jon Svaleson Smor served as regent

John	1483–1513 CE
Christian II	1513–1523 CE
Fredrick I	1524–1533 CE

Interregnum (1533–1537) in which Olaf Engelbrektsson served as regent

Christian III	1537–1559 CE
Fredrick II	1559–1588 CE
Christian IV	1588–1648 CE
Fredrick III	1648–1670 CE
Christian V	1670–1699 CE
Fredrick IV	1699–1730 CE

Christian VI	1730–1746 CE
Fredrick V	1746–1766 CE
Christian VII	1766–1808 CE
Fredrick VI	1808–1814 CE

Interregnum (1814–1814) in which Christian Frederick served as regent

Christian Frederick	1814–1814 CE

Interregnum (1814–1814) in which Marcus Gjoe Rosenkrantz served as prime minister

HOUSE OF HOLSTEIN-GOTTORD (1814-1818)

Charles II	1814–1818 CE

HOUSE OF BERNADOTTE (1818-1905)

Charles III John	1818–1944 CE
Oscar I	1844–1859 CE
Charles IV	1859–1872 CE
Oscar II	1872–1905 CE

CELTIC MONARCHS

This list is not exhaustive and dates are approximate. Where dates of rule overlap, emperors either ruled jointly or ruled in opposition to one another. There may also be differences in name spellings between different sources.

BEGINNINGS

The Celts were thought to have originated in central Europe at around 1400 BCE. Migrations across Europe began around 900 BCE and saw the Celts migrate west to parts of France, Spain, Italy, Greece, and into Scotland, England, Ireland and Wales. Broadly speaking, a celt can be defined as someone speaking a Celtic language and being from a Celtic culture. The Celts that settled in Britain in around 300 BCE became the island's dominant ethnic group. The lists that follow chart major events and rulers of Celtic people in Britain.

KINGS OF BRITONS/BRYTHONS

Legendary Kings

This includes a selection of mythological rulers. There is much diversity of opinion over who the kings actually consisted of and the dates they ruled.

Brutus   c.1115 BCE (23 years)
Founder and first king of the Britons, Brutus is thought to be
a descendant of Troy. He divided the land between his three
sons: Albanactus who gained Albany (Scotland); Kamber who
gained Cambria (Wales); and Locrinus who gained Lloegr
(roughly England), and was also high king of Britain

Pwyll Pen Annwn	King of Dyfed
Pryderi fab Pywll	Son of Pwyll, succeeded his father as king of Dyfed
Leir/Llyr	c.950 BCE, possible inspiration for Shakespeare's King Lear
Beli ap Rhun	c. 500s, king of Gwenydd
King Arthur	5th–6th century, king of Britain, led the Knights of the Round Table

Historical Kings of Briton (c. 54 BCE–50 CE)

This section mainly covers people of England, Wales and
southern Scotland.

Cassivellaunus	54 BCE; led the defence against Julius Caesar's second invasion
Tasciovanus	20 BCE–9 CE
Cunobeline	9–40 CE
Tiberius Claudius	40–43 CE
Caractacus	43–50 CE

Roman Rule of Briton (50–383 CE)

This section mainly covers people of England, Wales and
southern Scotland. These rulers may have only governed part

of Briton, with many being based in and ruler of Wales, which itself was split into several kingdoms. Some are disputed.

Vortigern	mid-5th century
Riothamus	*c.* 469 CE
Ambrosius Aurelianus	late 5th century
Maelgwn Gwynedd	mid- to late-5th century
Selyf ap Cynan	*c.* 613 CE
Ceretic of Elmet	*c.* 614 – 617 CE
Cadwallon ap Cadfan	*c.* 634 CE
Idris ap Gwyddno	*c.* 635 CE
Eugein I of Alt Clut	*c.* 642 CE
Cadwaladr	*c.* 654–664 CE
Ifor	683–698 CE
Rhodri Molwynog	*c.* 712–754 CE
Cynan Dindaethwy	798–816 CE
Merfyn Frych	825–844 CE
Rhodri ap Merfyn 'the Great'	844–878 CE
Anarawd ap Rhodri	878–916 CE
Idwal Foel ap Anarawd	916–942 CE
Hwyel Dda 'the Good'	942–950 CE
Dyfnwal ab Owain	930s–970s CE
Maredudd ab Owain	986–999 CE
Llywelyn ap Seisyll	1018–1023 CE
Iago ab Idwal	1023–1039 CE
Gruffyd ap Llywelyn	1039/1055–1063 CE

MONARCHS OF ENGLAND (886-1066 CE)

House of Wessex (c. 886-924 CE)

The House of Wessex was founded when Alfred became King of the Anglo-Saxons.

Alfred 'the Great'	c. 886–899 CE
Edward 'the Elder'	899–924 CE
Aethelstan 'the Glorious'	924–939 CE
Edmund I 'the Magnificent'	939–946 CE
Eadred	946–955 CE
Eadwig	955–959 CE
Edgar 'the Peaceful'	959–975 CE
Edward 'the Martyr'	975–978 CE
Aethelred II 'the Unready'	978–1013 CE

House of Denmark (c. 1013-1014 CE)

England was invaded by the Danes in 1013. Aethelred abandoned the throne to Sweyn Forkbeard.

Sweyn Forkbeard	1013–1014 CE

House of Wessex (restored, 1014-1016 CE)

Aethelred II was restored to the English throne after the death of Sweyn Forkbeard.

Aethelred II 'the Unready'	1014–1016 CE
Edmund Ironside	1016–1016 CE

House of Denmark (restored, 1016–1042 CE)

Cnut became king of all England apart from Wessex after signing a treaty with Edmund Ironside. He became king of all England following Edmund's death just over a month later.

Cnut 'the Great' (Canute)	1016–1035 CE
Harold Harefoot	1035–1040 CE
Harthacnut	1040–1042 CE

House of Wessex (restored, second time, 1042–1066 CE)

Edward 'the Confessor'	1042–1066 CE

House of Goodwin (1066 CE)

Harold II Godwinson	1066–1066 CE

Following Harold II's death in the Battle of Hastings, several claimants emerged to fight over the English throne. William the Conqueror of the House of Normandy was crowned king on 25 December 1066.

HIGH KINGS OF IRELAND

Mythological High Kings of Ireland

Dates and rulers are different depending on the source.

Nuada	?–1897 BCE; first reign
Bres	1897–1890 BCE
Nuada	1890–1870 BCE; second reign

Lug	1870–1830 BCE
Eochaid Ollathair (the Dadga)	1830–1750 BCE
Delbaeth	1750–1740 BCE
Fiacha	1740–1730 BCE
Mac Cuill	1730–1700 BCE

Ireland was split into several kingdoms until the national title of High King began, despite mythological stories of unbroken lines of High Kings.

Semi-historical High Kings (c. 459–831 CE)

Most of these kings are thought to be historical figures, but it is disputed whether they were all High Kings.

Ailill Molt	459–478 CE
Lugaid mac Loegairi	479–503 CE
Muirchertach mac Ercae	504–527 CE
Tuathal Maelgarb	528–538 CE
Diarmait mac Cerbaill	539–558 CE
Domhnall mac Muirchertaig	559–561 CE; joint ruler
Fearghus mac Muirchertaig	559–561 CE; joint ruler
Baedan mac Muirchertaig	562–563 CE; joint ruler
Eochaidh mac Domnaill	562–563 CE; joint ruler
Ainmuire mac Setnai	564–566 CE
Baetan mac Ninnedo	567 CE
Aed mac Ainmuirech	568–594 CE
Aed Slaine	595–600 CE; joint ruler
Colman Rimid	595–600 CE; joint ruler
Aed Uaridnach	601–607 CE
Mael Coba mac Aedo	608–610 CE
Suibne Menn	611–623 CE

Domnall mac Aedo	624–639 CE
Cellach mac Maele Coba	640–656 CE; joint ruler
Conall mac Maele Coba	640–656 CE; joint ruler
Diarmait	657–664 CE; joint ruler
Blathmac	657–664 CE; joint ruler
Sechnassach	665–669 CE
Cenn Faelad	670–673 CE
Finsnechta Fledach	674–693 CE
Loingsech mac Oengusso	694–701 CE
Congal Cennmagair	702–708 CE
Fergal mac Maele Duin	709–718 CE
Fogartach mac Neill	719 CE
Cinaed mac Irgalaig	720–722 CE
Flaithbertach mac Loingsig	723–729 CE
Aed Allan	730–738 CE
Domnall Midi	739–758 CE
Niall Frossach	759–765 CE
Donnchad Midi	766–792 CE
Aed Oirdnide	793–819 CE
Conchobar mac Donnchada	819–833 CE
Feidlimid mac Crimthainn	832–846 CE

Historical High Kings of Ireland (*c*. 846–1198 CE)

It is disputed whether these were all High Kings.

Mael Sechnaill mac Maele-Ruanaid	846–860 CE
Aed Findliath	861–876 CE
Fiann Sinna	877–914 CE
Niall Glundub	915–917 CE
Donnchad Donn	918–942 CE

Congalach Cnogba	943–954 CE
Domnall ua Neill	955–978 CE
Mael Sechnaill mac Domnaill	979–1002 CE; first reign
Brian Boruma	1002–1014 CE
Mael Sechnaill mac Domnaill	
	1014–1022 CE; second reign
Donnchad mac Brian	died 1064
Diarmait mac Mail na mBo	died 1072 CE
Toiredelbach Ua Briain	died 1086 CE
Domnall Ua Lochlainn	died 1121 CE
Muirchertach Ua Briain	died 1119 CE
Toirdelbach Ua Conchobair	1119–1156 CE
Muirchertach Mac Lochlainn	1156–1166 CE
Ruaidri Ua Conchobair	1166–1198 CE

RULERS OF SCOTLAND

Legendary kings

Fergus I	c. 330 BCE
Feritharis	305 BCE
Mainus	290 BCE
Dornadilla	262 BCE
Nothatus	232 BCE

Some of the significant rulers between 200 BCE and 800 CE are listed here.

Caractacus	King of the Britons, he was also considered king of Scotland in legend

| Donaldus I | Some consider him to be the first Christian king of Scotland |
| Fergus Mor | c. 500 CE; possible king of Dal Riata |

The list ends around the time of Kenneth MacAlpin, who founded the House of Alpin. Following the Roman departure from Britain, Scotland split into four main groups: the Picts, the people of Dal Riata, the Kingdom of Strathclyde and the Kingdom of Bernicia. The Picts would eventually merge with Dal Riata to form the Kingdom of Scotland.

Monarchs of Scotland (c. 848–1286 CE)

House of Alpin (848–1034 CE)

Kenneth I was the son of Alpin, king of Dal Riata, a Gaelic kingdom located in Scotland and Ireland.

Kenneth I MacAlpin	843/848–13 February 858 CE; first King of Alba thought to be of Gaelic origin
Donald I	858–13 April 862 CE
Causantin mac Cinaeda (Constantine I)	862–877 CE
Aed mac Cinaeda	877–878 CE
Giric 'mac Rath'	878–889 CE
Donald II	889–900 CE
Causantin mac Aeda (Constantine II)	900–943 CE
Malcolm I	943–954 CE
Indulf	954–962 CE
Dub mac Mail Coluim	962–967 CE
Cuilen	967–971 CE
Amlaib	973–977 CE

Constantine III	995–997 CE
Kenneth III	997–25 March 1005 CE
Malcolm II	1005–1034 CE

House of Dunkeld (1034–1286)

Duncan was the grandson of Malcolm II. He founded the House of Dunkeld.

Duncan I	1034–1040 CE
Macbeth	1040–1057 CE
Lulach	1057–1058 CE
Malcolm III	1058–1093 CE
Donald III	1093–1097 CE
Duncan II	1094 CE
Edgar	1097–1107 CE
Alexander I	1107–1124 CE
David I	1124–1153 CE
Malcolm IV	1153–1165 CE
William I	1165–1214 CE
Alexander II	1219–1249 CE
Alexander III	1249–1286 CE

SLAVIC NATIONS TIMELINE
& KEY LEADERS

This list is not exhaustive and dates are approximate. The legitimacy of some kings is also open to interpretation. Where dates of rule overlap, kings either ruled jointly or ruled in opposition to one another. There may also be differences in name spellings between different sources.

ORIGINS AND MIGRATIONS

Thought by many to have originated in Polesia, a region encompassing parts of Central and Eastern Europe and southwestern Russia, the Slavic people were made up of tribal societies. Many of these societies migrated across Europe integrating with Czech, Russia, Bulgaria, Croatia, Bosnia, Poland, Hungary and other countries and cultures.

While their beliefs and myths diverge, some believe the legend of three brothers who founded three of the main Slavic peoples. The three brothers, Lech, Czech and Rus', were on a hunting trip when they took different directions to hunt their own prey. Lech travelled to the north, where he would eventually found Poland; Czech travelled west to found Czech;

and Rus' travelled east to found Russia, Ukraine and Belarus.

The timelines that follow chart the main migrations, key events and major rulers of several branches of the Slavic people.

WESTERN STEM

Czech

?	Czech founds what is now the Czech Republic (mythological)
623 CE	Samo, the first King of the Slavs, founds Samo's Empire which includes the kingdom of Moravia
626 CE	Samo leads the Slavs against the Avars
631	Samo leads his realm in the Battle of Wogastisburg, defeating the Franks
658	Samo dies. His sons do not inherit and the Slavic kingdom dissolves
?	Little is known about this period but it might have fallen under Avar rule
820s	Mojmir I founds the House of Mojmir and converts to Christianity
833	Mojmir unifies Moravia and Nitra (Slovakia) as the state of Great Moravia
846	Mojmir I is deposed. Ratislav becomes the second prince of Moravia
862	Prince Ratislav of Moravia converts to Christianity
872	Ratislav is dethroned by his nephew, Svatopluk I, who succeeds him as prince of Moravia
870/874	Borivoj I becomes prince of Bohemia, founding the House of Premysl

880	Svatopluk I 'the Great' is crowned king of Great Moravia
882	The Moravians invade Bohemia and Pannonia
895	The dukes of Bohemia under Spytihnev I separate from the Moravian kingdom
902/907	The Moravian kingdom collapses
912	Vratislav I becomes duke of Bohemia
921	Wenceslas I (posthumously declared patron saint of Czech) becomes duke of Bohemia
929	Boleslav I 'the Cruel' becomes duke of Bohemia after murdering Wenceslas I Bohemia conquers Moravia (Slovakia)
972	Boleslav II 'the Pious' becomes duke of Bohemia
999	Boleslav III 'the Red' becomes duke of Bohemia (first reign)
1003	After a brief revolt, Boleslav III is restored to the dukedom (second reign)
1003	Poland conquers Moravia and Boleslaw I (also duke of Poland) becomes duke of Bohemia
1013	Bohemia reconquers Moravia from Poland under Ulrich, duke of Bohemia
1038	Bohemia under Bretislav I invades Poland conquers Silesia and Wroclaw
1061	Vratislav II becomes duke of Bohemia
1085	Henry IV (Holy Roman emperor) makes Vratislav II the first king of Bohemia (non-hereditary title) The House of Premysl continues to rule Bohemia
1158	German emperor Friedrich I Barbarossa makes Duke Vladislav II of Bohemia the second king of Bohemia (non-hereditary title)

1198	The duchy of Bohemia officially becomes a kingdom
1253	Ottakar II becomes king of Bohemia and the kingdom grows
1278	Wenceslas II becomes king of Bohemia
1300	Wenceslas II of Bohemia becomes king of Poland
1305	Wenceslas III becomes king of Bohemia and Poland
1306	Wenceslas III of Bohemia is murdered, ending the House of Premysl

Poland

?	Lech founds what is now Poland (mythological)
c. 8thC CE	Krak I or Krok founds Kracow (mythological)
c. 8thC	Krak II founds Kracow (mythological)
c. 9thC	Piast 'the Wheelwright' founds the Piast dynasty and names his state Polska (semi-mythological)
960?	Mieszko I founds the duchy of Poland
966	Mieszko I converts to Christianity
992	Boleslaw I 'the Brave' succeeds his father Mieszko I on his death
999	Poland becomes a Christian kingdom
1000	Poland becomes part of the German empire under Emperor Otto III
1025	Boleslaw I is crowned first Polish king by the Pope
1025	Mieszko II becomes king of Poland
1034/1040	Casimir 'the Restorer' becomes king of Poland
1058	Boleslaw II 'the Generous' becomes duke, then king of Poland
1079	Wladyslaw I becomes duke of Poland
1102	Boleslaw III 'the Wry-mouthed' becomes duke, then king of Poland

1138	Boleslaw III dies. The kingdom is divided among his sons, which begins the fragmentation of Poland
1226	Konrad I of Masovia asks the Teutonic Order (crusading knights based in Germany) to help subdue the pagan tribes of Prussia
1240/1241	The Mongols invade Poland, defeating a joint army of Henry I of Silesia and the Teutonic Order at the Battle of Legnica
1290	The Teutonic Order conquer all of Prussia
1295	Premysl II returns Poland to a kingdom with a hereditary title. Vytenis become grand duke of Lithuania and unites the country
1300	Wenceslas II of the house of Premysl, Bohemia, becomes king of Poland
1315/1316	Vytenis' brother Gediminas expands Lithuania to span from the Baltic Sea to the Black Sea
1320	Wladyslaw I Lokietek (known as Wladyslaw the Short) reunites the kingdom of Poland

EASTERN STEM

Russia and Former Soviet Republics

?	Rus' founded the Rus' people (mythological)
c. 800 CE	The Varingian Rus' found the state of Kiev
c.862/870	The Varingian Rus prince Rurik begins the Rurik dynasty by founding Novgorod
879	Rurik's son, Oleg 'the Wise', becomes ruler of Novgorod

882	Oleg of Novgorod conquers Kiev and later unifies it with Novgorod to form what would become Kievan-Rus'
912	Oleg dies and Igor 'the Old', Rurik's younger son, becomes the ruler of Kiev-Novgorod
921	Igor moves the capital of the duchy to Kiev
941 & 944	Igor besieges Constantinople
945	Igor is assassinated and his widow, Olga, succeeds him
962	Olga of Kiev is succeeded by Sviatoslav I, her son
964–968	Sviatoslav launches a military campaign to the east and south, conquering first the Volga Bulgars and then the Khazar empire
972	Sviatoslav dies. His son Yaropolk I is given Kiev, but civil war soon breaks out
980	Vladimir I 'the Great' of Novgorod conquers Kiev and creates a unified Rus. He soon begins a campaign to conquer the Baltic people
988	Vladimir, previously a pagan, converts to Greek-Orthodox Christianity. His kingdom now extends from Ukraine to the Baltic Sea
1015	Vladimir dies and civil war erupts again under the dubious claim of Sviatopolk I
1019	Yaroslav I 'the Wise' becomes the new ruler of Kiev
1054	Yaroslav dies, splitting the kingdom among his sons and leaving it weakened. He leaves Kiev and Novgorod to Iziaslav I
11–12thC	The kingdom remains divided. The Crusades further weaken the Baltic states and Constantinople
1237	The Mongols invade Kievan Rus'

1237–1239	Mongol leader Batu Khan raids Kiev before sacking Vladimir, Moscow, and many other Kievan Rus' cities
1253	Danylo Halitski of Galicia is crowned king by the Pope
1283	Daniil Alexsandrovich becomes the first prince of Moscow and establishes the grand duchy of Moscow

Illyrico-Servian branch

South Slavs migrate and begin to settle in countries including what are known today as Bosnia, Montenegro, Serbia and Croatia.

up to the late 500s	South Slavic tribes remain fragmented. Invasions on territories take place, including the Balkans, Dalmatia and Greece
558 CE	Several South Slavic tribes are defeated by the Avars. Many of the Slavs move east from the Russian steppes
600s–700s	South Slavs begin to settle along the Danube, in the Balkans, Bulgaria, Montenegro and Serbia. There is some assimilation of the cultures; South Slavs invade Greece, reaching Macedonia and Thessalonica; States or kingdoms are formed but many are threatened by invasion
870	The Serbs begin to convert to Christianity
925	The kingdom of Croatia is formed under Tomislav, its first king
1042	Duklja in Montenegro gains independence from the Roman Empire
1168	Stefan Nemanja founds the Nemanjic dynasty in Serbia

1217   Stefan Nemanjic 'the First-Crowned', son of
            Stefan Nemanja, is crowned by the Pope as first
            king of Serbia. The kingdom of Serbia is formed

Mid-12thC The Banate of Bosnia is formed

Mid-14thC Principality of Zeta is formed, covering
            parts of what is today Montenegro

Magyars/Hungary

14 BCE   Pannonia which includes parts of Hungary
            is classed as part of the Roman Empire

5 CE   The Romans found Aquincum (now Budapest)

370–469   The Hunnic empire invades much of Central and
            Eastern Europe, including Hung

c.5thC   The Magyars migrate from the Ural
            Mountains in Russia. Some settle along
            the Don River in the Khazar Khanate

862   The Magyars raid the Frankish Empire and
            parts of Bulgaria and the Balaton principality

895/896   Arpad, head of the seven Magyar tribes and
            thought to be a descendant of Attila, founds the
            kingdom of Hungary with three Khazar tribes

906   The Hungarians defeat the Moravian
            kingdom and annex Slovakia

907   The Hungarians defeat the Bavarian
            army in the Battle of Pressburg

917–934   The Hungarians raid parts of France, Switzerland,
            Saxony, Italy and Constantinople

948   Bulcsu, a descendent of Arpad, signs a
            peace treaty with the Roman Empire
            and converts to Christianity

955	Bulcsu and his troops meet the German army led by Otto I 'the Great' and are defeated in the Battle of Lechfeld, resulting in an end to further Hungarian invasions
1001	Stephen I (Saint Stephen) is crowned king of Hungary and sets out to consolidate and extend his rule
1030	Stephen I repels an invasion led by the Holy Roman Emperor, Conrad II
1038	Stephen I of Hungary dies. There follows a series of civil wars
1077	King Ladislaus I becomes king of Hungary (he also becomes king of Croatia in 1091)
1095	Coloman 'the Learned' becomes king of Hungary. Over the next few years, he annexes Croatia (becoming its king in 1097), Slavonia and Dalmatia
1116	Stephen II becomes king of Hungary and Croatia,
1141	Geza II becomes king of Hungary and Croatia and seeks to expand his borders. For the next century, the country faces both expansion and revolt
1241	Bela IV (who became king in 1235) refuses to surrender to the Mongols under Batu Khan, but the Hungarian army is defeated. However, the Mongols retreat in 1242
1242	With the country weakened, Bela IV concentrates on rebuilding, including the castle of Buda
1272	Ladislaus IV becomes king of Hungary and Croatia
1290	Ladislaus IV is murdered and his throne is taken by Andrew III, a descendant of the Arpads

| 1301 | Andrew II dies, causing the Arpad dynasty to become extinct in the male line. Charles Robert I of Anjou, a 13-year-old Catholic, inherits the throne of Hungary |

Bulgaria

6th century–479 BCE	The Achaemenid Empire controls parts of what is now Bulgaria
341 CE	Philip II of Macedon makes Bulgaria part of his empire
3rd century	Bulgaria is attacked by the Celts
45 CE	Bulgaria becomes part of the Roman Empire
c. 381	The Gothic (Wulfila) Bible is created in what is now northern Bulgaria
482	Following migration, the Turkic-speaking tribes of the Bulgars mainly reside northeast of the Danube River. The tribes are fragmented and remain so for the next century. Some are under the control of the Avars
584	Kubrat of the Dulo dynasty unifies the main Bulgarian tribes
619	Kubrat converts to Christianity
632	Kubrat unites all Bulgarian tribes and founds the state known as Old Great Bulgaria
650/665	Kubrat dies. Old Great Bulgaria largely disintegrates
680	Under Kubrat's sons, the Bulgars migrate across parts of Europe. Asparukh, one of Kubrat's sons and thought to be a descendant of Attila, travel west towards the Danube
680/681	Asparukh establishes the First Bulgarian Empire

700	Tervel becomes king of Bulgaria following Asparukh's death in battle. Terval is also given the title of Caesar in 705
753	Sevar, king of Bulgaria, dies, ending the reign of the Dulo dynasty
753/756	Vinekh begins the Ukil dynasty. The period is marked by the short reigns and murders of many of its kings, and by a series of attacks on Bulgaria by the Byzantine empire
777	Kardam becomes king of Bulgaria and restores order and power
c. 803	Krum 'the Fearsome' becomes king of the Bulgars, beginning the rule of the Krum dynasty
810	The Bulgars under Krum expand their empire and destroy the Avars
807–811	Krum's Bulgars are attacked by the Byzantine army, but defeat them in the Battle of Pliska, killing the Byzantine emperor, Nikephoros I
814/815	Krum dies while preparing to attack Constantinople. He is succeeded by his son Omurtag, who signs a 30-year peace treaty with the Byzantine Empire. This marks a period of peace and expansion in Bulgaria
852	Boris I becomes king of Bulgaria, marking a ten-year period of instability
864	Boris converts Bulgaria to Christianity and is regarded as a saint by the Eastern Orthodox Church
893	Boris' son, Simeon I 'the Great', becomes Bulgaria's first tsar. Under him, the state becomes among the most powerful in Eastern and Southeastern Europe

927	Simeon dies and is succeeded by his son, Peter I. This ushers in a golden age of peace and prosperity
934–965	A series of raids by Hungarians, coupled by political insecurity, causes the start of decline in Bulgaria
969	Boris II, Peter's son, becomes tsar when Peter abdicates. He spends most of his reign in captivity of the Byzantine emperor, Nikephoras II
997	Samuel becomes tsar. His reign is hindered by constant war with the Byzantines
1015	Ivan Vladislav becomes tsar
1018	Ivan dies, and the Byzantine Empire under Basil II annexes the kingdom of Bulgaria
1185	The Second Bulgarian Empire is established by Peter II. It remains a dominant power until the mid-1200s when the Mongols invade

SUMERIAN KING LIST

This list is based on the *Sumerian King List* or *Chronicle of the One Monarchy*. The lists were often originally carved into clay tablets and several versions have been found, mainly in southern Mesopotamia. Some of these are incomplete and others contradict one another. Dates are based on archaeological evidence as far as possible but are thus approximate. There may also be differences in name spellings between different sources. Nevertheless, the lists remain an invaluable source of information.

As with many civilizations, the lists of leaders here begin with mythological and legendary figures before they merge into the more solidly historical, hence why you will see some reigns of seemingly impossible length.

After the kingship descended from heaven, the kingship was in Eridug.

Alulim	28,8000 years (8 *sars**)
Alalngar	36,000 years (10 *sars*)

Then Eridug fell and the kingship was taken to Bad-tibira.

En-men-lu-ana	43,200 years (12 *sars*)
En-mel-gal-ana	28,800 years (8 *sars*)

Dumuzid the Shepherd (or Tammuz)   36,000 years (10 *sars*)

Then Bad-tibira fell and the kingship was taken to Larag.

En-sipad-zid-ana   28,800 years (8 *sars*)

Then Larag fell and the kingship was taken to Zimbir.

En-men-dur-ana   21,000 years (5 *sars* and 5 *ners*)

Then Zimbir fell and the kingship was taken to Shuruppag.

Ubara-Tutu   18,600 years (5 *sars* and 1 *ner**)

Then the flood swept over.

*A *sar* is a numerical unit of 3,600; a *ner* is a numerical unit of 600.

FIRST DYNASTY OF KISH

After the flood had swept over, and the kingship had descended from heaven, the kingship was in Kish.

Jushur	1,200 years
Kullassina-bel	960 years
Nangishlisma	1,200 years
En-tarah-ana	420 years
Babum	300 years

Puannum	840 years
Kalibum	960 years
Kalumum	840 years
Zuqaqip	900 years
Atab (or A-ba)	600 years
Mashda (son of Atab)	840 years
Arwium (son of Mashda)	720 years
Etana the Shepherd	1,500 years
Balih (son of Etana)	400 years
En-me-nuna	660 years
Melem-Kish (son of Enme-nuna)	900 years
Barsal-nuna (son of Enme-nuna)	1,200 years
Zamug (son of Barsal-nuna)	140 years
Tizqar (son of Zamug)	305 years
Ilku	900 years
Iltasadum	1,200 years
Enmebaragesi	900 years (earliest proven ruler based on archaeological sources; Early Dynastic Period, 2900–2350 BCE)
Aga of Kish (son of Enmebaragesi)	625 years (Early Dynastic Period, 2900–2350 BCE)

Then Kish was defeated and the kingship was taken to E-anna.

FIRST RULERS OF URUK

Mesh-ki-ang-gasher (son of Utu)   324 years (Late Uruk Period, 4000–3100 BCE)

Enmerkar (son of Mesh-ki-ang-gasher)	420 years (Late Uruk Period, 4000–3100 BCE)
Lugal-banda the shepherd	1200 years (Late Uruk Period, 4000–3100 BCE)
Dumuzid the fisherman	100 years (Jemdet Nasr Period, 3100–2900 BCE)
Gilgamesh	126 years (Early Dynastic Period, 2900–2350 BCE)
Ur-Nungal (son of Gilgamesh)	30 years
Udul-kalama (son of Ur-Nungal)	15 year
La-ba'shum	9 years
En-nun-tarah-ana	8 years
Mesh-he	36 years
Melem-ana	6 years
Lugal-kitun	36 years

Then Unug was defeated and the kingship was taken to Urim (Ur).

FIRST DYNASTY OF UR

Mesh-Ane-pada	80 years
Mesh-ki-ang-Nuna (son of Mesh-Ane-pada)	36 years
Elulu	25 years
Balulu	36 years

Then Urim was defeated and the kingship was taken to Awan.

DYNASTY OF AWAN

Three kings of Awan   356 years

Then Awan was defeated and the kingship was taken to Kish.

SECOND DYNASTY OF KISH

Susuda the fuller	201 years
Dadasig	81 years
Mamagal the boatman	360 years
Kalbum (son of Mamagal)	195 years
Tuge	360 years
Men-nuna (son of Tuge)	180 years
Enbi-Ishtar	290 years
Lugalngu	360 years

Then Kish was defeated and the kingship was taken to Hamazi.

DYNASTY OF HAMAZI

Hadanish   360 years

Then Hamazi was defeated and the kingship was taken to Unug (Uruk).

SECOND DYNASTY OF URUK

En-shag-kush-ana	60 years (c. 25th century BCE)
Lugal-kinishe-dudu	120 years
Argandea	7 years

Then Unug was defeated and the kingship was taken to Urim (Ur).

SECOND DYNASTY OF UR

Nanni	120 years
Mesh-ki-ang-Nanna II (son of Nanni)	48 years

Then Urim was defeated and the kingship was taken to Adab.

DYNASTY OF ADAB

Lugal-Ane-mundu	90 years (c. 25th century BCE)

Then Adab was defeated and the kingship was taken to Mari.

DYNASTY OF MARI

Anbu	30 years	Zizi of Mari, the fuller	20 years
Anba (son of Anbu)	17 years	Limer the 'gudug'	
Bazi the		priest	30 years
leatherworker	30 years	Sharrum-iter	9 years

Then Mari was defeated and the kingship was taken to Kish.

THIRD DYNASTY OF KISH

Kug-Bau (Kubaba)   100 years (*c.* 25th century BCE)

Then Kish was defeated and the kingship was taken to Akshak.

DYNASTY OF AKSHAK

Unzi	30 years	Ishu-Il	24 years
Undalulu	6 years	Shu-Suen (son of	
Urur	6 years	Ishu-Il)	7 years
Puzur-Nirah	20 years		

Then Akshak was defeated and the kingship was taken to Kish.

FOURTH DYNASTY OF KISH

Puzur-Suen (son of Kug-bau)	25 years (*c.* 2350 BCE)
Ur-Zababa (son of Puzur-Suen)	400 years (*c.* 2350 BCE)
Zimudar	30 years
Usi-watar (son of Zimudar)	7 years
Eshtar-muti	11 years
Ishme-Shamash	11 years
Shu-ilishu	15 years
Nanniya the jeweller	7 years

Then Kish was defeated and the kingship was taken to Unug (Uruk).

THIRD DYNASTY OF URUK

Lugal-zage-si   25 years (c. 2296–2271 BCE)

Then Unug was defeated and the kingship was taken to Agade (Akkad).

DYNASTY OF AKKAD

Sargon of Akkad   56 years (c. 2270–2215 BCE)
Rimush of Akkad (son of Sargon)   9 years (c. 2214–2206 BCE)
Manishtushu (son of Sargon)   15 years (c. 2205–2191 BCE)
Naram-Sin of Akkad (son of
  Manishtushu)   56 years (c. 2190–2154 BCE)
Shar-kali-sharri (son of Naram-Sin) 24 years (c. 2153–2129 BCE)

Then who was king? Who was not the king?

Irgigi, Nanum, Imi and Ilulu   3 years (four rivals who fought
                               to be king during a three-year
                               period; c. 2128–2125 BCE)
Dudu of Akkad   21 years (c. 2125–2104 BCE)
Shu-Durul (son of Duu)   15 years (c. 2104–2083 BCE)

Then Agade was defeated and the kingship was taken to Unug (Uruk).

FOURTH DYNASTY OF URUK

Ur-ningin	7 years (c. 2091?–2061? BCE)
Ur-gigir (son of Ur-ningin)	6 years
Kuda	6 years
Puzur-ili	5 years
Ur-Utu (or Lugal-melem; son of Ur-gigir)	6 years

Unug was defeated and the kingship was taken to the army of Gutium.

GUTIAN RULE

Inkišuš	6 years (c. 2147–2050 BCE)
Sarlagab (or Zarlagab)	6 years
Shulme (or Yarlagash)	6 years
Elulmeš (or Silulumeš or Silulu)	6 years
Inimabakeš (or Duga)	5 years
Igešauš (or Ilu-An)	6 years
Yarlagab	3 years
Ibate of Gutium	3 years
Yarla (or Yarlangab)	3 years
Kurum	1 year
Apilkin	3 years
La-erabum	2 years
Irarum	2 years
Ibranum	1 year
Hablum	2 years
Puzur-Suen (son of Hablum)	7 years

Yarlaganda	7 years
Si'um (or Si-u)	7 years
Tirigan	40 days

Then the army of Gutium was defeated and the kingship taken to Unug (Uruk).

FIFTH DYNASTY OF URUK

| Utu-hengal | 427 years / 26 years / 7 years |
| | (conflicting dates; *c.* 2055–2048 BCE) |

THIRD DYNASTY OF UR

Ur-Namma (or Ur-Nammu)	18 years (*c.* 2047–2030 BCE)
Shulgi (son of Ur-Namma)	48 years (*c.* 2029–1982 BCE)
Amar-Suena (son of Shulgi)	9 years (*c.* 1981–1973 BCE)
Shu-Suen (son of Amar-Suena)	9 years (*c.* 1972–1964 BCE)
Ibbi-Suen (son of Shu-Suen)	24 years (*c.* 1963–1940 BCE)

Then Urim was defeated. The very foundation of Sumer was torn out. The kingship was taken to Isin.

DYNASTY OF ISIN

| Ishbi-Erra | 33 years (*c.* 1953–1920 BCE) |
| Shu-Ilishu (son of Ishbi-Erra) | 20 years |

Iddin-Dagan (son of Shu-Ilishu)	20 years
Ishme-Dagan (son of Iddin-Dagan)	20 years
Lipit-Eshtar (son of Ishme-Dagan or Iddin Dagan)	11 years
Ur-Ninurta (son of Ishkur)	28 years
Bur-Suen (son of Ur-Ninurta)	21 years
Lipit-Enlil (son of Bur-Suen)	5 years
Erra-imitti	8 years
Enlil-bani	24 years
Zambiya	3 years
Iter-pisha	4 years
Ur-du-kuga	4 years
Suen-magir	11 years
Damiq-ilishu	23 years (son of Suen-magir)

ANCIENT GREEK MONARCHS

This list is not exhaustive and dates are approximate. Where dates of rule overlap, emperors either ruled jointly or ruled in opposition to one another. There may also be differences in name spellings between different sources.

Because of the fragmented nature of Greece prior to its unification by Philip II of Macedon, this list includes mythological and existing rulers of Thebes, Athens and Sparta as some of the leading ancient Greek city-states. These different city-states had some common belief in the mythological gods and goddesses of ancient Greece, although their accounts may differ.

KINGS OF THEBES (c. 753–509 BCE)

These rulers are mythological. There is much diversity over who the kings actually consisted of, and the dates they ruled.

Calydnus (son of Uranus)

Ogyges (son of Poseidon, thought to be king of Boeotia or Attica)

Cadmus (Greek mythological hero known as the founder of Thebes, known as Cadmeia until the reign of Amphion and Zethus)

Pentheus (son of Echion, one of the mythological Spartoi, and Agave, daughter of Cadmus)

Polydorus (son of Cadmus and Harmonia, goddess of harmony)

Nycteus (thought to be the son of a Spartoi and a nymph, or a son of Poseidon)

Lycus (brother of Nyceteus, thought to be the son of a Spartoi and a nymph, or a son of Poseidon)

Labdacus (grandson of Cadmus)

Lycus (second reign as regent for Laius)

Amphion and Zethus (joint rulers and twin sons of Zeus, constructed the city walls of Thebes)

Laius (son of Labdacus, married to Jocasta)

Oedipus (son of Laius, killed his father and married his mother, Jocasta)

Creon (regent after the death of Laius)

Eteocles and Polynices (brothers/sons of Oedipus; killed each other in battle)

Creon (regent for Laodamas)

Laodamas (son of Eteocles)

Thersander (son of Polynices)

Peneleos (regent for Tisamenus)

Tisamenus (son of Thersander)

Autesion (son of Tisamenes)

Damasichthon (son of Peneleos)

Ptolemy (son of Damasichton, 12 century BCE)

Xanthos (son of Ptolemy)

KINGS OF ATHENS

Early legendary kings who ruled before the mythological flood caused by Zeus, which only Deucalion (son of Prometheus) and a few others survived (date unknown).

Periphas (king of Attica, turned into an eagle by Zeus)

Ogyges (son of Poseidon, thought to be king of either Boeotia or Attica)

Actaeus (king of Attica, father-in-law to Cecrops I)

Erechtheid Dynasty (1556–1127 BCE)

Cecrops I (founder and first king of Athens; half-man, half-serpent who married Actaeus' daughter)	1556–1506 BCE
Cranaus	1506–1497 BCE
Amphictyon (son of Deucalion)	1497–1487 BCE
Erichthonius (adopted by Athena)	1487–1437 BCE
Pandion I (son of Erichthonius)	1437–1397 BCE
Erechtheus (son of Pandion I)	1397–1347 BCE
Cecrops II (son of Erechtheus)	1347–1307 BCE
Pandion II (son of Cecrops II)	1307–1282 BCE
Aegeus (adopted by Pandion II, gave his name to the Aegean Sea)	1282–1234 BCE
Theseus (son of Aegeus, killed the minotaur)	1234–1205 BCE
Menestheus (made king by Castor and Pollux when Theseus was in the underworld)	1205–1183 BCE
Demophon (son of Theseus)	1183–1150 BCE
Oxyntes (son of Demophon)	1150–1136 BCE
Apheidas (son of Oxyntes)	1136–1135 BCE
Thymoetes (son of Oxyntes)	1135–1127 BCE

Melanthid Dynasty (1126–1068 BCE)

Melanthus (king of Messenia, fled to Athens when expelled)	1126 – 1089 BCE
Codrus (last of the semi-mythological Athenian kings)	1089–1068 BCE

LIFE ARCHONS OF ATHENS (1068–753BCE)

These rulers held public office up until their deaths.

Medon	1068–1048 BCE	Pherecles	864–845 BCE
Acastus	1048–1012 BCE	Ariphon	845–825 BCE
Archippus	1012–993 BCE	Thespieus	824–797 BCE
Thersippus	993–952 BCE	Agamestor	796–778 BCE
Phorbas	952–922 BCE	Aeschylus	778–755 BCE
Megacles	922–892 BCE	Alcmaeon	755–753 BCE
Diognetus	892–864 BCE		

From this point, archons led for a period of ten years up to 683 BCE, then a period of one year up to 485 CE. Selected important leaders – including archons and tyrants – in this later period are as follows:

SELECTED LATER LEADERS OF ATHENS

Peisistratos 'the Tyrant of Athens'	561, 559–556, 546–527 BCE
Cleisthenes (archon)	525–524 BCE
Themistocles (archon)	493–492 BCE
Pericles	c. 461–429 BCE

KINGS OF SPARTA

These rulers are mythological and are thought to be descendants of the ancient tribe of Leleges. There is much diversity over who the kings actually consisted of, and the dates they ruled.

Lelex (son of Poseidon or Helios, ruled Laconia)   c. 1600 BCE
Myles (son of Lelex, ruled Laconia)   c.1575 BCE
Eurotas (son of Myles, father of Sparta)   c. 1550 BCE

From the Lelegids, rule passed to the Lacedaemonids when Lacedaemon married Sparta.

Lacedaemon (son of Zeus, husband of Sparta)
Amyklas (son of Lacedaemon)
Argalus (son of Amyklas)
Kynortas (son of Amyklas)
Perieres (son of Kynortas)
Oibalos (son of Kynortas)
Tyndareos (first reign; son of Oibalos, father of Helen of Troy)
Hippocoon (son of Oibalos)
Tyndareos (second reign; son of Oibaos, father of Helen of Troy)

From the Lacedaemons, rule passed to the Atreids when Menelaus married Helen of Troy.

Menelaus (son of Atreus, king of Mycenae,
    and husband of Helen)   c. 1250 BCE
Orestes (son of Agamemnon, Menelaus' brother)   c. 1150 BCE
Tisamenos (son of Orestes)
Dion   c. 1100 BCE

From the Atreids, rule passed to the Heraclids following war.

Aristodemos (son of Aristomachus, great-great-grandson of Heracles)

Theras (served as regent for Aristodemes' sons, Eurysthenes
  and Procles)
Eurysthenes   c. 930 BCE

From the Heraclids, rule passed to the Agiads, founded by Agis
I. Only major kings during this period are listed here.

Agis I (conceivably the first historical Spartan king) c. 930–900 BCE
Alcamenes   c. 740–700 BCE,
                                            during First Messenian War
Cleomenes I (important leader in the
  Greek resistance against the Persians)   524 – 490 BCE
Leonidas I (died while leading the
  Greeks – the 300 Spartans – against
  the Persians in the Battle of
  Thermopylae, 480 BCE)   490–480 BCE
Cleomenes III (exiled following the
  Battle of Sellasia)   c. 235 – 222 BCE

KINGS OF MACEDON

Argead Dynasty (808–309 BCE)

Karanos	c. 808–778 BCE	Alcetas I	c. 576–547 BCE
Koinos	c. 778–750 BCE	Amyntas I	c. 547–498 BCE
Tyrimmas	c. 750–700 BCE	Alexander I	c. 498–454 BCE
Perdiccas I	c. 700–678 BCE	Alcetas II	c. 454–448 BCE
Argaeus I	c. 678–640 BCE	Perdiccas II	c. 448–413 BCE
Philip I	c. 640–602 BCE	Archelaus I	c. 413–339 BCE
Aeropus I	c. 602–576 BCE	Craterus	c. 399 BCE

Orestes	c. 399–396 BCE	Perdiccas III	c. 368–359 BCE
Aeropus II	c. 399–394/93 BCE	Amyntas IV	c. 359 BCE
Archelaus II	c. 394–393 BCE	Philip II	c. 359–336 BCE
Amyntas II	c. 393 BCE	Alexander III 'the Great'	
Pausanias	c. 393 BCE	(also King of Persia and	
Amyntas III first reign	c. 393 BCE;	Pharaoh of Egypt by end of reign)	c. 336–323 BCE
Argeus II	c. 393–392 BCE	Philip III	c. 323–317 BCE
Amyntas III	c. 392–370 BCE	Alexander IV	c. 323/
Alexander II	c. 370–368 BCE		317–309 BCE

Note: the Corinthian League or Hellenic League was created by Philip II and was the first time that the divided Greek city-states were unified under a single government).

Post-Argead Dynasty (309–168 BCE, 149–148 BCE)

Cassander	c. 305–297 BCE
Philip IV	c. 297 BCE
Antipater II	c. 297–294 BCE
Alexpander V	c. 297–294 BCE

Antigonid, Alkimachid and Aeacid Dynasties (294–281 BCE)

Demetrius	c. 294–288 BCE
Lysimachus	c. 288–281 BCE
Pyrrhus	c. 288–285 BCE; first reign

Ptolemaic Dynasty (281–279 BCE)

Ptolemy Ceraunus (son of Ptolemy I of Egypt)	c. 281–279 BCE
Meleager	279 BCE

Antipatrid, Antigonid, Aeacid Dynasties, Restored
(279–167 BCE)

Antipater	c. 279 BCE
Sosthenes	c. 279–277 BCE
Antigonus II	c. 277–274 BCE; first reign
Pyrrhus	c. 274–272 BCE; second reign
Antigonus II	c. 272–239 BCE; second reign
Demetrius II	c. 239–229 BCE
Antigonus III	c. 229–221 9BCE
Philip V	c. 221–179 BCE
Perseus (deposed by Romans)	c. 179–168 BCE
Revolt by Philip VI (Andriskos)	c. 149–148 BCE

SELEUCID DYNASTY (c. 320 BCE–63 CE)

Seleucus I Nicator	c. 320–315, 312–305, 305–281 BCE
Antiochus I Soter	c. 291, 281–261 BCE
Antiochus II Theos	c. 261–246 BCE
Seleucus II Callinicus	c. 246–225 BCE
Seleucus III Ceraunus	c. 225–223 BCE
Antiochus III 'the Great'	c. 223–187 BCE
Seleucus IV Philopator	c. 187–175 BCE
Antiochus (son of Seleucus IV)	c. 175–170 BCE
Antiochus IV Epiphanes	c. 175–163 BCE
Antiochus V Eupater	c. 163–161 BCE
Demetrius I Soter	c. 161–150 BCE
Alexander I Balas	c. 150–145 BCE
Demetrius II Nicator	c. 145–138 BCE; first reign
Antiochus VI Dionysus	c. 145–140 BCE

Diodotus Tryphon	c. 140–138 BCE
Antiochus VII Sidetes	c. 138–129 BCE
Demetrius II Nicator	c. 129–126 BCE; second reign
Alexander II Zabinas	c. 129–123 BCE
Cleopatra Thea	c. 126–121 BCE
Seleucus V Philometor	c. 126/125 BCE
Antiochus VIII Grypus	c. 125–96 BCE
Antiochus IX Cyzicenus	c. 114–96 BCE
Seleucus VI Epiphanes	c. 96–95 BCE
Antiochus X Eusebes	c. 95–92/83 BCE
Demetrius III Eucaerus	c. 95–87 BCE
Antiochus XI Epiphanes	c. 95–92 BCE
Philip I Philadelphus	c. 95–84/83 BCE
Antiochus XII Dionysus	c. 87–84 BCE
Seleucus VII	c. 83–69 BCE
Antiochus XIII Asiaticus	c. 69–64 BCE
Philip II Philoromaeus	c. 65–63 BCE

Ptolemaic Dynasty (305–30 BCE)

The Ptolemaic dynasty in Greece was the last dynasty of Ancient Egypt before it became a province of Rome.

Ptolemy I Soter	7 305–282 BCE
Ptolemy II Philadelphos	284–246 BCE
Arsinoe II	c. 277–270 BCE
Ptolemy III Euergetes	246–222 BCE
Berenice II	244/243–222 BCE
Ptolemy IV Philopater	222–204 BCE
Arsinoe III	220–204 BCE
Ptolemy V Epiphanes	204–180 BCE

Cleopatra I	193–176 BCE
Ptolemy VI Philometor	180–164, 163–145 BCE
Cleopatra II	175–164 BCE, 163–127 BCE and 124–116 BCE
Ptolemy VIII Physcon	171–163 BCE, 144–131 BCE and 127–116 BCE
Ptolemy VII Neos Philopator	145–144 BCE
Cleopatra III	142–131 BCE, 127–107 BCE
Ptolemy Memphites	113 BCE
Ptolemy IX Soter	116–110 BCE
Cleopatra IV	116–115 BCE
Ptolemy X Alexander	110–109 BCE
Berenice III	81–80 BCE
Ptolemy XI Alexander	80 BCE
Ptolemy XII Auletes	80–58 BCE, 55–51 BCE
Cleopatra V Tryphaena	79–68 BCE
Cleopatra VI	58–57 BCE
Berenice IV	58–55 BCE

In 27 BCE, Caesar Augustus annexed Greece and it became integrated into the Roman Empire.

ANCIENT ROMAN LEADERS

This list is not exhaustive and some dates are approximate. The legitimacy of some rulers is also open to interpretation. Where dates of rule overlap, emperors either ruled jointly or ruled in opposition to one another. There may also be differences in name spellings between different sources.

KINGS OF ROME (753–509 BCE)

Romulus (mythological founder and first ruler of Rome)	753–716 BCE
Numa Pompilius (mythological)	715–672 BCE
Tullus Hostilius (mythological)	672–640 BCE
Ancus Marcius (mythological)	640–616 BCE
Lucius Tarquinius Priscus (mythological)	616–578 BCE
Servius Tullius (mythological)	578–534 BCE
Lucius Tarquinius Superbus (Tarquin the Proud; mythological)	534–509 BCE

ROMAN REPUBLIC (509–27 BCE)

During this period, two consuls were elected to serve a joint one-year term. Therefore, only a selection of significant consuls are included here.

Lucius Junius Brutus (semi-mythological)	509 BCE
Marcus Porcius Cato (Cato the Elder)	195 BCE
Scipio Africanus	194 BCE
Cnaeus Pompeius Magnus (Pompey the Great)	70, 55 and 52 BCE
Marcus Linius Crassus	70 and 55 BCE
Marcus Tullius Cicero	63 BCE
Caius Julius Caesar	59 BCE
Marcus Aemilius Lepidus	46 and 42 BCE
Marcus Antonius (Mark Anthony)	44 and 34 BCE
Marcus Agrippa	37 and 28 BCE

PRINCIPATE (27 BCE–284 CE)

Julio-Claudian Dynasty (27 BCE–68 CE)

Augustus (Caius Octavius Thurinus, Caius Julius Caesar, Imperator Caesar Divi filius)	27 BCE–14 CE
Tiberius (Tiberius Julius Caesar Augustus)	14–37 CE
Caligula (Caius Caesar Augustus Germanicus)	37–41 CE
Claudius (Tiberius Claudius Caesar Augustus Germanicus)	41–54 CE
Nero (Nero Claudius Caesar Augustus Germanicus)	54–68 CE

Year of the Four Emperors (68–69 CE)

Galba (Servius Sulpicius Galba Caesar Augustus)   68–69 CE
Otho (Marcus Salvio Otho Caesar Augustus)   Jan–Apr 69 CE
Vitellius (Aulus Vitellius Germanicus Augustus)   Apr–Dec 69 CE

Note: the fourth emperor, Vespasian, is listed below.

Flavian Dynasty (66–96 CE)

Vespasian (Caesar Vespasianus Augustus)   69–79 CE
Titus (Titus Caesar Vespasianus Augustus)   79–81 CE
Domitian (Caesar Domitianus Augustus)   81–96 CE

Nerva-Antonine Dynasty (69–192 CE)

Nerva (Nerva Caesar Augustus)   96–98 CE
Trajan (Caesar Nerva Traianus Augustus)   98–117 CE
Hadrian (Caesar Traianus Hadrianus Augustus)   138–161 CE
Antonius Pius (Caesar Titus Aelius Hadrianus
    Antoninus Augustus Pius)   138–161 CE
Marcus Aurelius (Caesar Marcus Aurelius
    Antoninus Augustus)   161–180 CE
Lucius Verus (Lucius Aurelius Verus Augustus)   161–169 CE
Commodus (Caesar Marcus Aurelius Commodus
    Antoninus Augustus)   180–192 CE

Year of the Five Emperors (193 CE)

Pertinax (Publius Helvius Pertinax)   Jan–Mar 193 CE
Didius Julianus (Marcus Didius Severus Julianus) Mar–Jun 193 CE

Note: Pescennius Niger and Clodius Albinus are generally regarded as usurpers, while the fifth, Septimius Severus, is listed below

Severan Dynasty (193–235 CE)

Septimius Severus (Lucius Septimius Severus Pertinax)	193–211 CE
Caracalla (Marcus Aurelius Antonius)	211–217 CE
Geta (Publius Septimius Geta)	Feb–Dec 211 CE
Macrinus (Caesar Marcus Opellius Severus Macrinus Augustus)	217–218 CE
Diadumenian (Marcus Opellius Antonius Diadumenianus)	May–Jun 218 CE
Elagabalus (Caesar Marcus Aurelius Antoninus Augustus)	218–222 CE
Severus Alexander (Marcus Aurelius Severus Alexander)	222–235 CE

Crisis of the Third Century (235–285 CE)

Maximinus 'Thrax' (Caius Julius Verus Maximus)	235–238 CE
Gordian I (Marcus Antonius Gordianus Sempronianus Romanus)	Apr–May 238 CE
Gordian II (Marcus Antonius Gordianus Sempronianus Romanus)	Apr–May 238 CE
Pupienus Maximus (Marcus Clodius Pupienus Maximus)	May–Aug 238 CE
Balbinus (Decimus Caelius Calvinus Balbinus)	May–Aug 238 CE
Gordian III (Marcus Antonius Gordianus)	Aug 238–Feb 244 CE
Philip I 'the Arab' (Marcus Julius Philippus)	244–249 CE
Philip II 'the Younger' (Marcus Julius Severus Philippus)	247–249 CE
Decius (Caius Messius Quintus Traianus Decius)	249–251 CE
Herennius Etruscus (Quintus Herennius Etruscus Messius Decius)	May/Jun 251 CE

Trebonianus Gallus (Caius Vibius Trebonianus Gallus)   251–253 CE

Hostilian (Caius Valens Hostilianus Messius
   Quintus)   Jun–Jul 251 CE

Volusianus (Caius Vibius Afinius Gallus
   Veldumnianus Volusianus)   251–253 CE

Aemilian (Marcus Aemilius Aemilianus)   Jul–Sep 253 CE

Silbannacus (Marcus Silbannacus)   Sep/Oct 253 CE

Valerian (Publius Licinius Valerianus)   253–260 CE

Gallienus (Publius Licinius Egnatius Gallienus)   253–268 CE

Saloninus (Publius Licinius Cornelius
   Saloninus Valerianus)   Autumn 260 CE

Claudius II Gothicus (Marcus Aurelius Claudius)   268–270 CE

Quintilus (Marcus Aurelius Claudias
   Quintillus)   Apr–May/Jun 270 CE

Aurelian (Luciua Domitius Aurelianus)   270–275 CE

Tacitus (Marcus Claudius Tacitus)   275–276 CE

Florianus (Marcus Annius Florianus)   276–282 CE

Probus (Marcus Aurelius Probus Romanus;
   in opposition to Florianus)   276–282 CE

Carus (Marcus Aurelias Carus)   282–283 CE

Carinus (Marcus Aurelius Carinus)   283–285 CE

Numerian (Marcus Aurelius Numerianus)   283–284 CE

DOMINATE (284–610)

Tetrarchy (284–324)

Diocletian 'Iovius' (Caius Aurelius Valerius Diocletianus)   284–305

Maximian 'Herculius' (Marcus Aurelius Valerius
   Maximianus; ruled the western provinces)   286–305/late 306–308

Galerius (Caius Galerius Valerius Maximianus; ruled the eastern provinces)	305–311
Constantius I 'Chlorus' (Marcus Flavius Valerius Constantius; ruled the western provinces)	305–306
Severus II (Flavius Valerius Severus; ruled the western provinces)	306–307
Maxentius (Marcus Aurelius Valerius Maxentius)	306–312
Licinius (Valerius Licinanus Licinius; ruled the western, then the eastern provinces)	308–324
Maximinus II 'Daza' (Aurelius Valerius Valens; ruled the western provinces)	316–317
Martinian (Marcus Martinianus; ruled the western provinces)	Jul–Sep 324

Constantinian Dynasty (306–363)

Constantine I 'the Great' (Flavius Valerius Constantinus; ruled the western provinces then whole)	306–337
Constantine II (Flavius Claudius Constantinus)	337–340
Constans I (Flavius Julius Constans)	337–350
Constantius II (Flavius Julius Constantius)	337–361
Magnentius (Magnus Magnentius)	360–353
Nepotianus (Julius Nepotianus)	Jun 350
Vetranio	Mar–Dec 350
Julian 'the Apostate' (Flavius Claudius Julianus)	361–363
Jovian (Jovianus)	363–364

Valentinianic Dynasty (364–392)

Valentinian I 'the Great' (Valentinianus)	364–375
Valens (ruled the eastern provinces)	364–378

Procopius (revolted against Valens)	365–366
Gratian (Flavius Gratianus Augustus; ruled the western provinces then whole)	375–383
Magnus Maximus	383–388
Valentinian II (Flavius Valentinianus)	388–392
Eugenius	392–394

Theodosian Dynasty (379–457)

Theodosius I 'the Great' (Flavius Theodosius)	Jan 395
Arcadius	383–408
Honorius (Flavius Honorius)	395–432
Constantine III	407–411
Theodosius II	408–450
Priscus Attalus; usurper	409–410
Constantius III	Feb–Sep 421
Johannes	423–425
Valentinian III	425–455
Marcian	450–457

Last Emperors in the West (455–476)

Petronius Maximus	Mar–May 455
Avitus	455–456
Majorian	457–461
Libius Severus (Severus III)	461–465
Anthemius	467–472
Olybrius	Apr–Nov 472
Glycerius	473–474
Julius Nepos	474–475
Romulus Augustulus (Flavius Momyllus Romulus Augustulus)	475–476

Leonid Dynasty (East, 457–518)

Leo I (Leo Thrax Magnus)	457–474
Leo II	Jan–Nov 474
Zeno	474–475
Basiliscus	475–476
Zeno (second reign)	476–491
Anastasius I 'Dicorus'	491–518

Justinian Dynasty (East, 518–602)

Justin I	518–527
Justinian I 'the Great' (Flavius Justinianus, Petrus Sabbatius)	527–565
Justin II	565–578
Tiberius II Constantine	578–582
Maurice (Mauricius Flavius Tiberius)	582–602
Phocas	602–610

LATER EASTERN EMPERORS (610–1059)

Heraclian Dynasty (610–695)

Heraclius	610–641
Heraclius Constantine (Constantine III)	Feb–May 641
Heraclonas	Feb–Nov 641
Constans II Pogonatus ('the Bearded')	641–668
Constantine IV	668–685
Justinian II	685–695

Twenty Years' Anarchy (695–717)

Leontius	695–698
Tiberius III	698–705

Justinian II 'Rhinometus' (second reign)	705–711
Philippicus	711–713
Anastasius II	713–715
Theodosius III	715–717

Isaurian Dynasty (717–803)

Leo III 'the Isaurian'	717–741
Constantine V	741–775
Artabasdos	741/2–743
Leo V 'the Khazar'	775–780
Constantine VI	780–797
Irene	797–802

Nikephorian Dynasty (802–813)

Nikephoros I 'the Logothete'	802–811
Staurakios	July–Oct 811
Michael I Rangabé	813–820

Amorian Dynasty (820–867)

Michael II 'the Amorian'	820–829
Theophilos	829–842
Theodora	842–856
Michael III 'the Drunkard'	842–867

Macedonian Dynasty (867–1056)

Basil I 'the Macedonian'	867–886
Leo VI 'the Wise'	886–912
Alexander	912–913
Constantine VII Porphyrogenitus	913–959
Romanos I Lecapenus	920–944

Romanos II	959–963
Nikephoros II Phocas	963–969
John I Tzimiskes	969–976
Basil II 'the Bulgar-Slayer'	976–1025
Constantine VIII	1025–1028
Romanus III Argyros	1028–1034
Michael IV 'the Paphlagonian'	1034–1041
Michael V Kalaphates	1041–1042
Zoë Porphyrogenita	Apr–Jun 1042
Theodora Porphyrogenita	Apr–Jun 1042
Constantine IX Monomachos	1042–1055
Theodora Porphyrogenita (second reign)	1055–1056
Michael VI Bringas 'Stratioticus'	1056–1057
Isaab I Komnenos	1057–1059